DAVID F. ADDLESTONE, a Washington, D.C., attorney, has done extensive work in the area of military law. He is coauthor, with Susan Hewman, of the ACLU PRACTICE MANUAL ON MILITARY DISCHARGE UPGRADING. He was a staff attorney with the Lawyers Military Defense Committee in Saigon and served as an Air Force Judge Advocate. Mr. Addlestone is director of the ACLU's National Military Discharge Review Project and a member of the Ethics Investigations Committee of the Court of Military Appeals. He is currently on the steering committee of the Individual Rights Section of the District of Columbia Bar.

SUSAN H. HEWMAN is a graduate of Smith College and Georgetown University Law Center. She was a Prettyman Fellow at Georgetown after she received her J.D., and was a staff attorney with the ACLU Military Rights Project and the National Military Discharge Review Project.

FREDRIC J. GROSS is a lawyer and anthropologist who specializes in subvertebrate bureaucracies. He has been concerned with military and veterans' law for many years.

Also in this Series

THE RIGHTS OF MENTAL PATIENTS	36574	$1.75
THE RIGHTS OF MILITARY PERSONNEL	33365	$1.50
THE RIGHTS OF YOUNG PEOPLE	31963	$1.50
THE RIGHTS OF ALIENS	31534	$1.50
THE RIGHTS OF STUDENTS	32045	$1.50
THE RIGHTS OF MENTALLY RETARDED PERSONS	31351	$1.50
THE RIGHTS OF CANDIDATES AND VOTERS	28159	$1.50
THE RIGHTS OF GAY PEOPLE	24976	$1.75
THE RIGHTS OF HOSPITAL PATIENTS	22459	$1.50
THE RIGHTS OF THE POOR	28001	$1.25
THE RIGHTS OF SUSPECTS	28043	$1.25
THE RIGHTS OF TEACHERS	25049	$1.50
THE RIGHTS OF WOMEN	27953	$1.75

Where better paperbacks are sold, or directly from the publisher. Include 25¢ per copy for mailing; allow three weeks for delivery.

Avon Books, Mail Order Dept., 250 West 55th Street, New York, N.Y. 10019

AN AMERICAN
CIVIL LIBERTIES
UNION HANDBOOK

THE RIGHTS OF VETERANS

THE BASIC ACLU GUIDE TO A VETERAN'S RIGHTS

David F. Addlestone
Susan Hewman
Fredric Gross

General Editors of this series:
Norman Dorsen, *Chairperson*
Aryeh Neier, *Executive Director*

 A DISCUS BOOK/PUBLISHED BY AVON BOOKS

*To those who through the folly
of many of our political leaders
did not survive to become veterans
and to Gussie Lee Davis, Jr.
who was driven to the brink by all of it.*

This book is a combination of the experiences the three of us have
faced over the past ten years. Probably our greatest inspiration,
and unfortunately practical experience, came from clients who
sought our help. What we learned from their suffering hopefully
will be put to good use to change the future. Jon Landau of
the CCCO in Philadelphia was responsible for the excellent
and thorough chapter on AWOL's.

THE RIGHTS OF VETERANS is an original publication of
Avon Books. This work has never before appeared in book form.

AVON BOOKS
A division of
The Hearst Corporation
959 Eighth Avenue
New York, New York 10019

First Avon Printing, April, 1978

AVON TRADEMARK REG. U.S. PAT. OFF. AND IN
OTHER COUNTRIES, MARCA REGISTRADA, HECHO EN
U.S.A.

Printed in the U.S.A.

Contents

Preface

This guide sets forth your rights under present law and offers suggestions on how you can protect your rights. It is one of a continuing series of handbooks published in cooperation with the American Civil Liberties Union.

The hope surrounding these publications is that Americans informed of their rights will be encouraged to exercise them. Through their exercise, rights are given life. If they are rarely used, they may be forgotten and violations may become routine.

This guide offers no assurances that your rights will be respected. The laws may change and, in some of the subjects covered in these pages, they change quite rapidly. An effort has been made to note those parts of the law where movement is taking place but it is not always possible to predict accurately when the law *will* change.

Even if the laws remain the same, interpretations of them by courts and administrative officials often vary. In a federal system such as ours, there is a built-in problem of the differences between state and federal law, not to speak of the confusion of the differences from state to state. In addition, there are wide variations in the ways in which particular courts and administrative officials will interpret the same law at any given moment.

If you encounter what you consider to be a specific abuse of your rights you should seek legal assistance. There are a number of agencies that may help you, among them ACLU affiliate offices, but bear in mind that the

ACLU is a limited-purpose organization. In many communities, there are federally funded legal service offices which provide assistance to poor persons who cannot afford the costs of legal representation. In general, the rights that the ACLU defends are freedom of inquiry and expression; due process of law; equal protection of the laws; and privacy. The authors in this series have discussed other rights in these books (even though they sometimes fall outside the ACLU's usual concern) in order to provide as much guidance as possible.

These books have been planned as guides for the people directly affected: therefore the question and answer format. In some of these areas there are more detailed works available for "experts." These guides seek to raise the largest issues and inform the non-specialist of the basic law on the subject. The authors of the books are themselves specialists who understand the need for information at "street level."

No attorney can be an expert in every part of the law. If you encounter a specific legal problem in an area discussed in one of these handbooks, show the book to your attorney. Of course, he will not be able to rely *exclusively* on the handbook to provide you with adequate representation. But if he hasn't had a great deal of experience in the specific area, the handbook can provide helpful suggestions on how to proceed.

> Norman Dorsen, Chairperson
> American Civil Liberties Union
>
> Aryeh Neier, Executive Director
> American Civil Liberties Union

The principal purpose of these handbooks is to inform individuals of their rights. The authors from time to time suggest what the law should be. When this is done, the views expressed are not necessarily those of the American Civil Liberties Union.

Introduction

This book is not intended to be an exhaustive list of all the rights and privileges that veterans have acquired through their status as former members of an armed force. Rather, it is a guide for those veterans who are experiencing difficulties with the Veterans Administration, who have less than fully honorable discharges, or who have entries in their military records that they wish to have changed. For example, Chapter III describes how a court-martial conviction, seemingly long since finalized, can still be appealed. Chapter VIII discusses employment discrimination, and Chapter IX discusses back-pay claims.

Cautious individuals should obtain a copy of their service records and be certain that they are satisfied with the information contained therein. Chapter IV provides such guidance.

Almost anyone who has come in contact with a government bureaucracy has experienced frustration. This is particularly true for Vietnam-era veterans who must deal with the Veterans Administration. Chapters X through XVII contain discussions of little-known rights that vets have when dealing with the VA. Specific VA regulations are discussed. Armed with this guide, you need no longer accept the word of a VA bureaucrat as final. Fight back if you feel you are right.

It may seem odd that Chapter I deals extensively with AWOL, but we feel that "self-retired veterans" should have their rights explained. Furthermore, the law of AWOL is relevant to many of the subsequent chapters.

While each chapter may not contain information with which every veteran is concerned, a sizable percentage of the 29 million veterans have had and will have problems with the VA, have bad discharges or codes on their discharge papers, have had court-martial convictions, or are or have been AWOL.

Some of the guidance provided in this book is subject to the changing law and regulations, and some advice is based on our best judgment. Many on the "legal" issues discussed are simplified; otherwise, this would have been a legal textbook and not a guide for lay persons. Appendix I lists many counseling organizations that can provide referrals for representation. The *Military Law Reporter* published by the Public Law Education Institute in Washington, D.C. also provides a complete description of the changing aspects of military and veterans' law.

This book reflects our feeling that a highly formalized federal criminal system such as the military justice system should be more than adequate—it should be a model. We also feel that the VA should no longer shut out outside counsel and lawyers (currently, there is a $10 limit on attorneys' fees) and that it should be subject to judicial review as are all other agencies.

David F. Addlestone
Susan H. Hewman
Frederic J. Gross

I

AWOL Military Personnel

Despite the passage of several years since the United States military left Vietnam, there remain thousands of Vietnam-era military AWOLs.[1] In addition, people continue to go AWOL in unprecedented numbers during peacetime.[2] Time works against long-term AWOLs. As the months pass and the AWOL period increases, the risk of severe punishment increases. Some AWOLs will elect to remain exiled, underground, or simply "back home," but some will eventually be arrested. Many others will decide to return voluntarily to face their AWOL charges. This chapter is intended to assist returning AWOLs so that they may have some control over their situation when and if they return to military control.

Are you an AWOL or a deserter?

One of the first steps you can take as an AWOL to improve your legal situation is to avoid thinking of yourself and referring to yourself as a "deserter." All people absent without leave for 30 days or more are classified for military administrative purposes as "deserters." However, legally a deserter is an AWOL who intended or intends never to return to the military. While a few unfortunate AWOLs have made desertion charges possible by writing letters to their commanding officers stating that they are leaving and never coming back, in general, desertion is rarely charged at court-martial and is extremely difficult to prove.

11

Since the maximum sentence for AWOL includes 1 year of confinement, and the maximum for desertion can include up to 5 years of confinement, it is important to avoid desertion charges if possible. While some Presidents and top military officials regularly and inaccurately refer to all long-term AWOLs as deserters, it is only when AWOLs have referred to themselves as deserters that this has been regarded as evidence of the crime of desertion.[3]

Even an AWOL period of many years is not *alone* sufficient evidence to support a desertion charge,[4] but several pieces of incriminating evidence taken together can lead to a desertion charge. Generally, you face a serious risk of desertion charges only if you have been gone for several years *and* you are arrested or are known to have become a resident of a foreign country or to have changed your identity.[5] To minimize the risk, hold on to military papers, ID, and uniforms if you have them; avoid being caught using an alias or a phony social security number; and let your family and friends know of your intention to return eventually. If you turn yourself in to state police, be sure someone knows you turned yourself in; frequently, state police list a voluntary returnee as an arrestee so they can collect the AWOL bounty.

Will the military dismiss AWOL charges against you while you are still AWOL?

There are all sorts of rumors about AWOLs receiving good discharges without having to return to the military, but the sad truth is that it almost never happens. The only two exceptions at present involve Army AWOLs who can prove that their enlistments were illegal[6] and nonlocatable Army AWOLs who were called to active duty from the Reserves and have been AWOL more than a year.[7] Undesirable discharges* are sometimes given to alien AWOLs who are known to be outside the United States[8] and to AWOLs convicted of civilian crimes who are in civilian confinement,[9] but in addition to the normal difficulties with undesirable discharges, aliens receiving these discharges can be

---

*The term "undesirable discharge" was recently changed to "other than honorable discharge" for enlisted people. For officers it has always been "under other than honorable conditions." We still use the term "undesirable" as it is the most familiar.

listed as undesirable aliens and thus effectively be permanently exiled from the United States. For the vast majority of AWOLs, the only way to clear up military charges is for them to return to the military, prepared to present their best case.

What about clemency or amnesty?

The "clemency" program begun by President Ford in 1974 is over. The only people who might still benefit from it are people who can prove that they applied for the program before April 1, 1975, and that their case was not properly processed. Even when the clemency program was around, it was not much of a deal for most AWOLs. It applied only to periods of AWOL that *began* between August 4, 1964, and March 28, 1973. For those who qualified, up to twenty-four months of low-paying alternative civilian services was required before a "clemency discharge" was granted. The clemency discharges replaced an undesirable discharge the AWOL received when s/he first entered the program, but the clemency discharge itself is no guarantee against employment discrimination, and does not automatically result in veterans' benefits (*see* Chapter X). It is, in effect, another name for an undesirable discharge. Most people who entered the program did not complete their alternative service as the obligation was unenforceable. However, those who received a clemency discharge may be eligible for a discharge upgrade under President Carter's program (*see* Chapter VII).

On April 5, 1977, the Pentagon announced a program somewhat similar to President Ford's earlier program. Absentees who went AWOL between August 4, 1964, and March 28, 1973, had six months to turn themselves in and receive other than honorable discharges which could later be upgraded (*see* Chapter VII). At this writing, the six-month period had not been extended. Excluded are those people who went AWOL from a combat zone or while on leave, TDY, or other authorized absence and did not return to their assignment in a combat zone. Failure to report for an initial assignment in or embarkation to a combat zone does not exclude an absentee from the program. Offenses other than absence offenses can still be prosecuted.

An absentee may inquire about his or her status if the program is extended by telephoning collect the appropriate military department numbers below:

US Army 317-542-3354
US Navy 202-694-2386
US Air Force 800-531-7500
US Marine Corps 202-694-2180
US Coast Guard 202-426-1317

How can you find out the best way to deal with the AWOL charges against you?
To begin with, never blindly follow the advice of a local recruiter or FBI agent. Even when they mean well, they rarely have reliable information on the treatment of AWOLs. There are experienced civilian counselors and lawyers located throughout the country who can advise you on the best way to return to military control. Counseling or a referral can be obtained by contacting one of the counseling groups listed in Appendix I. These groups can advise you the best base to return to, advise you as to roughly how much punishment to expect when you return, refer you to an experienced lawyer if necessary, and begin to prepare a case with you for your eventual return.

Can you begin to prepare for your return while still AWOL?
Now is the time to begin to prepare a case for your eventual return. Once you are back in the military, the process of obtaining documentation and support becomes much more difficult. Maintain a file of your military records. Whether or not you have a legal defense for your AWOL, there frequently are compelling reasons for an AWOL that can be documented.

You may have left the military because of extreme emotional or financial hardship involving your family, or because of medical difficulties inadequately treated by the military. Or maybe you left because your contract was broken and no one would listen, or because you became a conscientious objector, or because you were under strong psychological pressure. A counselor can help you to gather evidence, such as notarized letters from people aware of

14

your family problems, and letters from doctors or psychiatrists, and can help you to prepare a discharge application from the military.

It is best to obtain a copy of your military records to use in preparing for your return. The records may show that the military does not have evidence against you to prove AWOL (AWOL is sometimes technically hard to prove), or that you have a good defense that you did not realize. Counselors and lawyers can obtain a copy of your records with your power of attorney, by sending a request to one of the addresses listed at the end of this chapter.[10]

Where is the best place to return?

With base conditions changing continually, often the best advice counselors can give you is advice on where to return. In any case, surrendering to the local recruiting office, Reserve center, or FBI agent is a mistake. Typically, you will wind up deposited in a local jail, sometimes for several wasted weeks, until you are finally transported to a base where your case will be considered.

In the Air Force and the Marine Corps, the place of return is normally not important, since AWOLs are always returned to the area from which they left. However, even in these cases, you may have medical or psychological problems that justify return to a military hospital, or you may have a federal court case that could be brought closer to home. In the Army and Navy, if the AWOL period is more than 30 days, any base you return to with facilities for processing long-term AWOLs will process your case. If you choose a base on your own, you may choose one that will be much harder on you than some other base. Counselors will be aware of these differences in bases.

Will you be confined when you return?

The decision to keep an AWOL in pretrial confinement must be based on "probable cause" that a crime has been committed, and a decision that pretrial confinement is necessary to ensure his or her presence at trial.[11] Probable cause is not difficult to show in most AWOL cases; but where an AWOL has returned voluntarily, it is very hard to argue that confinement will be necessary to ensure his or her presence at trial.

15

As a result, many long-term AWOLs are not confined when they return. Those who are not confined are usually assigned to legal hold areas (Personnel Control Facilities in the Army). These are housing facilities for servicemembers facing legal charges, and you cannot be denied any of your rights simply because you are housed there. (*See* Chapter IX for a discussion of pay entitlement during this period.)

If a decision is made to confine you, this decision must be reviewed promptly by a magistrate.[12] If the magistrate agrees that you should be confined, you can appeal that decision or file an extraordinary writ in the Court of Military Appeals.[13] Your civilian attorney or assigned military attorney can assist with this.

Do you have a right to a lawyer?

You have a right to two lawyers. You are always entitled to be represented by a civilian lawyer (if you pay for it), and, in addition, the military must provide you with a military lawyer if you are facing a special or a general court-martial. No matter how much confidence you might have in your civilian laywer, you will almost always want to have a military lawyer as well. Since the military lawyer will be knowledgeable about local information, s/he should have experience that could prove an invaluable aid to your civilian lawyer.

If you cannot arrange to have a civilian lawyer, the choice of a good military lawyer becomes critical. According to military law, you are entitled to the military lawyer of your choice, and if this lawyer is "reasonably available," s/he must be provided to you. You might want to have a lawyer from some other base, particularly if you previously had a good one. If you are black, you might want to request a black lawyer. You can even request a lawyer from another service. There is no guarantee that the lawyer you request will be available, but there is no harm in making a written request.

Unfortunately, the right to military counsel of one's choice is far too often of no value since AWOLs do not generally know one military lawyer from the next. The right to counsel of your choice means you have a right to make a meaningful choice. If you are not confined, go to other courts-martial and watch the lawyers in action. Insist on speaking with a number of defense lawyers if you are not sure you are satisfied with the one assigned to you. Often civilian counselors will have the names of military lawyers who are known to be good.

Will the military insist on court-martialing you?

Many returning AWOLs are offered deals: the chance to confess guilt and take an administrative discharge rather than going to court-martial. This process (referred to as a "Chapter 10" in the Army) normally leads to an undesirable discharge about a month to two from the time you return. You can always apply for this discharge in lieu of any court-martial where the offense could lead to a bad conduct or dishonorable discharge. Whether or not the military will approve your request will depend primarily on (1) the branch of the military you are in, (2) the length of your AWOL, (3) your previous record in the military, and (4) the policy of the base to which you have returned. Since conditions change frequently, the best way to find out if and where you might be offered this deal is to check with one of the counselors listed in Appendix I.

Keep in mind, however, that this discharge in lieu of court-martial may not be your best deal. You may have a good defense at your court-martial. Maybe the charges against you are not too severe, and you can take your punishment and then apply for a good discharge. Once you receive an undesirable discharge in lieu of court-martial, the discharge will be very difficult to upgrade (*see* Chapter VI), so think carefully before you accept this discharge, which can amount to a life sentence.

Is it possible that you may have a defense to the AWOL charge against you?

Contrary to popular myth, there are a number of good defenses to the crime of AWOL. The military legal system is badly overburdened with large numbers of AWOL servicemembers returning daily, and as a result individual AWOL cases often fail to get the attention they deserve. Typically, the "lucky" long-term AWOLs sign waivers and are released with undesirable discharges, while the others plead guilty at courts-martial and are sentenced to time in prison and a bad discharge. Accepting an undesirable discharge or pleading guilty to AWOL may prove the best course in some situations, but these choices should only be resorted to after possible AWOL defenses have been carefully reviewed and determined not to apply to you. *Remember, the undesirable discharge is a serious, lifetime stigma.*

If applicable to your situation, the defenses listed below might lead to dismissal of the charges against you, and at least will put you in a better bargaining position in seeking an administrative discharge or a reduced sentence through plea bargaining.

1. *Lack of jurisdiction.* Even if you did leave the military without authorization, you can only be court-martialed and punished if you were legally a member of the military at the time you left.

If you were drafted, there is some chance that you were drafted improperly and cannot now be court-martialed.[14] You may also have a good defense if you were enlisted improperly. If, for example, you were too young when you enlisted,[15] or you were ordered by a judge to enlist or go to jail,[16] or you can prove that your recruiter acted illegally,[17] you may never have had a legally binding contract with the military, at least not to the extent that the military has jurisdiction over you. Recently, the Court of Military Appeals has been strictly interpreting recruiters' obligations, and all military attorneys are aware of these defenses. Since the military must pay witness fees and since many of these defenses involve calling witnesses from far away, the military may be more willing to discuss a "deal" if a defense of this nature is raised.

Similarly, a large percentage of Reservists who are activated into the active military are not properly activated, and this will serve as a defense to AWOL charges.[18] Proper activation requires that your Reserve unit have justification for considering you an unsatisfactory participant in the Reserves (usually missing too many meetings without excuse), be given notice of your unsatisfactory participation and your right to appeal, and that any appeal that you make be considered fairly.

2. *Improper denial of your discharge request.* Many people go AWOL for a long time because of pressing per-

sonal problems that often have been compounded when the military failed to provide requested help. Many of these problems would have resulted in discharges if proper counseling had been given on how to file a discharge application, but many requests for discharge were illegally denied, and still more GIs with serious problems were misled into believing that it would be impossible or futile to file a discharge request.[19] Each year, hundreds of people are discharged, upon their request, with honorable discharges for conscientious objection, hardship, or medical reasons.

If you are in this situation, you should consider carefully either raising this as a defense at court-martial or going directly to federal court and seeking a *habeas corpus* discharge on the grounds that the military illegally denied you a discharge.[20] The latter course may be the best, for military law does not currently permit failure to discharge for conscientious objection, hardship, or medical reasons as defense to a court-martial's jurisdiction. However, the Court of Military Appeals has recently begun to reconsider many of its past rulings. This is one area where it may reverse itself.

3. *Mistake of fact*. In order to find you guilty of AWOL, the military must show that you knew you were to be on duty at a specific place and time and yet you were not there. If at any time you had reason to be confused about or unaware of your time and place of duty, you might have a defense to your AWOL. While this might happen in any number of situations, in the past it has occurred most frequently in situations where GIs believed they were to wait home indefinitely for discharge papers or transfer orders that never came,[21] and where Reservists never received activation orders.[22] In the instance of the GIs, the "bad time" may have to be made up through assessment of lost time pursuant to 10 United States Code, Section 972.

4. *Constructive discharge*. When for a period of time a servicemember and the military act as if the servicemember has been discharged, a constructive discharge takes place,[23] and the servicemember cannot be charged with AWOL. One example of this would be where a servicemember was told s/he was discharged and should go

home, and then the military discovers some time later that s/he was never officially discharged.

5. *Physical incapacity.* Even if you know when and where you were supposed to be on duty, if you were physically incapable of getting to your place of duty you may have an AWOL defense. The most common example of this defense occurs when a servicemember is arrested and confined in a civilian jail but is never convicted of the civilian charge. If you were found guilty of the civilian charge, you might still have a defense if you gave the military notice of the civilian charges and the military did nothing to regain custody of you and just listed you as AWOL.

6. *Mental incapacity.* In order to be convicted of AWOL, you must have understood at the time of your AWOL that you were not where you were supposed to be, and you must be competent to stand trial. Legal insanity at the time of the AWOL is a defense; and, short of this, if it can be shown at the time of the AWOL that you were acting under an "irresistible impulse," this too will provide a defense.[24]

7. *Failure to pursue.* If the military knew your correct address throughout your AWOL and still allowed your AWOL to continue, with no effort made either to warn you of the seriousness of your crime or to arrest you, it is possible that you may not be held responsible for the full length of your AWOL.[25]

8. *AWOL reporting errors.* This is the most frequently used of all AWOL defenses. In order to prove AWOL, the military normally produces reports from the time you went AWOL and from the time you returned. Since these records most often represent the entire case against you, it is vital that they be procedurally correct. Occasionally, records of AWOLs will be lost and the military may have to drop the case. Often, the AWOL records will contain errors. For example, the records may list you as AWOL from the wrong duty station, or they may not be properly signed, or they may list you as AWOL for a time when you were actually there. These errors occurred frequently at overseas replacement stations.[26]

9. *Statute of limitations.* Except during "time of war," the statue of limitations is 2 years on AWOL and 3 years

on desertion. This means that charges must be brought against you, ("preferred") within 2 years for AWOL and within 3 years for desertion, or you cannot be found guilty of these crimes. The "time of war" exception has been ruled to apply to the Vietnam war,[27] and therefore Vietnam-era AWOLs commencing before January 27, 1973,[28] are not governed by the 2- and 3-year limitations. Keep in mind also that charges are usually brought while a person is still AWOL, so you cannot simply stay away 2 or 3 years and assume that you are safe.

10. *Constructive condonation.* If the military knows when you return that you have been AWOL and yet you are returned to duty without action on AWOL or desertion charges, the military has constructively condoned your AWOL or desertion, and you cannot later be court-martialed on these charges.[29]

11. *Speedy trial.* Denial of a speedy trial has become an important defense in all courts-martial. Following your return, if 90 days pass without court-martial and with continued confinement, the military must show extraordinary circumstances, or the charges will be dismissed for lack of a speedy trial.[30] Keep in mind, however, that the 90-day rule does not include time used up by defense delays, and that there is only a hard 90-day rule if you are confined (or perhaps if you are restricted). If you are not confined, you can still make a written request for a speedy trial when your case seems to be dragging and thus force the military to act promptly. If they do not act promptly, dismissal for denial of a speedy trial may still be a possibility.

If you have no defense, must you plead guilty and accept your punishment?

You may decide to plead guilty, but during the extenuation and mitigation portion of your court-martial, you should still attempt to show that you should not be punished severely. This is where the documentation explaining the difficulties that led to your AWOL may be most important, and also where you can present evidence of any particular hardship that imprisonment or a bad discharge would create for you and your family. But documentation is often not the most effective way of presenting your case.

Witnesses can be very important if they can present a

21

convincing story on your behalf. If you know of some people who might be effective witnesses for you, even if their sole contribution would be a description of you as a fine person who should not be punished severely, you should call them to the attention of your lawyer. The military has an obligation to call people with important testimony for you as witnesses and to pay for their expenses.[81]

How can you be certain that the military will comply with laws and regulations in handling your AWOL case?

Abuses of rights occur even more frequently for those returning from AWOL than for others in the military. Facilities for returning AWOLs tend to be understaffed and overcrowded. AWOL processors have an unfortunate tendency of treating returning AWOLs as if they have already been convicted and are serving sentences.

Having a civilian lawyer or counselor often leads to more careful processing of your case. However, regardless of whether you have counseling, there is a great deal that you can do to ensure that your rights are respected. Sometimes your representative from Congress will be helpful, particularly if you present a hardship case. Keep a record of the names of people you feel have mistreated you. If you make a request and it is denied, present your request in writing and keep a copy.

Finally, be prepared when important rights are denied to you to file an Article 138 Complaint. An Article 138 Complaint can be brought for all sorts of wrongs, for example, failure to pay you, illegal pretrial confinement, unsanitary housing conditions, failure to process a discharge claim, or failure to allow you to see a lawyer. The procedure for bringing an Article 138 Complaint is simple.

The complaint must be against an officer who has wronged you, and you must first explain the wrong to the officer in writing and give him or her a reasonable amount of time to right the wrong (normally 3 working days would be plenty of time). Also explain in writing that if s/he does not right the wrong, you will file an Article 138 Complaint. If the wrong is not righted, go ahead and submit the complaint; entitle it "Article 138 Complaint," and simply explain how the officer wronged you. Submit the complaint to his or her commanding officer and send a copy to your congressperson. Keep a copy for yourself also. All such complaints must be fully investigated, with a copy sent to the Secretary of your military branch, so at times just the threat of a complaint will get you the relief you seek. Unfortunately, this important right has been diluted by some Secretarys' delegating their authority to the Judge Advocates General and thereby leaving the final decision to military, not civilian, decision-makers.

What can you do if the local police or FBI think you are still AWOL even though you have been discharged?
The names of military personnel who have been AWOL more than 30 days are reported to the FBI. The FBI adds the names to the Wanted Person File of the National Crime Information Center (NCIC) to which most police have access. NCIC requires that the military keep its entries up to date. Every 4 months, the FBI furnishes the Department of Defense (DOD) with a listing of the records of wanted persons entered by DOD, in order that the accuracy of the file may be assured.

NCIC requires that a police department that receives a positive response from NCIC concerning a wanted person make an immediate follow-up with the military if the person is listed as a deserter. Likewise, the military has an obligation to reply promptly to the police department with confirmation of wanted status and with other pertinent details requested and to remove the wanted person's record from NCIC promptly following his or her identification and apprehension. Thus, if the military has not promptly notified the FBI of the resolution of an AWOL case, the FBI may still list the former GI as a deserter. This was a fairly frequent problem until recently when DOD promulgated procedures by which NCIC would be promptly notified of case results.[32]

It is clear, then, that the FBI and the military departments have a regulatory obligation to remove a nonwanted person's name from the Wanted Persons List. Negligent failure to do so that causes a false arrest can make the U.S. government liable for financial damages.[33] It would also seem that a police department that fails to follow up a NCIC listing with the military could also be liable.

If your name continues to appear on the Wanted List,

write the Director of the FBI, your congressperson, and the Deserter Information Point at the addresses given at the end of this chapter.[34]

NOTES

1. The Department of Defense (DOD) listed 4,560 AWOLS eligible for the Presidential Clemency Program as still AWOL after the program ended on April 1, 1975. The program records also show that the DOD had no listing on roughly 25% of the returning AWOLs.
2. There were 81,271 AWOL offenses in the first half of military fiscal year 1975. In the Marine Corps in 1975, there were 30 AWOL offenses for every 100 Marines.
3. *U.S.* v. *Clower*, 23 USCMA* 15, 48 CMR* 307 (1974).
4. *U.S.* v. *Cothern*, 8 USCMA 158, 23 CMR 382 (1957); *U.S.* v. *Simmons*, 42 CMR 543 (ACMR 1970).
5. Even in these situations, you may not have to worry about desertion charges at particular bases. Always check with a counselor to find out what your chances are.
6. Army Regulation 635-200, paragraph 5-31e.
7. Department of Army Message Changes 271400Z, May 1975, and 061952Z, June 1975.
8. DOD Directive 1332.14.
9. Army Regulation 635-200, Chapter 15, Section III; BUPERSMAN 3850220 (Navy).
10. Records of AWOL servicemembers can be obtained from:
    USADIP
    U.S. Army Enlisted Records Center
    Ft. Benjamin Harrison, IN 46249

    Commandant of the Marine Corps
    (Code MMO HQ) U.S. Marine Corps
    Washington, DC 20380

    Chief of Naval Personnel
    PERS 83

* "USCMA" refers to decisions of the U.S. Court of Military Appeals reported in volumes containing their decisions. "CMR" refers to cases of that court or lower military courts reported in *Court-Martial Reports*. After volume 23 USCMA and volume 50 CMR, military decisions began to be reported in the *Military Justice Reporter* ("M.J."). The *Military Law Reporter* ("MLR"), however, provides a more complete service as it does not confine itself to "published" military criminal cases.

Navy Department
Washington, DC 20370
ATTN: Deserter Section

Air Force Military Personnel
  Center/DPMAKE
Randolph Air Force Base
Texas 78148

Commandant of the Coast Guard (PE)
Washington, DC 20590

11. *Courtney* v. *Williams,* 24 USCMA 87, 51 CMR 260, —
    M.J.— (1976); *U.S.* v. *Heard,* 3 M.J. 14 (1977).
12. *Ibid.*
13. *Ibid. Fletcher* v. *Commanding Officer,* —M.J.— (February
    18, 1977).
14. *U.S. ex rel. Vacca* v. *Commanding Officer,* 446 F.2d 1079
    (2d Cir. 1971); *U.S. ex rel. Brown* v. *Resor* 429 F.2d
    1340 (10th Cir. 1970); *Talmage* v. *Froehlke,* 345 F. Supp.
    1361 (D.N.C. 1972).
15. *U.S.* v. *Graham,* 22 USCMA 75, 46 CMR 75 (1972).
16. *U.S.* v. *Catlow,* 23 USCMA 142, 48 CMR 758 (1974).
17. *U.S.* v. *Russo,* 23 USCMA 511, 50 CMR 650 (1975);
    U.S. v. *Barrett,* 23 USCMA 474, 50 CMR 493 (1975);
    U.S. v. *Little,* 24 USCMA 328, 52 CMR 39, —M.J.—
    (1976) (recruiter improperly assisted recruit with Armed
    Forces Qualification Test); 4 MLR 1026.
18. *U.S.* v. *Kilbreth,* 22 USCMA 390, 47 CMR 327 (1973).
19. *Epstein* v. *Commanding Officer,* 327 F. Supp. 1122 (E.D.
    Pa. 1971).
20. *Parisi* v. *Davidson,* 405 U.S. 34 (1972); *Baldwin* v. *Commanding Officer,* 368 F. Supp. 580 (E.D. Pa. 1973); *Vallecillo* v. *David,* 360 F. Supp. 896 (D.N.J. 1973). *But see*
    Apple v. *Greer,* 554 F. 2d 105 (3rd Cir. 1977).
21. *Forbes* v. *Laird,* 340 F. Supp. 193 (E.D. Wis. 1972); *U.S.*
    v. *Davis,* 22 USCMA 241, 46 CMR 241 (1973); *U.S.* v.
    Hale, 20 USCMA 150, 42 CMR 342 (1970).
22. *U.S.* v. *Moore,* 44 CMR 496 (ACMR 1971).
23. Department of Army Pamphlet 27-21, paragraph 3-57.
24. Jerry Kinchy, *CCCO Military Counselor's Manual*
    (1974), p. D1-16. A more liberal insanity rule was adopted
    on July 25, 1977, U.S. v. Frederick, 3 M.J. 230 (1977).
25. *U.S.* v. *Birckhead,* 45 CMR 832 (CGCMR 1972).
26. *U.S.* v. *Mahan,* 24 USCMA 109, 51 CMR 299, —M.J.—
    (1976). (Lack of record of accused at overseas replacement station does not prove he did not report. Actual record
    of AWOL is needed.)

27. *U.S.* v. *Anderson*, 17 USCMA 588, 38 CMR 386 (1968).
28. *U.S.* v. *Reyes*, 48 CMR 832 (ACMR 1974).
29. *Manual for Courts-Martial* (1969, Rev. Ed.), paragraph 68 (f).
30. *U.S.* v. *Marshall*, 22 USCMA 431, 47 CMR 409 (1973); *U.S.* v. *Burton*, 21 USCMA 112, 44 CMR 166 (1971).
31. *Manual for Courts-Martial* (1969, Rev. Ed.), paragraph 115. *U.S.* v. *Willis*, 3 M.J. 94 (1977).
32. DOD Directive 1325.2, paragraph V.C.3. Army Regulation 630-10 requires USADIP at Fort Benjamin Harrison to request the removal of a name from NCIC within 2 days after a request for records after return to military control.
33. 28 U.S. [U.S.C.] § 2680(h) (amended March 16, 1974) *Dupree* v. *Village of Hempstead*, 401 F. Supp. 1398 (E.D.N.Y. 1975).
34.   Air Force Military Personnel Center/DPMAKE
Randolph Air Force Base
Texas 78148
(512) 652-5774

U.S. Marine Corps
Headquarters (Code MPS-50)
Washington, DC 20380
(202) 694-2927

Bureau of Naval Personnel
PERS 38-R
Navy Department
Washington, DC 20370
ATTN: Deserter Section
(202) 694-1522

USADIP
U.S. Army Enlisted Records Center
Ft. Benjamin Harrison, IN 46249
(317) 542-2547

Commandant (G-015)
U.S. Coast Guard
Washington, DC 20590
(202) 426-1969

II

Jurisdiction by the Military
After Active Duty

Can you be court-martialed after you have left active duty?

Generally not. However, the Uniform Code of Military Justice (UCMJ), on its face, permits a court-martial to try persons who have left active duty and:

1. who fraudulently obtained their discharge (for the fraudulent discharge and offenses that occurred before that time);[1]
2. who cannot be tried by another state, federal, or territorial court and who committed an offense that is punishable by confinement of over 5 years[2] (this section of the UCMJ was declared unconstitutional by the Supreme Court in the case of *Toth* v. *Quarles*, 350 U.S. 11 (1955), and therefore is no longer usable by the military);
3. who are retired regulars who are entitled to pay;[3]
4. who are in the Fleet Reserve and Fleet Marine Corps Reserve;[4]
5. who are retired Reservists who are receiving hospitalization from an armed force;[5] or
6. who are Reservists on inactive duty training who voluntarily accept orders that specify that they are subject to the UCMJ.[6]

Court-martial jurisdiction has been exercised very sparingly in the case of retired people and is generally precluded by service policies[7] unless the offense has some military significance. The case of *O'Callahan* v. *Parker,* 395 U.S. 258 (1969), which limits court-martial jurisdiction to "service-connected" offenses would even more severely limit the offenses for which a court-martial would have jurisdiction over persons not on active duty. Thus, the possibility of a court-martial exercising jurisdiction over retired people is minimal.

The situation for those in the Reserves is a bit different. When you spend your 2 weeks a year on active duty, you are subject to court-martial jurisdiction for service-connected offenses committed during that time. However, you cannot be recalled to active duty for a court-martial unless the case was being processed properly before you were released.[8] You can also be court-martialed for conduct at weekend drills (1) during that drill session or (2) later, if the proper procedural steps are taken "with a view to trial" before the drill is over.[9] In the second case you can be tried at a subsequent drill session without steps being taken to try you at the first session.[10] The Army and Air Force limit such trials to cases involving the use of dangerous or expensive equipment.[11]

Standby Reservists or ready Reservists do not attend drills and would not be subject to court-martial jurisdiction.

It is not certain, however, that the current Court of Military Appeals (COMA) would permit the exercise of court-martial jurisdiction over retired personnel or Reservists. If you fall in one of these categories and are facing a court-martial, you should test the court-martial's jurisdiction by seeking an order from COMA barring your trial.

Can you be given a general or undesirable discharge for your actions while you are in the Reserves?

Yes. If you remain in the Reserves even if it is just to complete your obligation after active duty, the armed forces claim to have jurisdiction to issue bad administrative discharges. This usually occurs when a report of a civilian conviction reaches the Reserve unit responsible for your personnel file. (Note that the Privacy Act of 1974 may prohibit transfer of such information to your Reserve unit.)

If this occurs, you will be notified that unless you are in jail, you are entitled to be present at a hearing before a board of officers to submit statements or evidence in your own behalf, to retain civilian counsel, and to have military counsel (a lawyer, if one is reasonably available) appointed to represent you. You must bear all expenses, except that the military counsel is free. It is not clear what interest of the military is served by giving less than fully honorable discharges for civilian-related conduct to Reservists. Since it is clear that such procedures are on shaky legal grounds,[12] you should obtain the assistance of a civilian attorney who should challenge the authority of the military to give you a bad discharge. Strong inquiries from attorneys and congresspersons in such cases have in the past resulted in fully honorable discharges for Reservists.

What are the restrictions on your use of your uniform once you are a civilian?

Obviously, it's unlawful to impersonate military personnel in order to obtain benefits not due you.[13] It also is unlawful for *anyone* to wear "the uniform [of the armed forces of the U.S.] or a distinctive part thereof or anything similar to a distinctive part of the uniform" without authority within the jurisdiction of the United States or Canal Zone. The penalty is 6 months of confinement and/or a fine of $250.[14] The constitutionality of this section has been upheld.[15] Convictions have been upheld even when a person believed it was lawful to wear his old uniform.[16] The statute literally prohibits the wearing of old fatigues if the original military buttons are still on them.[17]

Sometimes that statute must be read together with others[18] that prohibit the wearing of the uniform or a "distinctive part thereof" except:

1. by National Guard members as permitted by the Guard;
2. by retired *officers* wearing the uniform of their retired grade;
3. by a person who served honorably in time of war in accordance with regulations prescribed by the President;
4. by a person with an honorable or general discharge

on his or her way from the place of discharge to home (within 3 months);

5. by a person portraying a member of the military in a theatrical or motion picture production (the phrase "if the portrayal does not tend to discredit that armed force" was eliminated by the Supreme Court,[19] but still appears by inference in *Once a Veteran*, the DOD publication given to separating service members);

6. by a resident of a VA home as prescribed by regulations; and

7. by a person attending a course of military instruction conducted by an armed force.

Persons with honorable or general discharges who are members of a "military society" and certain ROTC instructors may wear a uniform, in accordance with Secretarial regulations, if they wear insignia distinguishing the uniform from a military uniform.

Federal regulations[20] permit former members of the armed forces, who served honorably during a declared or undeclared war if their last period of service was terminated under honorable conditions, to wear the uniform in the highest grade held during such war service only on the following occasions (unless the above-described statutes permit otherwise) and during travel to and from:

1. military funerals, memorial services, weddings, and inaugurals;

2. parades on national or state holidays, or other parades or ceremonies of a patriotic character in which any active or Reserve U.S. military unit is taking part.

Medal of Honor winners may wear the uniform at any time, with some exceptions.

Some of the conditions and restrictions on the wearing of a uniform appear to be unduly restrictive and offensive to the notion of freedom of expression. However, it is unlikely that the current Supreme Court would hold any of them unconstitutional.

NOTES

1. 10 U.S.C. § 803(b).*
2. 10 U.S.C. § 803(a).
3. 10 U.S.C. § 802(4), *U.S.* v. *Hooper*, 9 USCMA 637, 26 CMR 417 (1958).
4. 10 U.S.C. § 802(6).
5. 10 U.S.C. § 802(5).
6. 10 U.S.C. § 802(3).
7. *Air Force Manual* 111–1, paragraph 2-6; *Manual of the Judge Advocate General of the Navy*, paragraph 0107d(1) (a); *U.S.* v. *Bowie*, 34 CMR 808 (AFBR 1964).
8. *Manual for Courts-Martial* (1969, Rev. Ed.), paragraph 11d.
9. *Ibid.*
10. *U.S.* v. *Schuering*, 16 USCMA 324, 36 CMR 480 (1966).
11. Opinion of Judge Advocate General of the Army 1967/4322 and Opinion of the Judge Advocate General of the Air Force 1953/9, 2 Dig. Ops. 163 (1953).
12. *Harmon* v. *Brucker*, 355 U.S. 579 (1958), and *Stapp* v. *Resor*, 314 F. Supp. 475 (S.D.N.Y. 1970). A class action suit, *Wood* v. *Secretary*, civil action No. 77-0684 (D.D.C.), challenging these discharges is currently in litigation.
13. 18 U.S.C. § 912.
14. 18 U.S.C. § 702. Members on active duty are governed by DOD regulation, 32 C.F.R. 53.2(a).
15. *Schacht* v. *U.S.*, 398 U.S. 58 (1970).
16. *Gaston* v. *U.S.*, 143 F.2d 10, *cert. den.* 322 U.S. 764 (1944).
17. *U.S.* v. *Krahower*, 86 F.2d 111 (2nd Cir. 1936).
18. 10 U.S.C. § 771 ,771a, 772, and 773.
19. *Schacht* v. *U.S.*, 398 U.S. 58 (1970).
20. 32 C.F.R. § 53.2(b).*

---

* "U.S.C." refers to the United States Code. "C.F.R." refers to the Code of Federal Regulations. Both can be found in most law libraries and often in public libraries.

III

Consequences and Appeal of Court-Martial Convictions After Release from Active Duty

Courts-martial currently make up approximately one-third of all federal prosecutions. During the Vietnam war, they made up an even higher percentage, and during World War II, one out of every eight GIs was court-martialed. It is safe to estimate that since 1940 there have been over 3 million convictions at courts-martial. Many veterans are unaware of the effect of these convictions and what can be done to overturn them or to reduce the adverse effects caused by a court-martial conviction.

This chapter cannot go into great detail about all of the possible errors that could occur at a court-martial for that would require volumes. The aim of this chapter is to alert a veteran who has been convicted at a court-martial to possible legal consequences of the conviction and to what, if anything, can be done about it. Chapter X deals with the effect that a punitive discharge awarded by a court-martial can have on veterans' benefits; Chapter VI deals with the procedures for seeking a change in the nature of a punitive discharge without an actual appeal of the conviction; and Chapter VIII deals with employment discrimination based on bad discharges or court-martial convictions.

What effect does a court-martial conviction have on a veteran once s/he becomes a civilian?

A court-martial conviction may have varied effects, ranging from those strictly legal to those resulting from the attitudes of the community toward one who has been convicted of a crime. A court-martial conviction is a federal criminal conviction because courts-martial are criminal prosecutions brought on behalf of the United States. However, a court-martial conviction is not generally viewed with the same disfavor as would be a civilian court conviction. One reason may be that most people know that a court-martial may involve a wide variety of offenses, many of which are as petty as being late to work. However, almost any offense can be tried by any one of three types of courts-martial. Clearly, anything tried at a summary court-martial is a minor offense.[1] A special court-martial, which can give up to 6 months confinement and a bad conduct discharge, would be viewed as more serious, and a general court-martial would be viewed as the most serious.

It is important to know which court-martial convictions are equal to felony convictions, which often create civil disabilities such as the loss of the right to vote, hold office, or obtain certain professional licenses. There is very little law on the books that allows a definite answer as to whether a particular court-martial conviction is a felony conviction. Many factors such as the nature of the offense, the type of court-martial involved, the maximum potential sentence, the actual sentence, or the potential sentence for an equivalent state or federal offense must be taken into consideration. Also, each state has its own method for determining what constitutes a felony conviction. As a rule of thumb, it can be said that a court-martial conviction is likely to be considered a felony conviction if a general court-martial awarded a dishonorable discharge or if the offense was a serious civilian-type offense (for example, robbery or grand larceny) and was tried by a general court-martial. It is a very good possibility that convictions for serious civilian-type offenses tried by a general or special court-martial that result in a bad conduct discharge will be considered to have been felony convictions. It is also possible that any conviction resulting in confinement for more than 1 year, or any offense for which the punishment under state law could have exceeded 1 year, will be considered to be a felony conviction. A strong argument can be made, however, that any conviction for a purely military offense (for example, AWOL or disrespect to an NCO) should never be considered to be a felony. These general rules would probably also apply if a veteran were being sentenced by a civilian court and the judge were deciding whether to consider the court-martial conviction as a prior conviction that would warrant imposing a stiffer sentence.

A court-martial conviction may jeopardize a veteran's right to obtain licenses for certain occupations, to take advantage of government employment opportunities, to be bonded, etc. According to a recent survey,[2] few state licensing boards, employers, universities, and unions would automatically reject an applicant because s/he had received a punitive discharge from a court-martial. The real concern is with the type of crime for which the former servicemember was convicted.[3] Thus, while a positive response may be required to the question "Have you ever been convicted of a crime?" it would be wise to include an explanation if it was for a court-martial, particularly if it was for a military offense. For example, questions on Civil Service Commission application forms ask if you were ever convicted by a *general* court-martial.

Does a dishonorable discharge awarded by a general court-martial carry any specific disabilities?

Federal law prohibits the receipt, *possession*, or transportation of *any* firearms by any person who has been discharged from military service under dishonorable conditions if the transaction is even remotely connected to interstate commerce. The maximum penalties are $10,000 or 2 years imprisonment, or both.[4] Presumably this statute refers only to a dishonorable discharge resulting from a conviction by a general court-martial; however, the phrase "dishonorable conditions" may include discharges under other circumstances.[5]

The Emergency Employment Act provides funds for local governmental units to hire Vietnam-era veterans on a preferential basis unless they have dishonorable discharges.[6]

A dishonorable discharge automatically excludes the veteran who holds one from veterans' benefits, with a few minor exceptions (*see* Chapter X).

Are court-martial convictions, military arrests, and other purely military matters reported to the FBI?

Generally, they are not. When they are, they would be included in the National Crime Information Center's Computerized Criminal History (CCH) as are some *arrests* for AWOL made by civilian authorities. Since it is sometimes virtually impossible to trace the ever-changng administrative practices of each service back more than 10 to 15 years, what follows is a generalized statement of the reporting practices of each service. If you have some doubt about what might have been reported to the FBI about you, you should request to see your FBI file, particularly the CCH ("rap sheet") file, under the Freedom of Information Act.[7] If the information is inaccurate, you can request a change in your file, or its destruction, under the Privacy Act.[8]

Navy and Marine Corps. It has never been their practice to volunteer to the FBI any information concerning arrests, court-martial convictions, or less than fully honorable discharges.[9]

Air Force. Since 1968, and probably since 1953, the Air Force has not reported arrests to the FBI (unless the FBI was called into the case), and has reported only those convictions where the servicemember was still in jail when the final approved sentence (after all appeals) included a bad conduct or dishonorable discharge.[10] Since 1965, no report of bad discharges, except those mentioned above, has been made to the FBI. Practice prior to that time is unknown. It is possible that reports were made to the FBI in special cases or upon request of the FBI.[11]

Army. It has never been Army practice to report *arrests* to the FBI except in unusual cases.[12] Information about less than honorable discharges has never been routinely sent to the FBI. Some undesirable discharges for "the good of the service" given after a court-martial conviction for an offense that would be reported to the FBI (discussed below) have been reported to the FBI since November 1972.[13]

The Army's practice of reporting court-martial convictions to the FBI has changed drastically over the years. The procedure has been as follows:

1. The Army policy of submitting fingerprint cards to the FBI was first started in Change 2, SR 210-188-1, *Installations-Guardhouses, Stockades, and Hospital Prison Wards*, dated September 16, 1952. Paragraph 9c(5) of that regulation provided as follows:

A sentenced [after all appeals] prisoner whose sentence includes a bad conduct [and presumably dishonorable] discharge, suspended or executed, will be fingerprinted on the Federal Bureau of Investigation, United States Department of Justice, arrest fingerprint card [and forwarded to the FBI].

This procedure remained substantially the same until November 1972.

2. DA Message 221315Z, November 1972, later superseded by AR 190-4 and AR 190-47, has permitted an extremely liberal reporting of convictions. It, with some modifications to make it more readable, is as follows (note that minor changes in the procedure have been left out; while it is still confusing, it clearly permits the reporting of many convictions):

a. On receipt of a final judicially approved sentence that meets any of the three criteria set forth below, action will be taken to report a prisoner's offense(s) and sentence for entry on FBI records:

(1) Civil-type offense criteria. The offense is punishable by confinement for 1 year or more under the Table of Maximum Punishments, *Manual for Courts-Martial* (MCM), and the final judicially approved sentence by any military court includes confinement.

(2) Military offense criteria. The offense is punishable by confinement for 1 year or more and a punitive discharge under the Table of Maximum Punishments, MCM, and the final judicially approved sentence by a general court-martial includes confinement or a punitive discharge.

(3) Multiple charges/specifications criteria. The fi-

nal judicially approved sentence includes confinement for 1 year or more regardless of the nature of the offense(s).

b. As an exception and in addition to part a, above, the following offense(s) will also be reported to the FBI:

(1) Felony offenses punishable by confinement for more than 1 year under the Table of Maximum Punishments, MCM, which are not prosecuted due to lack of jurisdiction, mental competency, or for other reasons not indicative of a finding of lack of criminal responsibility.

(2) Offenders who otherwise meet the criterion of part a (1), (2), or (3), above, but who are separated or placed on excess leave without pay pending a completion of appellate review.

(3) Offenders who otherwise meet the criterion of part a (1), (2), (3), above, but who are separated for the good of the service (an administrative discharge) subsequent to the sentence of a court-martial that includes confinement and/or a punitive discharge and prior to completion of appellate review.

(4) Offenders whose offense(s) meet the criteria set forth in part a (1), (2), or (3), above, and whose sentence to confinement expires prior to completion of appellate review and affirmation of sentence. In such cases, the words "pending appellate process" will be entered in the final disposition section of the FBI form. On receipt of final appellate process and affirmation of sentence, final disposition data will be forwarded to the FBI.

How can a veteran obtain a copy of the record of trial of his or her court-martial?

Every accused military person is entitled to a free transcript (record of trial) of his or her court-martial. The record is almost always given to the accused immediately after the local commander (convening authority) acts on the findings and sentence. However, there is rarely any transcript made at a summary court-martial (one-officer court), and the only documents available are a copy of the formal-charge sheets and sometimes witness statements. Special and general courts-martial not resulting in a discharge or a sentence to confinement of over 6 months often result in only a summarized record of trial. Other courts-martial records and most Air Force courts-martial records are verbatim. If you have lost your record of your trial, you may obtain information about how to obtain another copy (you will have to pay for it unless it can be called up for you to read and not copy) by writing the following offices and supplying your name (at the time of the trial), service number, type of court-martial, date and place of the court-martial, and the sentence adjudged:

Army	Clerk, Army Court of Military Review U.S. Army Judiciary Nassif Building 5611 Columbia Pike Falls Church, VA 22041
Navy and Marines	Clerk, Navy Court of Military Review Navy Appellate Review Activity Washington Navy Yard, Building 200 Washington, DC 20390
Air Force	Clerk, Air Force Court of Military Review Forrestal Building Washington, DC 20314
Coast Guard	Commandant U.S. Coast Guard (G-LMJ) Washington, DC 20590

These offices have access to the ever-changing regulations dealing with retention and storage of records of trial. It should be noted that many records of trial are not kept for more than 10 years.

How can a conviction by court-martial be "appealed" once the servicemember is discharged?

Strictly speaking, once a person is discharged, there is no appeal in the sense of a direct appeal from a conviction. There are, however, several steps that can be taken that might produce the same results. Obviously, this book cannot be as detailed as a textbook for lawyers, so you should, if possible, consult an attorney experienced with military law. Many of the groups listed in Appendix I can make such referrals as can bar-association referral services. For example, the District of Columbia Bar, which has many members specializing in military law, has a lawyer referral service and a bar directory where lawyers list their specialties.

1. *Article 69 appeals.* In 1968, Congress amended the Uniform Code of Military Justice. Among other liberalizing changes, a procedure was instituted for the first time by which people with summary and special court-martial convictions (not resulting in a bad conduct discharge) could appeal those convictions.[14] These are cases that were never reviewed by a Court of Military Review (or Board of Review, before 1969). Now, any such court-martial (even one from World War I) can be appealed to the Judge Advocate General of the appropriate service.

Appeals may be based on "newly discovered evidence, fraud on the court, lack of jurisdiction over the accused or the offense, or error prejudicial to the substantial rights of the accused." The last category is the most important and covers just about any issue the former accused wishes to raise.

There is no time limit on Article 69 appeals; therefore, a person can file an Article 69 appeal no matter when the conviction occurred. The procedures for Article 69 appeals are set forth in Appendix II. The procedures are simple, and if some of the required information is unknown, this should be stated. It should be noted that the person appealing must sign the appeal before a notary public except in the case of the Air Force, where the applicant's lawyer may sign the appeal under oath. Army applications can, but need not, be made on Department of Army Form 3499.

The applications should be sent to:

Army	The Judge Advocate General Department of the Army ATTN: Examination and New Trials Division U.S. Army Judiciary Nassif Building Falls Church, VA 22041
Navy and Marines	The Judge Advocate General Department of the Navy Washington Navy Yard, Washington, DC 20374
Air Force	The Judge Advocate General Hq. USAF/JAG Forrestal Building Washington, DC 20314
Coast Guard	Commandant U.S. Coast Guard (G-LMJ) Washington, DC 20590

2. *The Boards for Correction of Military or Naval Records (BCMR).* Applications to these Boards are discussed in more detail in Chapters VI and VII.

Sometimes it will be appropriate to ask the BCMR to act on a court-martial conviction. While it is not clear if all the BCMRs have *authority* to expunge a conviction (the Air Force BCMR feels it has such authority), they can act on the sentence. This applies to all court-martial cases. Thus, even if the particular BCMR does not "reverse" or expunge a conviction, it can grant relief as to the sentence if it feels it would be "unjust" not to do so. Such relief (other than discharge upgrading) by a BCMR is rare and, in general, the Article 69 appeal would be the preferred route if the case is within the jurisdictional limits of Article 69.

3. *Extraordinary relief from the Court of Military Review or Court of Military Appeals (COMA).* Recently, COMA has been willing to hear more cases than it had in the past. In particular, it has begun to entertain more cases by way of a procedure called writ of error *coram nobis.* This means that COMA will sometimes rehear cases that

have been before it in the past or that it has, in the past, refused to hear. This is particularly true when a jurisdictional error is later discovered;[15] the law has changed in favor of the accused;[16] or the court earlier "misperceived or improperly assessed a material fact."[17] Late in 1976, COMA held in a wide-ranging opinion, *McPhail* v. *U.S.*,[18] that it has jurisdiction to hear an "appeal" from *any* court-martial by way of a writ of error *coram nobis* even though its normal appellate jurisdiction is limited (with a few exceptions) to cases in which the sentence included a bad conduct or dishonorable discharge and/or confinement for over a year. In the *McPhail* case, COMA ordered the Judge Advocate General of the Air Force to vacate Sergeant McPhail's conviction and restore all of his "rights, privileges and property affected by the execution of the sentence imposed by the court-martial" that convicted him. (The order was never actually issued; for in an effort to moot the effect of the opinion, the Judge Advocate General of the Air Force granted relief to Sergeant McPhail before the mandate of COMA was issued.) It is too early to tell how far COMA is willing to go in hearing such cases, but the language of the opinion indicates that where a military accused's constitutional or statutory rights under the Uniform Code of Military Justice were violated and relief could not be had anywhere else (for example, if the Judge Advocate General refused to grant relief under Article 69), COMA can and will grant relief. Attorneys experienced in military law are closely watching COMA to see how *McPhail* will be interpreted. If it is interpreted broadly, the recent concern COMA has shown for rights of the accused (ironically unlike the Burger Supreme Court) may benefit many of those who in the past suffered from convictions sanctioned by a court less inclined to be concerned with the rights of individuals. Perhaps the Judge Advocates General will also heed the warning and follow strictly the decisions of COMA when acting on Article 69 appeals.

4. *The federal courts.* Convictions by a court-martial can be reviewed by the federal district courts and the Court of Claims. However, normally only constitutional errors will be reviewed.[19] Also, the Burger Supreme Court has shown that it will generally defer to the judgment of

the military in almost all cases[20] (which usually equals exactly what the government argues but not necessarily proves in court). The lower federal courts have shown an inclination to fall in line (COMA need only follow the Supreme Court and not the lower federal courts). Such litigation in the federal courts is also expensive and takes a long time. Before any such suit is instituted, the means of relief discussed above should be explored.

What type of errors in a court-martial might be grounds for an appeal?

This question would take volumes to answer in full; however, some general guidance can be provided. Normally, the fact that someone feels s/he is innocent, that a witness lied, or that other people were not tried for similar offenses are not grounds for appeal. Innocent (or the "least guilty") people can be and are convicted, and sometimes the error is never overturned. Also, except as noted below, a plea of guilty is hard to undo on appeal. The following list is by no means all-inclusive, but it points out some common errors that can occur. Most of the cases discussed apply retroactively, that is, to all convictions that occurred before the case in question was decided. Where retroactivity is not mentioned, it means that that particular issue is still an open legal question.

1. *Jurisdictional errors.* Since the whole court-martial system was created by statute (the UCMJ), courts-martial are unlike most other federal courts, which are "constitutional courts." One consequence of this is that if the statutory procedures are not followed, the court-martial is normally without jurisdiction to try the accused. In other words, if the statute requires X numbers of things to occur and X minus one things occur, the court-martial is without power to act in the case. Legal prejudice usually need not be shown as the omission itself is considered to be automatically fatal to the court-martial's jurisdiction. Jurisdictional errors are almost always retroactive. A discussion of some of the more obvious jurisdictional errors follows.

Since August 1, 1969, an accused could request trial by military judge alone in special and general courts. COMA has held that this request must be in *writing—U.S.* v.

Dean, 40 USCMA 212, 43 CMR 52 (1970). Sometimes there is a written request, but the name of the judge is left blank at the time the accused signs the request. This is an error—*U.S.* v. *Brown*, 21 USCMA 516, 45 CMR 290 (1972). Sometimes judges are changed after the request. This is an error unless a new written request is executed—*U.S.* v. *Rountree*, 21 USCMA 62, 44 CMR 116 (1971). The written request must be submitted before assembly of the court—*U.S.* v. *Nix*, 21 USCMA 76, 44 CMR 130 (1971), and *U.S.* v. *Fife*, 20 USCMA 218, 43 CMR 58 (1970). *Dean* has been held to be fully retroactive to August 1, 1969—*Belichesky* v. *Bowman*, 21 USCMA 146, 44 CMR 200 (1972).

If the accused requested enlisted members, they must have made up at least one-third of the court after challenges, and the request must have been in *writing*—*U.S.* v. *White*, 21 USCMA 583, 45 CMR 357 (1972). This was held retroactive in *U.S.* v. *Gallagher*, 22 USCMA 191, 46 CMR 191 (1973). Refusal to allow an accused to withdraw a request for enlisted members before the pretrial session ends in an error—*U.S.* v. *Stipe*, 23 USCMA 11, 48 CMR 267 (1974).

Other possible errors that may result in a conviction being overturned are: lack of qualified lawyer-counsel at a general court-martial, a general court-martial with less than five members at any time during the trial, a special court-martial with less than three members at any time, a summarized record so inadequate that it was incapable of being reviewed meaningfully, failure to swear in the law officer (military judge) or court members in each others' presence; and a nonverbatim transcript (this would apply to bad conduct and dishonorable discharge cases only and also includes cases where part of the transcript had to be reconstructed due to the loss of the reporter's notes or tapes)—*U.S.* v. *Boxdale*, 22 USCMA 414, 47 CMR 351 (1973).

If the accused was 16 or 17 at the time of trial, with no parental consent to enlist, there is no jurisdiction. There are other variations of this problem.

National Guard or Reservist call-ups that are improper render any subsequent court-martial without jurisdiction —*U.S.* v. *Kilbreth*, 22 USCMA 390, 47 CMR 327 (1973).

The same is true with improper inductions or enlistments. *See* Chapter I for a discussion of this and similar issues in the context of defenses to AWOL. They apply equally to other cases.

COMA has held in effect that hundreds of Navy and Marine special courts-martial convening authorities had improperly delegated authority to convene special courts-martial.[21] (The improper designation began in June 1961 and ceased on or about May 29, 1970.) Since these officers did not have the lawful power to convene these special courts-martial, all such courts convened by them were unlawful. If you have a conviction that occurred on a small ship or in a small Navy detachment or Marine advisory group, your conviction may have been unlawful. Many counselors have a list of these commands (which are too numerous to set out in this book), but you will probably need an experienced lawyer to assist you with an appeal.

2. *Non-service-connected cases.* In *O'Callahan* v. *Parker*, 395 U.S. 258 (1969), the Supreme Court held that for there to be court-martial jurisdiction the offense must be "service-connected." Non-service-connected offenses usually mean off-base, off-duty, out-of-uniform, and within the United States. The military courts had found "service connection" in all drug-related offenses except smuggling until September 24, 1976. On the date COMA decided that its past cases in the area of drugs and service connection were based on an improper analysis of *O'Callahan*, and that the specific facts in each case had to be analyzed to see if military jurisdiction was proper.[22] While it is too early to tell what this case means, it is clear that off-base incidents involving small amounts of drugs cannot normally be tried by a court-martial. Whether cases that occurred after the *O'Callahan* decision (June 2, 1969) but before September 24, 1976, can benefit from the new rule remains to be seen.

Another recent change in the law occurred in *U.S.* v. *Hedlund*, 25 USCMA 1, 54 CMR 1,—N.J.—(1976). Before that time the courts had decided that if another service-person was the victim of a crime, "service connection" was almost automatic. In *Hedlund*, COMA rejected that idea for a rule similar to that used in the drug cases. Again, it is too early to tell if this means that old convictions can be reversed.

O'Callahan affects cases where convictions were not final [appeal over] on June 2, 1969. While the Supreme Court did not actually hold *O'Callahan* nonretroactive to before that date, as COMA has, that is the practical effect of the decision in *Gosa* v. *Mayden*, 413 U.S. 665 (1973). Thus, at the present time, nothing can be done about *O'Callahan* errors that occurred when the conviction was final before June 2, 1969.

3. *Speedy trial.* If an accused was held in pretrial confinement (or perhaps on restriction) for over 90 days because of government inaction and the offense occurred *after* December 17, 1971, the charges should have been dismissed for lack of a speedy trial. *U.S.* v. *Burton*, 21 USCMA 112, 44 CMR 166 (1971). Defense-requested delays are subtracted from the total time to see if 90 days of confinement were caused by the government.

4. *Search and seizure.* The law of search and seizure fills volumes; however, this section will alert you to the issue. Searches in the military, as in civilian life, must be "reasonable," which normally means incident to arrest or as a result of a search warrant based on "probable cause." In addition, contraband found during the course of a legitimate "health and welfare inspection" can be seized and used at trial. On October 8, 1976, COMA ruled that "shakedown inspections" for drugs were unconstitutional searches and the evidence seized could not be used at a court-martial. This effectively "reversed" a District of Columbia Circuit Court case that upheld such a program of "inspections" in the Army in Germany.

Actual search warrants are usually not used in the military, as the GI's commanding officer usually has the power to authorize or conduct a search. If a search is not "reasonable" or is improperly authorized, the evidence seized cannot be used at trial. If this issue was raised at trial and rejected, there would be no harm in raising it by way of an Article 69 appeal if the case falls within the jurisdiction of Article 69. If the issue was not raised at trial, it is normally waived and cannot be raised successfully on appeal.

5. *Confessions.* Like search and seizure, this topic could fill a book. Suffice it to say that involuntary confessions or

statements cannot be admitted at trial; most statements obtained without the required *Miranda* warnings (right to remain silent, to counsel, and to free counsel if one cannot afford to retain counsel, and to be informed that anything said can be used at trial) have not been admissible at trials since June 16, 1966; and Article 31, UCMJ, must be read to any GI suspected of an offense before a statement by the GI can be used at trial. Such issues, like search and seizure, are worth raising on appeal, particularly if they were raised at the trial.

6. *Improvident guilty pleas.* Military law has a very strict rule about guilty pleas. If the accused at any time during the trial, including the sentencing portion, sets up any matter that would be a defense, the plea should be withdrawn as "improvident." An example is a guilty plea to ·assault, but during the sentencing portion the accused said, "He was coming at me with a knife." This clearly sets up the defense of self-defense. In order to be complete this section would have to cover the elements of and defenses to all crimes under the UCMJ, which is, of course, beyond the scope of this book. Thus, you should be aware that if a plea appears to be inconsistent with the facts in the record of trial, an appeal should be taken.[23]

7. *Pretrial agreements or negotiated guilty pleas.* In an extremely important case, *U.S.* v. *Holland*, 23 USCMA 442, 50 CMR 461 (1975), COMA held that certain pretrial agreements (written deals to plead guilty in exchange for a set maximum sentence) that had long been in use were in violation of public policy. These were agreements where the accused had agreed to enter the plea of guilty "prior to presentation of any evidence on the merits and/or presentation of motions going to matters other than jurisdiction." In other words, such an agreement effectively forced an accused to waive any pretrial motions that might have resulted in a dismissal of the charges. This case has been held to be retroactive—*U.S.* v. *Schmeltz*, 24 USCMA 93, 51 CMR 266,—N.J.—(1976). So if you entered into a similar pretrial agreement, your guilty plea should be invalidated.

8. *Convictions for violations of regulations.* If you were convicted of a violation of local or command regulations, several possible issues may be raised. Some regulations

have been held to be nonpunitive, that is, criminal sanctions were not contemplated if the regulations were violated. Some regulations are not self-implementing, that is, something must be done by lower commanders before the regulations are in effect. Also, some regulations have been found not to operate as "general" regulations as alleged.[24]

9. *Urinalysis.* An order to give a urine sample as part of a drug-detection program is an illegal order if a bad discharge could result from a "positive" sample—*U.S.* v. *Ruiz,* 23 USCMA 181, 48 CMR 797 (1974). Such a discharge could have resulted from an involuntarily supplied urine sample required as part of the "drug-exemption program" prior to January 1975. Thus, any conviction for a refusal to provide such a urine sample prior to January 1975 would be illegal.

How can someone receive a presidential pardon from a court-martial conviction?

Presidential pardons (unrelated to the Ford Vietnam-era Clemency Program) are possible with respect to court-martial convictions. Petitions for Executive Clemency are governed by 28 C.F.R. §§ 1.1 through 1.9. Information and instructions, plus the necessary forms—Petition, Personal Oath, and Character Affidavit form—may be obtained from the Pardon Attorney, Department of Justice, Washington, DC 20530. Petitions regarding courts-martial are to be directed to the service concerned rather than to the Attorney General, although the Department of Justice (DOJ) forms, with appropriate modifications, may be used. There is a 3-year waiting period after release from confinement (or date of conviction, if no confinement) before such a petition may be submitted. Persons familiar with such applications have noted that a good post-service record is extremely important.

Applications should be sent (certified mail is suggested) in envelopes clearly marked "Executive Clemency Petition" to:

Army   Commander, USARCPAC
                           9700 Page Boulevard
                           St. Louis, MO 63132

Air Force	HQ USAF/JAJR Washington, DC 20314
Navy and Marines	Secretary of the Navy Navy Department Washington, DC 20350
Coast Guard	Commandant (G-P/62) U.S. Coast Guard Washington, DC 20590

What good is such a pardon?

A pardon does not expunge an offense, but it removes all remaining consequences, such as loss of voting privileges. A pardon is also helpful if the recipient is seeking a change of the character of his or her discharge, veterans' benefits, a job, or a professional license. It can't hurt to ask.

NOTES

1. The Supreme Court recently decided that a summary court-martial is not a criminal prosecution for purposes of the Sixth Amendment's requirement of counsel—*Middendorf* v. *Henry*, 425 U.S. 25 (1976). This might support an argument that a summary court-martial is not a criminal conviction for any purpose. COMA is considering this argument as this book goes to press—*U.S.* v. *Redmond* (No. 32,049 argued September 25, 1976).
2. Charles E. Lance, *A Punitive Discharge—An Effective Punishment?* The Army Lawyer, DA Pamphlet, 27-50-43, July 1976.
3. *Ibid.* at p. 27.
4. 18 U.S.C. App. § 1202(a) (2).
5. *U.S.* v. *Day*, 476 F.2d 562 (6th Cir. 1973).
6. 29 U.S.C. § 845(c) (5) (A). *Thompson* v. *Gallagher*, 489 F.2d 443 (5th Cir. 1973).
7. 5 U.S.C. § 552. Write to the Director, FBI, 10th & Pennsylvania Avenues, N.W., Washington, DC 20535, saying that this is a request under the Freedom of Information Act and specifying what you want. You can also make a request through a local law enforcement agency, but the agency will ask for your fingerprints unless it already has a set—20 C.F.R. § 20.34(a).

8. 5 U.S.C. § 552a. While the FBI may be exempt from the correction and expungement sections of the Privacy Act, the FBI does regularly process requests for expungement of arrest records. You can also request the agency that supplied the information to the FBI to supply the FBI with a correction—20 C.F.R. § 20.34(b).

9. Letter to David Addlestone from G. F. Dooley, Bureau of Naval Personnel.

10. Air Force Regulation 125-18 ¶ 2-3a, b, and c. Letter to David Addlestone from Myron L. Birnbaum, Office of the Judge Advocate General of the Air Force.

11. Letter from Mr. Birnbaum.

12. Letter to David Addlestone from Col. Wayne E. Alley, Office of Judge Advocate General of the Army.

13. *Ibid.* and DA Message 2213152; Army Regulation 635-10 ¶ 3-17 (29 Aug. 1973); Army Regulation 190-47 ¶ 5-2 (15 Dec. 1975); and Army Regulation 635-120 ¶ 2-9 (3 Aug. 1973).

14. Article 69, UCMJ, 10 U.S.C. § 869.

15. *U.S.* v. *Gallagher*, 22 USCMA 191, 46 CMR 191 (1973).

16. *U.S.* v. *Johnson*, 24 USCMA 115, 51 CMR 305, —M.J.— (1976); *Schmeltz* v. *U.S.*, 24 USCMA 93, 51 CMR 266, —M.J.— (1976).

17. *Del Prado* v. *U.S.*, 23 USCMA 132, 48 CMR 748 (1974); *McPhail* v. *U.S.* 24 USCMA 304, 52 CMR 15, —M.J.— (1976).

18. 24 USCMA 304, 52 CMR 15, —M.J.— (1976).

19. *Schlesinger* v. *Councilman*, 420 U.S. 738 (1975).

20. *Parker* v. *Levy*, 417 U.S. 733 (1974); *Middendorf* v. *Henry*, 425 U.S. 25 (1976).

21. The cases involved are *U.S.* v. *Ortiz*, 15 USCMA 505, 36 CMR 3 (1965), *rehearing denied*, 16 USCMA 127, 36 CMR 283 (1966); *U.S.* v. *Greenwell*, 19 USCMA 460, 42 CMR 62 (1970); and *U.S.* v. *Ferry*, 22 USCMA 339, 46 CMR 339 (1973). *Ferry* held *Greenwell* retroactive in the context of using an invalid *Greenwell* conviction to increase the sentence in a subsequent case. In *Brown* v. *U.S.*, 508 F.2d 618 (3rd Cir. 1974), a federal court held the cases not to be retroactive. The Navy has been strictly interpreting *Ferry*; however, we feel that COMA might ignore the Third Circuit case and hold the cases fully retroactive should a case be presented to it. COMA is not bound by any federal court except the Supreme Court.

22. *U.S.* v. *McCarthy*, 25 USCMA 30, 54 CMR 30, —M.J.— (1976).

23. A good recent example is the agency theory of drug sale. If one pleaded guilty to sale and then testified s/he was

merely a conduit who was making no profit, this would be an improvident plea. Also, possession is not a lesser included offense of sale under military law. The *Manual for Courts-Martial* (1969, Rev. Ed.) lists all the elements of the offenses, and it can be purchased from the U.S. Government Printing Office for $7.30. An excellent treatise on military law is *Justice and The Military*, P.L.E.I., 1972, 1346 Connecticut Ave., N.W., Washington, DC 20036.

24. For example, in *U.S.* v. *Tassos*, 18 USCMA 12, 39 CMR 12 (1968), MACV Directive 10-4, December 11, 1965, and I Corps Coordinator Instruction 1050.5B, January 27, 1967, were held not to be general regulations as to establishing off-limits areas in Vietnam; and in *U.S.* v. *Scott*, 22 USCMA 35, 46 CMR 25 (1972), U.S. Army Pacific Reg. (USARPAC) 190-30, November 24, 1969, was held to be nonpunitive (possession of drugs and drug paraphernalia).

IV

Privacy and Military Records

The military, like other branches of government, has indulged in an excessive amount of record keeping about individuals. Of particular interest to veterans should be what is contained in their military records, how they can see the contents, how the records can be changed, and who has access to these records.

What is contained in your military records?

Many things. Military records (sometimes called a "201 file" or "service record book") contain complete information on enlistment or induction, assignments, training, medals and awards, letters of commendation, promotions and demotions, efficiency and conduct ratings, and copies of the many official forms and orders relating to your service. Naturally, many bad things are also included: information concerning court-martial convictions and acquittals, non-judicial punishments (Article 15), reprimands, bad time assessment, involuntary discharge actions, and notations as to "counseling" by commanders. Even copies of letters written to Congress that were referred to the military can find their way into your military records. Most medical records (including psychiatric records) are also kept with your military records. These can contain information about treatment for drug abuse, even voluntary treatment under the "exemption program."

How can you see what is in these records?

Every person with an honorable or general discharge is automatically entitled to a free copy of his or her complete service records. If you have a discharge under other than honorable conditions, you can obtain a free copy of your records if you are seeking a change in discharge or financial benefits.[1] If this is the case, state it when you ask for a copy of your records.

To obtain your service records, get a copy of Standard Form 180 from a Veterans Administration (VA) office (these are listed in Appendix III). On the line where you are asked what documents you want, put "complete service records to include medical records." Mail the form to the address on the back of the form, which indicates where your records are stored. You can indicate on Form 180 the name of an attorney or anyone else to whom you wish to release your records, and they will be sent directly to that person. Should you not get complete records or for any other reason have cause to complain, write to:

The Director
National Personnel Records Center
9700 Page Boulevard
St. Louis, MO 63132

On July 12, 1973, there was a fire at the Records Center that damaged or destroyed the following categories of records:

1. Army personnel discharged between November 1, 1912, and December 31, 1959: 2.5 million of 20 million can be salvaged.
2. Air Force personnel discharged between September 25, 1947, and December 31, 1963, last names beginning with the letters "I" through "Z"; 423,000 of 1.4 million can be salvaged.
3. Army personnel discharged between January 1, 1973, and time of fire; 314,000 of 316,000 can be salvaged.

Thus, in some cases, the Records Center will have to try to reconstruct military records by writing to other agencies such as the VA. In some cases, no records will be available.

Records of drug abuse and treatment are not releasable to anyone but you and your attorney. If you have reason to believe such records exist, request them specifically or they will not be sent. A special release form, which the Records Center will send you on request, is needed before these records will be released to your attorney. Also, sometimes records of treatment at military hospitals are kept only at those hospitals and not in your records. If your records are at the VA (and they are if you applied for benefits), it is more difficult to obtain copies. However, free copies are obtainable from the VA.[2]

Investigations concerning you by military investigation divisions (CID, OSI, NIS, or ONI) will not be included in your military records; however, you may be able to obtain copies of these under the Freedom of Information Act (FOIA) or Privacy Act. Merely write the head of the agency involved, stating that your request is an FOIA and Privacy Act request, and specifying what you want.

Everyone should obtain a copy of his or her records!

Who else has access to your military records?

There are restrictions on the release of military records. Normally federal, state, and local governmental agencies can obtain them without a court order or a release from you. If you apply for a job with the federal government, there is a chance that your military records will be reviewed. United States Attorneys, probation officers, and other law enforcement agencies usually can obtain copies. Private individuals, businesses, insurance companies, and credit bureaus cannot obtain copies unless you sign a release form.

Many employers, such as the U.S. Postal Service, require such a release as a part of the job application process. In some places this may be unlawful.[3] Also, errors can and do occur. We have seen records released to an individual who was not entitled to them without a release. In such a case, a suit for invasion of privacy would lie against the requestor and a Federal Tort Claims Act[4] or Privacy Act[5] suit could be brought against the government.

How can errors in my military record be corrected?

Routine errors like misspellings and wrong dates can be corrected by writing to the Records Center. Other errors can be corrected by way of an application to the Board for Correction of Military or Naval Records. Each service has one. These boards can correct "any error or injustice"[6] such as changing the character of discharges, date of rank, actual rank, length of service, etc. In short, the boards can do anything (with some exceptions) or recommend almost anything to correct "any error or injustice." The application procedures are described in Chapter VI. Keep in mind that these boards are swamped with applications, have small staffs, and rarely grant personal-appearance hearings. Your application should be as complete as possible with relevant supporting documents attached, for your records are likely to contain only information about the other side of the dispute. In many cases it would be a good idea to consult an attorney to assist you. The application form for these boards is DD Form 149, which can be obtained from any VA office (see Appendix III).

Another method to correct errors in your record is by use of the Privacy Act of 1974. Although the act has been little used in cases involving military records, it clearly seems to apply.[7] Among other things, the act permits an individual to inspect his or her records that are kept by a government agency. A person can then request that the record be corrected because the person believes it "is not accurate, relevant, timely, or complete." The agency must act promptly to change the record or explain why not, and inform the requesting individual how to appeal the denial. The appeal must be completed in 60 days. The individual can have included in the record his or her explanation of why s/he believes the record to be in error. Should the requesting individual be dissatisfied, s/he may file suit in federal district court. The issue in dispute is then considered by the court on the basis of the matters submitted to the court with the agency determination not being presumed to be accurate. That is, a trial over the issue in dispute can occur. Attorneys' fees can be awarded if the requestor "substantially prevails." Damages are also possible if inaccurate information was disseminated after the effective date of the Privacy Act, September 30, 1975.

What are SPN codes?

In the early 1950s, the services started to use two- and three-digit figures (and sometimes letters) on the DD Form 214, the document each service member receives upon discharge or separation from active duty. These figures appeared in the block reserved for "reason and authority," usually block 11c. The figure was usually preceded by "SPN" (separation program number) or "SDN" (separation designation number, for the Air Force). Sometimes SPN or SDN was omitted. In the 1960's the codes were computerized so that the names of people who received certain codes could be located. Block 11c also contained the specific regulation and paragraph under which a person was discharged, and block 15 (these block numbers may have changed over the years) contained a reenlistment code that indicated whether a person was eligible to reenlist. Any code other than RE-1 might cause an employer to wonder about your military service, since that is the code that has most always been given to those eligible to reenlist, even though some non-RE-1 codes do not actually stand for something bad. The most common SPN codes are listed in Appendix IV.

This practice of including these RE and SPN codes on the DD 214 ceased on May 1, 1974. After that date, people could request a separate statement of the reason for their separation. If you were discharged before that date, you can have the two codes and the notation as to the regulatory authority for discharge removed by writing to:

ARMY
Commander
Reserve Components Personnel
 and Administration Center
Box 12479
Olivette Branch
St. Louis, MO 63132

AIR FORCE
Air Force Military Personnel Center (DPMDR)
Randolph Air Force Base
Texas 78148

or
through a local base personnel office

NAVY
Chief
Bureau of Naval Personnel
(Pers 38)
Department of the Navy
Washington, DC 20370

MARINE CORPS
Commandant
U.S. Marine Corps (MSRB-10)
Headquarters, U.S. Marine Corps
Washington, DC 20380

COAST GUARD
Commandant
U.S. Coast Guard (G-PS)
Washington, DC 20590

Include your name, social security number, any military service identification number, dates of service, and a copy of the DD Form 214. Also, as was previously available on the request of a former servicemember, a narrative description of the reason for discharge will be provided if requested. You should state specifically that you do *not* want a photocopy of your old DD 214 with the codes blacked out. If your code does not appear in Appendix IV, write to the appropriate address above and ask the meaning of your code.

Why should you have your SPN code removed?

Other than to prevent people who see your DD Form 214 from being supplied with information about you (most big employers have a list of the codes),[8] there are several good reasons. The codes were revised over the years so that some old but good codes became bad codes, at least on some lists that may not reflect the changes. We have seen such cases and have tried to obtain the old lists, but our requests have been refused. Some employers are confused about the codes and think that any number on the 214 form is "the code." The block near 11c contains a place for a number that stands for the type of discharge certificate issued. These numbers are often mistaken for SPN codes that indicate involuntary discharges. Sometimes a typographical error creates the wrong code or one that does not exist. What will an employer think if your code does not appear on his or her list?

The DD Form 214 has much more information on it that can be harmful. If you think some of it is inaccurate, apply for correction to the appropriate correction board. If you do not understand what the information means, write to the address listed above for your service. Also a Privacy Act claim could be made to correct an "inaccuracy."

If your DD Form 214 does not contain a SPN or RE code, does that mean employers will not be able to learn the reason for your discharge?

No. The services will supply you, upon request, with a "narrative" giving a brief description of your reason for discharge; for example, "Unfitness, drugs." Thus, an employer can require you to furnish this document unless the state or city in which you are applying for employment has forbidden employers by law or regulation to ask you about your discharge.

It is also possible that if you request a new DD Form 214 that does not contain any reference to these codes, a potential employer will think you have something to hide. The only real solution would be for DOD to recall all discharge certificates. However, it has refused a request that it do so.

On balance, however, requesting a "clean" DD Form 214 is probably the best course of action for you to take.

What if the local police think that your military records still show you as AWOL?

This problem is discussed in Chapter I.

What if your military records contain information about your legitimate First Amendment activities?

There were many cases, particularly during the Vietnam war, where military records included notations as to arrests, "counseling," loss of a security clearance, or other personnel actions resulting from legitimate petitioning or other First Amendment activities. The courts and Congress have recognized that military personnel have First Amendment rights.[9] In one case, when a veteran filed suit to have a notation of a change in job (due to a petition he circulated) removed from his records, the Army Board for Correction of Military Records changed his records before the suit was decided.[10] The Privacy Act also prohibits any government agency from "maintain[ing any] record describing how any individual exercises rights guaranteed by the First Amendment unless expressly authorized by statute or by the individual about whom the record is maintained or unless pertinent to and within the scope of an authorized law enforcement activity."

NOTES

1. DOD Instruction 7230.7 ¶ IV.D.
2. VA Regulation 256E, 38 C.F.R. § 1.526.
3. For example, the Washington State Human Rights Commission Employment Regulations prohibit such a request—WAC 162-12-140 (3) i.
4. 28 U.S.C. § 2671.
5. 5 U.S.C. § 552a.
6. 10 U.S.C § 1552.
7. *Beller* v. *Middendorf,* No. 75-2747GBH N.D. Calif. April 15, 1976 (unpublished). *See also* 4 MLR 6008-9.
8. *Congressional Record,* Nov. 28, 1973, survey by Congressman John F. Seiberling.
9. 10 U.S.C. § 1034 (permits unfettered petition to Congress). *Carlson* v. *Schlesinger,* 511 F.2d 1237 (D.C. Cir. 1975) (arrests for petitioning could be expunged, but an exception was made for this combat-zone petitioning); *Huff* v. *Secretary,* 413 F. Supp. 863 (D.D.C. 1976) (petitions permitted on base in Japan); *Greer* v. *Spock,* 424 U.S. 828 (1976) (partisan political campaign could be kept off military installation); *Glines* v. *Wade,* 401 F. Supp. 127 (N.D. Calif. 1975) (petitions permitted in Guam); and *Allen* v. *Monger,* 404 F. Supp. 1081 (N.D. Calif. 1975) (petitions permitted on aircraft carrier). Appeals are pending in *Huff, Glines* and *Allen.*
10. *Malone* v. *Secretary,* Civil Action No. 1103-73 (D.D.C.).

V

The Military Discharge System

This chapter discusses briefly the military discharge system, and the significance of the various types of discharges to the veterans who have them.

What types of discharges does the military issue?

There are now six types of military discharges issued by all the services.

The first three categories are administratively issued: honorable, general, and undesirable ("under other than honorable conditions" for officers and after January 1, 1977, "other than honorable discharge" for enlisted persons). For clarity we will use undesirable throughout the book). Prior to 1947, today's undesirable discharge was called a "Blue Discharge" by the Army. A new type of discharge is the clemency discharge, issued by an administrative process to certain categories of Vietnam-era veterans.

There are two types of discharges that can be issued only as part of a sentence imposed by a court-martial. These are bad conduct and dishonorable discharges (or "dismissal" for officers).

What do the various types of discharges mean?

Approximately 90% of discharges issued are fully honorable. The honorable discharge is given routinely at the expiration of a term of enlistment. It also may be issued in other routine separations, in cases of hardship, minority or conscientious objector discharge, or even in cases of involuntary discharge for cause.

The general discharge ("under honorable conditions," in the case of an officer) is considered to be "under honorable conditions." It is occasionally issued at the expiration of enlistment (such as for low marks in the Navy or Marines). Most often, however, it is issued in "unsuitability" cases, which include the following: inaptitude; character and behavior disorders (now called personality disorders), apathy, defective attitudes and inability to expend efforts constructively; alcohol abuse; "homosexual and other aberrant tendencies;" financial irresponsibility; drug abuse upon voluntary admission for treatment or through detection by urinalysis prior to July 1974.

An undesirable discharge is presumed in cases involving discharge for "misconduct," "unfitness,"[1] and "resignation for the good of the service." Misconduct cases are those involving conviction by a civilian or foreign court, fraudulent enlistment, or in some cases an AWOL of more than 1 year's duration. Unfitness includes the following specifics: frequent involvement of a discreditable nature with civil or military authorities; "sexual perversion" (usually homosexuality); drug abuse; established pattern of shirking; established pattern of showing dishonorable failure to pay debts or support dependents. A general or honorable discharge may occur in such cases if there are mitigating factors.

Resignation for the good of the service (commonly known in the Army as a "Chapter 10") is a resignation in lieu of trial by a court-martial, which could issue a bad conduct or dishonorable discharge. This type of discharge occurred in great numbers during and after the Vietnam war.

Bad conduct and dishonorable discharges are given only as sentences following a court-martial conviction and a subsequent appeal to military appellate courts.

The clemency discharge is a new type of discharge created by the Presidential Clemency Program established by President Ford on September 16, 1974. The three-part program provided for the issuance of "clemency discharges" for two categories of cases: (1) Those servicemembers in deserter (or AWOL) status on September

16, 1974, whose absence began between August 4, 1964, and March 28, 1973, could turn themselves in and be immune from prosecution if they did so by March 31, 1975. Virtually all who did so were given undesirable discharges by the Joint Alternate Service Board and a period of up to 24 months of "alternate service" to perform, which, if completed, permitted the substitution of a "clemency discharge" for the undesirable discharge. Alternate service meant securing a low-paying "public service" job that did not compete with the normal job market. The job had to be approved by the Selective Service. (2) Those former servicemembers who had received undesirable, bad conduct, or dishonorable discharges between August 4, 1964, and March 28, 1973, for absence-related offenses, were entitled to a review of their cases by the specially created Presidential Clemency Board, if they applied by March 31, 1975. That board could recommend to the President that he issue a "pardon" and/or a clemency discharge, which also could be conditioned upon completion of up to 24 months of alternate service.

The clemency discharge is not an upgraded discharge, but is considered by the Department of Defense to be under "other than honorable conditions." While the pardon could help if the bad discharge was based on a court-martial conviction that could be considered to have been a felony conviction (*see* Chapter III), the clemency discharge is little more than an undesirable discharge with a nicer name. However, under the Carter program to review Vietnam-era discharges these clemency discharges became easy to upgrade (*see* Chapter VIII).

How does the military discharge system work?

Only about 10% of less than fully honorable discharges are a direct result of a conviction by a court-martial. The remainder are general and undesirable discharges issued through an administrative process. Although the UCMJ, which governs the system of criminal justice in the military, does not provide procedures to govern administrative discharges, the less than fully honorable discharge has been used by the services as an integral part of the disciplinary process.

The administrative process, which brands veterans with

stigmatizing discharges, does not contain the same level of safeguards as the UCMJ. In the 1950s, regulations regarding the administrative discharge contained virtually no procedural safeguards at all. Since 1959, there has been a steady expansion of procedural rights. Each service has regulations promulgated under the authority of Department of Defense Directive 1332.14, December 29, 1976. Hearings and counsel are accorded most service personnel when discharge action is initiated that could result in an undesirable discharge. Even if a general discharge could result, a hearing is afforded the individual in all Army cases (and in Navy and Air Force cases if the GI has had more than 8 years of service and in some other cases). In recent years, lawyer counsel has been provided in most cases. Nonetheless, the safeguards are still inadequate and have resulted in thousands of less than honorable discharges that were unwarranted and unjust. Chapters VI and VII discuss discharge upgrading.

Does the character of discharge that one holds have any consequences in later civilian life?

Yes. The type of discharge one holds does affect eligibility for veterans' benefits and some employment possibilities. Generally, an honorable or general discharge automatically entitles you to all veterans' benefits. If you hold an undesirable discharge or a bad conduct discharge issued by a special court-martial, your eligibility for most benefits depends on a determination by the Veterans Administration. If you have a bad conduct discharge given by a general court-martial or a dishonorable discharge, you are not entitled to any VA benefits (with minor exceptions). The following chart details eligibility by character of discharge. "E" represents eligible; "A" means that you may be eligible pending VA or other agency administrative action; and "NE" means definitely not eligible. (Discharge upgrading normally makes one eligible for VA benefits. Upgrades in certain Vietnam-era and AWOL cases present a different problem. See Chapters VII and X.) Chapters X and XII discuss VA adjudication procedures in detail, and Chapter VIII discusses employment discrimination.

	Dishonorable	Bad Conduct (General c-m)	Bad Conduct (General c-m)	Undesirable	General	Honorable
Education Assistance	NE	NE	A	A	E	E
Hospital Care	NE	NE	A	A	E	E
Vocational Rehabili- tation	NE	NE	A	A	E	E
Home Loans	NE	NE	A	A	E	E
Civil Service Employ- ment Preference	NE	NE	NE	NE	E	E
Reemployment Benefits	NE	NE	NE	NE	E	E
Unemployment Benefits	NE	NE	A	A	E	E

NOTES

1. Effective in 1976, the terms of unfitness and misconduct were placed under the one category of "misconduct"—DOD Directive 1332.14, September 30, 1975.

VI

The Discharge Review System

This chapter describes the process by which a veteran can obtain relief if s/he holds a less than fully honorable discharge. The following discussion describes how the discharge review system of the various services works and what steps the veteran should take to ensure a successful appeal of his/her "bad paper." Be aware, however, that legislation enacted on October 8, 1977, requires the DOD to establish a somewhat different review system. The details are not yet known, but it is unlikely that the following discussion will be greatly affected. Also, when signing the bill, the President said he will seek additional legislation in the discharge review area.

How can a bad discharge be changed?
File an application for change with the Discharge Review Board or the Board for Correction of Military (or Naval) Records.

Who may seek a recharacterization, or upgrade, of a discharge?
Any veteran who leaves the service with a discharge other than fully honorable has the right to seek a discharge upgrade.

How do you start the process?
The process is initiated in most cases by filing an application on DD Form 293 with the appropriate Discharge

Review Board (DRB)—Army, Air Force, Navy (includes Marine Corps), or Coast Guard. You file a DD 149 with the appropriate Board for Correction of Military Records (BCMR) if your discharge was the result of a sentence of a general court-martial or if you lost at the DRB or if the DRB will not hear your case. These forms can be obtained from any VA office listed in Appendix III or from any of the veterans' assistance organizations listed in Appendix I.

Do not send in your DD Form 293 or 149 before you obtain a copy of your military records. You can get a copy of your military personnel file free of charge by sending a Standard Form 180 (available from the VA or the groups listed in Appendix I) to the appropriate address listed on the back of the 180. Once you send a DD 293 to a DRB or a 149 to a BCMR, you can no longer obtain a copy of your records since the originals will be sent to the DRB or BCMR.

Before you initiate the process, it would be best for you to contact a veterans' assistance organization (*see* Appendix I) or an attorney for advice as to how to proceed. (*See* Chapter IV for more information about your military records.)

What is the Discharge Review Board?

The DRB of each service is established by the Secretary of that service under authority of a law passed by the Congress in 1944 (10 U.S.C. 1553). The boards have the authority to review the type and nature of discharges at the request of the veteran of his/her representative, or the DRB can act on its own motion without an application.

A DRB panel consists of five members who are high-ranking active-duty officers, usually in the rank or equivalent rank of Lieutenant Colonel or Colonel. The board members are generally not lawyers, although the Army and Navy Boards have legal advisors who sometimes sit, and one lawyer will generally sit on each Air Force panel. Similarly, doctors are available to sit if a case raises a medical issue. The Air Force permits an applicant to request that an NCO be on the panel.

The Marine Corps board is combined with that of the Navy, but at least three Marine officers will sit on any Marine case.

Do you have to appear in person before the board to have your case heard?

No. Each board has the authority to review a case based on the application (DD Form 293) submitted and your military personnel file, which is obtained by the board in each case.

However, each veteran has a right to appear before the board, and your chances of success *more than triple* if you make a personal appearance. The boards are greatly influenced by a veteran's appearance because it shows sincerity and gives the board members the opportunity to ask questions that simply are not answered by the papers they have before them. It is clear that your records alone generally are not going to present your side of the case.

Do you have to go to Washington in order to appear before the board?

No. The DRBs have started a system of regional and traveling panels to make it possible for most veterans seeking discharge review to make a personal appearance without undue hardship.

The Army has two panels that meet in the Pentagon in Washington, D.C., and has established a system of traveling panels and hearing examiners that will hear cases in any city (including prisons) where there are a sufficient number of pending applications. For example, in 1977, cases were heard in at least 27 cities.[1]

When the Army DRB dispatches a traveling panel, that panel has final authority to decide the case. When a hearing examiner is sent, s/he hears the case, and records the hearing on videotape. That tape is then reviewed by a five-member panel in Washington, which then decides the case.

The Air Force has a permanent panel in Washington that also travels on a regular basis to hear cases in St. Louis, Missouri; San Francisco, California; Coswell AFB, Texas; Dobbins AFB, Georgia; Lowry AFB, Colorado; Maguire AFB, New Jersey; L. G. Hanscomb Field, Maine; Norton AFB (Los Angeles), California; Dayton, Ohio; and Minneapolis, Minnesota.

The Air Force will also send its panel to additional cities if there is sufficient demand.

The Navy (and Marine) board meets in Washington, D.C., and meets on a regular basis in San Francisco, California; New Orleans, Louisiana; and Chicago, Illinois, and has gone to San Diego, California; Seattle, Washington; Columbus, Ohio; Albany, New York; Boston, Massachusetts; Pittsburgh, Pennsylvania; Detroit, Michigan; and San Antonio, Texas. When the Navy (Marine) board meets outside Washington, D.C., it is composed of two to three permanent board members from Washington, D.C. The panel is then completed by active-duty officers from the location where the cases are being heard.

The Coast Guard board meets only in Washington, D.C.

What powers does a Discharge Review Board have?

A Discharge Review Board can only change a discharge to a higher one and issue a new discharge. It cannot reinstate an individual. Nor can it change a discharge to or from one issued on grounds of physical disability. Only the Air Force DRB can change a reenlistment code, which can make a veteran eligible for reenlistment (but does not guarantee it). Nor can a DRB review a discharge resulting from a general court-martial. All other such relief can be obtained from the appropriate Board for Correction of Military Records.

What are your chances of receiving a discharge upgrade if you apply to one of these boards?

Your chances are very good. The DRBs are upgrading the discharges of a higher percentage of applicants each year. If you seek the assistance of a discharge-upgrade counselor (see Appendix I) or attorney and cooperate fully in the preparation of your case, you probably have about a 50% or better chance of success.

Can you apply for a discharge upgrade at any time after your discharge?

No. You must apply to the DRB within 15 years of the date of discharge. This statute of limitations set by 10 U.S.C. 1553 cannot be waived. However, interpretations of the statute of limitations by the various boards differ, resulting in some situations in the possibility of a *rehearing* if you have already been turned down and it is now beyond the 15-year period: [2]

1. The Navy strictly interprets the 15-year rule. If 15 years since discharge have passed, a hearing or rehearing is not possible under any circumstances.

2. The Army interprets the 15-year rule more liberally. If the veteran made an application for review within the 15 years, s/he is eligible for a rehearing at any time within 15 years of the filing of the last application considered by the board, if the board grants a request for a rehearing (Usually such a request will be granted if you will appear and did not do so the first time *or* now have an attorney *or* have new arguments to present).

3. The Air Force may also grant a rehearing beyond the 15-year period since discharge if the board completed one review within the 15 years *and* the new application is filed within 15 years of the first. Rehearing will be granted if the applicant did not make a personal appearance before but will now; or if s/he did make a personal appearance but now has new evidence to present (including evidence of post-service rehabilitation); or, in the case of a bad conduct discharge, if either of the above criteria are met or if significant changes have been made in the UCMJ since the court-martial that resulted in the discharge.

Recent legislation required the DOD to open the review system to all veterans with other than honorable administrative discharges for one year, thereby waiving the statute of limitations for these veterans for one year and in effect permitting *automatic rehearings* for many of these veterans.

If your case has already been reviewed by a DRB and relief was denied, can you apply for an upgrade again?

Yes. All DRBs, by regulation, will grant a rehearing if material evidence not available at the first hearing will be presented. Also, if you did not appear personally at the first hearing, and will appear this time, the boards will generally grant a rehearing with no further evidence. Moreover, if you did appear personally the first time but were not assisted by a veterans' counselor or lawyer, but will be assisted the second time, the boards will sometimes grant a second review of your case. (*See* discussion immediately before this question as it relates to the new DOD program.)

In any case, it cannot hurt to reapply. Chances are good that you will be granted a rehearing, sometimes simply because policies regarding upgrades have been liberalized in the last few years. Your good post-service record may now be enough to get you an upgrade. Also, the BCMR (see discussion below) infrequently grants personal appearance hearings; therefore, take advantage of the rehearing opportunity if possible so you can plead your case in person.

How long does it take from the time you send in your application until a hearing is held?

This varies depending on the board and how difficult it is to obtain your service records. Recently, the Air Force has been taking only about 4 months, while the Marines can take up to a year. This, however, is subject to change.

What evidence do the boards consider?

The DRBs will consider your military personnel records as well as all evidence you submit. Such evidence may include affidavits or statements by you and other persons familiar with aspects of your case, character references, letters from your employers, legal briefs, etc. At the hearing itself, the board will hear testimony from you and from others at your request, and arguments from your lawyer or counselor. Evidence tending to show that there were extenuating or mitigating circumstances that bear on your acts or offenses can be important.

Will the boards gather any evidence or pay for your appearance or the appearance of witnesses?

The boards will usually secure only your military personnel file. Any other evidence you wish them to consider will have to be supplied by you. The DRBs will not pay any expenses involved in your appearance or that of any witnesses. Further, the boards do not have subpoena power. Thus, any witnesses you wish the board to hear must come voluntarily and at their own or your expense.

Do you have to appear at the hearing alone?

No—and you shouldn't. The regulations of the DRBs

provide that you may be represented by "counsel." Counsel may be an attorney, a member of an accredited veterans' organization (listed on the back of the application form, DD Form 293), and such other individuals whom the board considers to be competent to present your case. (*See* Appendix I for a list of organizations that provide counsel in addition to the traditional veterans' organizations.) In practice, the boards will normally approve as your "counsel" anyone you designate from any veterans' assistance organization. Counsel from the organizations listed on the back of the DD Form 293 are generally not lawyers and take on all cases where applicants designate them as counsel. They normally do not submit written briefs in support of your application or obtain a copy of your records before filing a 293 form. Caution should be exercised if one of these groups is your counsel.[3] Under President Carter's Special Program military lawyers were provided for holders of undesirable discharges. It is unknown whether the new program will have this feature. Legal services or legal aid offices frequently provide free counsel for veterans who request their services.

How do you go about gathering the evidence that will be needed to win your case?

The most important step is for you to enlist the help of a veterans' counselor (*see* Appendix I) or a lawyer. The veterans' assistance groups do not charge for their services. They will review your case, evaluate the issues, and tell you what evidence will be necessary and helpful. If there are legal issues in your case, they can prepare a legal "brief" to be submitted to the board. The counselor will also help you prepare for the hearing, will attend the hearing with you, and guide you through it to make sure that the board has all the information favorable to you.

You can also obtain the 306-page *ACLU Practice Manual on Military Discharge Upgrading* from the American Civil Liberties Union, Literature Department, 22 East 40th Street, New York, NY 10016. The cost is $10. If you are in prison, the *Manual* will be provided to you free of charge if a copy is not in the prison library. Also, many law libraries have a copy of the *Manual*. The most recent edition is November 1975 with a 1977 supplement.

How important is it to submit evidence to the DRBs?

It is often the difference between winning and losing. Often you will be able to submit medical evidence or affidavits that will inform the DRB of circumstances surrounding your discharge that are not clear from the military records. It also helps to have employer and general character references to show what you have done since your discharge. Post-service conduct is quite influential, especially at the Air Force board.

Will your family and employer find out that you have applied for an upgrade if you don't want them to know?

No. The board proceedings are closed. The hearing is open to observers only if you so request (except DRB personnel). The board's records are completely confidential and are not made available to anyone except the board, its staff, you, and your counsel. Thus, if your family or employer are unaware of your bad discharge, they will not learn about it because you apply to a DRB for a discharge upgrade. Remember, though, to use a post office box or a friend's address for correspondence from the board if you want it to remain a secret.

Do the DRBs ever decide a case without holding a hearing?

Yes. In some cases, because of general changes in policies or regulations since a veteran's discharge, the board will offer an upgrade by letter without a hearing. Such offers are called "tender offers" or "conditionals."

Should you accept such an offer if it is for a general rather than an honorable discharge?

In a case in which the offer is for a general discharge, you will be given the choice of accepting the offer or appearing at a hearing to seek a fully honorable discharge. If you appear at a hearing, the board does reserve the power to withdraw the offer completely if adverse information comes out at the hearing. Such action is extremely rare, so the risk is not great. On the other hand, sometimes the general discharge offered will be upgraded to an honorable discharge at a hearing. Your decision will generally depend on how important an honorable discharge is to you,

71

the nature of the evidence not already before the board that you could present at a hearing, the hardship that attending a hearing would present to you, or the immediate need for obtaining VA benefits. *See* Chapters X to XII for details about retroactive payment after an upgrade. Your counselor can advise you as to the best course of action in such a case. In many cases, you can accept the general discharge and apply for an honorable discharge at a later date. If you plan to do that, be sure to inform the board of why you cannot appear at this time.

How much notice will you get of the hearing date?
At least 30 days, and you can always request a more convenient date. Your request will almost always be granted.

What is a DRB hearing like?
The hearings are relatively informal and brief. You will have a full opportunity to tell your story, guided by your counselor or lawyer. The board members will question you at the conclusion of your testimony or sometimes will break in to ask questions. Your counselor will have an opportunity to develop any legal issues and to summarize the case. The most important thing to remember is to go over your story in great detail with your counsel. If s/he does not want to spend the time to do this, you should consider getting assistance elsewhere. You can request a new hearing date, even at the last minute.

If you make a personal appearance at a DRB hearing, will the board tell you the results right away?
The boards differ in their practices. The Army will sometimes tell you if you win. The Air Force and Navy (Marines) will not tell you the results on the day of the hearing. You will hear from the Air Force in 3 to 4 weeks, the Navy in about 2 months, and the Marines may take as long as 4 months to inform you of the results. The Secretary of the Navy reviews some of the recommendations of the Navy (Marine) board. Past practice was not to permit you to see this recommendation until after the Secretary has acted; however, the practice ended in 1977.

Since there is a long waiting period, be sure to notify the board of a new address if you move after the hearing.

Do the boards prepare findings and reasons for their decisions?

As a result of a lawsuit, they (and the BCMRs) have started doing so effective April 1, 1977. (The Navy DRB and some BCMRs have prepared findings in some cases over the years. Always request to see them if you are seeking a rehearing.) If you are not given the complete relief you request, all of the arguments you make must be answered unless the board determines you would not prevail even if they bought your position. State your arguments carefully if you want the board to deal with them. The boards also maintain reading rooms with old decisions (names and identifying data are left out) which can be cited as precedent. A detailed discussion of these new and important procedures appears at 4 MLR 6001 and 4 MLR 6038-6042.

If your discharge is upgraded, will your new DD 214 indicate that you originally held a bad discharge?

No. Your new DD 214 will indicate only the new type of discharge issued to you and will be dated as of the date of your original discharge from the service.

Will you be entitled to any money if your discharge is upgraded?

An individual who is discharged with an undesirable, bad conduct, or dishonorable discharge is not entitled to accrued leave, mustering-out pay, or travel pay for dependents. Once the discharge has been upgraded, a claim for such entitlements can be made to the finance center of the appropriate branch of service (see Chapter IX). In old cases, you may have to prove you were never paid; as the official records will have been destroyed.

The most significant financial awards are available through eligibility for VA benefits after a bad discharge has been upgraded to general or honorable. A veteran with an honorable *or* general discharge is entitled to all benefits if s/he is otherwise eligible. (see Chapter X).

73

If you have received a clemency discharge through the President's Clemency Program, can you still apply to a DRB to have your discharge upgraded to honorable or general?

Yes, and you should do so. A clemency discharge is still a discharge under other than honorable conditions. It does not automatically entitle you to VA benefits and probably will not free you from employment discrimination. The policy of the DRBs regarding the clemency discharge is not clear. However, it certainly cannot hurt you in the review of your case, and probably will be considered by the boards to be a factor in your favor, since they do consider post-service circumstances. Anyone who had a clemency discharge and applied under President Carter's special discharge upgrade program (*see* Chapter VII) probably got an upgrade. If you were unaware of this program, tell the board this. The program was poorly advertised due to administration non-involvement and a congressional ban on paid advertising of the program.

If you were required to do a term of alternate service by the Presidential Clemency Board or the Joint Alternate Service Board as a condition of getting a clemency discharge, but did not complete the term, should you still apply for a discharge upgrade?

Yes. Failure to comply with the requirements set for obtaining clemency discharge does not preclude review of your original discharge by a DRB. Be sure to explain to the DRB the reason you did not complete your alternate service; for example, you were unable to find an approved alternate service job; you were unable to support your family on the salary paid you in your low-paying alternate service job; Selective Service did not help you locate a job, etc.

Can you apply for a discharge upgrade if you are currently in prison?

Yes. Many of the veterans' assistance organizations listed in Appendix I will prepare cases for imprisoned veterans in their geographical area. You may also obtain the *ACLU Practice Manual on Military Discharge Upgrading* free of charge from the American Civil Liberties

Union, Literature Department, 22 East 40th Street, New York, NY 10016 if you cannot afford to pay for it. The *Manual* will give you specific guidance in case preparation. Each federal prison and many other prisons already have copies in their libraries. Please use the library copy if possible.

If you are an Army veteran, the Army DRB or a hearing examiner may even come to the prison so that you can have a personal hearing. The other services have not stated that they would provide this service, but you could request that they come to the facility in which you are incarcerated. Even if you cannot have a personal-appearance hearing, a counselor or lawyer could appear at a hearing in your behalf.

If you cannot find any group to assist you, you should nonetheless write to the DRB of your service or the VA and obtain the following forms: SF 180, DD 293, and DD 149. Write for your records, and prepare your case as best you can, using the *ACLU Manual* as a guide, unless you think it best to wait until you get out of prison. Maybe a "jailhouse lawyer" can help. File your 293 form with any evidence you can gather, including letters from the prison staff about your good behavior. You do have a chance for an upgrade. An upgrade may improve your parole chances.[4]

If you do not obtain relief from the Discharge Review Board, can you appeal their decision?

If the decision of the DRB is unfavorable, you can apply for a completely new review of your case at the Board for Correction of Military Records (BCMR) of your former service. A recent change in Navy DRB regulations permits an "appeal" of an adverse final decision of the DRB to the secretary of the navy.

What powers do the BCMRs have?

The BCMRs are authorized by statute (10 U.S.C. 1552) to correct *any* error or injustice. Their jurisdiction is very broad and not limited to review of less than honorable discharges. They can even change an undesirable discharge to a medical retirement with a pension and back pay. Their review function as it applies to discharges is fivefold.

First, the BCMR may review a discharge after relief has been denied by the DRB, acting, in effect, as a board of appeal. Further, even if the DRB upgrades a discharge, it cannot (except in the case of the Air Force DRB) change the reenlistment (RE) code that governs the ability to return to service. In the case of an individual who wishes to reenlist, application for change in the RE code can be made to the BCMR subsequent to a favorable ruling by the DRB on the discharge itself. Also, the BCMR can change a discharge to or from a medical discharge.

Second, unlike the DRBs, the BCMRs can review and recharacterize discharges awarded by general courts-martial.

Third, the BCMRs hear cases that the DRBs 15-year statute of limitations preclude them from considering. Although there is a 3-year statute of limitations governing the BCMRs, unlike the DRBs, the BCMRs may, and generally do, waive the time limit "in the interests of justice." Lack of knowledge of review remedies is usually an adequate reason for waiver of the statute of limitations. Should your application be rejected as untimely, demand to know when such a policy to do this was instituted and what the policy states.

Fourth, the BCMRs have the power to correct or change military records. This authority includes, but is not limited to, the expungement of nonjudicial punishment and court-martial convictions (only the Air Force BCMR can expunge a court-martial conviction) or elimination of poor efficiency ratings. It is thus advisable in some cases to apply to the BCMR to have such changes made, if there are legal grounds for so doing, before making an application to the DRB for a discharge upgrade. If offenses have been expunged, or efficiency ratings changed, the DRB will be reviewing a better record.

Fifth, as discussed in Chapter VII, recent legislation gives the BCMR and the VA concurrent powers to remove certain bars to veterans' benefits in cases of some upgraded discharges.

The BCMRs will not review a case within 15 years from the date of discharge unless the DRB has already

heard it and, in some cases, will return a case to the DRB
if a rehearing at the DRB is possible.

What evidence will the BCMRs consider?

The BCMRs will accept the same type of evidence as
described above in the discussion of the DRBs.

Are you entitled to a personal appearance hearing at the BCMR?

No. The granting of a hearing by a BCMR, unlike a
DRB, is discretionary and hearings are rarely granted.
Thus, it is important that you file an affidavit and brief or
description of your arguments with your BCMR application setting forth every fact you wish the BCMR to consider. It is unlikely that you will have the opportunity to
tell the BCMR story in person. The BCMRs often get advisory opinions from other agencies, *so you should request
to see those opinions* and be given an opportunity to rebut
them before the BCMR sees them.

How do you initiate a review by the BCMR?

The review process is started by filing a DD Form 149,
available at all VA offices or from any of the veterans' assistance organizations listed in Appendix I.

How long does it take to get results from the BCMRs?

The BCMRs all have serious backlogs. You can expect
to wait approximately 6 months for results from the Army
and up to 18 months from the other boards. (These waiting times are subject to change.)

If your case has been heard once by a BCMR, will it grant a second review?

The BCMRs will grant reconsideration only if new evidence is presented. Each board has its own interpretation
of new evidence. If you were not represented by counsel
the first time, a legal brief by a lawyer or counselor the
second time may be sufficient to fill the new-evidence requirement. If you were turned down before, be sure to
request a copy of any advisory opinions, staff memoranda,
record of proceedings, and any other documents that the
board has pertaining to your previous application(s). With

information such as this, and a good brief, an upgrade is possible even though you were turned down more than once before. Also, policies do change.[5]

What if you lose at the BCMR?

You can then take your case to federal court. Federal court relief is granted only if the military did not follow its own regulations, violated your constitutional rights, or if the BCMR was acting in an arbitrary manner ("unsupported by substantial evidence") in denying you relief. You must file in federal court within 6 years after being denied relief at the BCMR.[6]

How are applications for other relief made to the BCMR's?

In just about the same manner as above. Remember, the main rules are that boards with crowded dockets have little time for most applications, so make yours as complete and as readable as possible.

NOTES

1. These cities are: Los Angeles, Calif.; Salt Lake City, Utah; Jackson, Miss.; Pittsburgh, Pa.; Minneapolis, Minn.; Seattle, Wash.; Austin, Tex.; St. Petersburg, Fla.; Boston, Mass.; Kansas City, Mo.; Mobile, Ala.; Syracuse, N.Y.; Phoenix, Ariz.; Omaha, Neb.; Buffalo, N.Y.; Helena, Mont.; Raleigh, N.C.; Oklahoma City, Okla.; Boise, Idaho; Portland, Maine; Spokane, Wash.; Las Vegas, Nev.; Shreveport, La.; Madison, Wis.; Norfolk, Va.; El Paso, Tex.; Flint, Mich. Panels will also travel to Alaska, Hawaii, and Puerto Rico if sufficient applications are received.
2. The boards have tended to change these interpretations, so check the current rule before you give up.
3. We do not mean to disparage the work of these organizations; however, recently it appeared that they were burdened with too many cases to handle all of them effectively.
4. *The Rights of Prisoners* is another handbook in this series; Also, the ACLU National Prison Project at 1346 Connecticut Avenue, Washington, D.C. 20036, can provide referrals for prisoners with prison-related problems.
5. Over the years, the Army BCMR had a policy of letting staff members deny requests for reconsideration. This vio-

lated their own regulations. If this happened to you (read your letter from them closely to see if the board is not mentioned as having acted on your request), you are entitled to a determination as to reconsideration by the board. This was the result of a settlement in a class action lawsuit, *Heiler* v. *Williams*, Civil Action No. 76-0912 (D.D.C.).

6. 28 U.S.C. 2401(a). *But see Mathis* v. *Laird*, 324 F. Supp. 885 D. Fla. 1971, *aff'd* 457 F. 2d 926, *cert. den.* 409 U.S. 871 and *Saffron* v. *Department of Navy*, No. 75-1794 (D.C. Cir., July 1, 1977) which suggests that suit must be filed within six years after the claim first arose. Thus, caution may dictate filing in federal court if six years from discharge is close.

VII

Upgrading Bad Discharges, Particularly Those Related to Drugs, Alcohol, Homosexual Acts, and Certain Vietnam-era Discharges

This chapter outlines some common reasons for bad discharges, and discusses approaches to upgrading such cases. It also discusses the recently instituted special Vietnam-era discharge review program of the Carter administration. Many of these approaches apply as general approaches to all cases.

What are your chances for a discharge upgrade if you have an undesirable, bad conduct, or dishonorable discharge because of drugs?

If your discharge resulted from drug use or possession of drugs for your personal use and your case was in process before July 7, 1971, an upgrade is almost assured.

On July 7, 1971, Secretary of Defense Melvin Laird established a policy exempting military members from prosecution or the issuance of a less than general discharge for drug use or possession on the basis of evidence developed from either mandatory random urinalysis or voluntary admission to a drug-treatment program. On August 13, 1971, Laird issued a memorandum instructing the Secretary of each service to review applications through the DRBs, for recharacterization of those other than honorable discharges issued solely on the basis of use of drugs or possession of drugs for personal use in all cases processed before July 7, 1971, or in process on or before that date. On April 28, 1972, that policy was extended to punitive discharges (bad conduct and dishonorable discharges) issued as a result of court-martial convictions for the use or possession of drugs.

The purpose of the August 13, 1971, and April 28, 1972, policies was to put veterans with bad discharges for drugs in the same position they would have been in if the drug-rehabilitation policy of July 7, 1971, had been effective when they were in service. Since vets earlier than July 7, 1971, never had the opportunity to turn themselves in, be treated, and be discharged honorably or under honorable conditions, they are now given an opportunity to improve the character of their discharges.

The drug policy applies to the use and possession of all types of drugs—hard drugs, hallucinogens, "uppers," "downers," as well as marijuana. The policy also applies to individuals addicted to drugs as well as experimenters and casual users. It also applies if the discharge was the result of a civilian court conviction for drug possession. Thus, the upgrade of a discharge for drug use or possession for personal use is virtually certain unless the person had a terrible service record unrelated to drug use.

The policy does not apply to individuals involved or seeming to be involved in the sale of drugs.

How do you qualify under the Laird memo?

It is essential to dispel any notion of sale that may be inferred from the circumstances of the case. This means putting to rest not only any implication that the individual was selling drugs, but also the idea that s/he had the intent to sell because of possession of a large quantity of drugs. For example, it has been argued in a case involving possession of a large quantity of drugs that the cost of drugs in Vietnam was so low that the individual often bought large amounts at one time for his or her own use to avoid having to make frequent purchases: in other words, "wholesale" purchases were made.

If the veteran was charged with sale or possession with intent to sell and accepted an undesirable discharge in lieu of trial, and if the veteran is now denying involvement in the sale of drugs, the reasons for accepting the discharge must be explained. If the veteran cannot show that the charges were erroneous and provide plausible reasons for not contesting the mistaken charges at a court-martial, the acceptance of an undesirable discharge may appear to have been an admission of guilt. Although sale of drugs is not covered by the policy, an upgrade may be possible if there are mitigating circumstances. Sale of small amounts where no profit is involved, such as between friends, is often made an exception. We know that the Navy DRB and Army BCMR have decided such cases favorably. Also, a drug seller may, because of his or her rehabilitation, qualify for an upgrade.

What is discharge "solely" for drugs?

Although the policy statement is clear that sale or intent to sell excludes the individual from the policy's application, the interpretation of the term "solely for use and possession" has not been equally clear. In a memorandum dated September 17, 1971, Undersecretary of the Army Thaddeus Beall, by way of guidance for the review of less than honorable discharges held by drug users, wrote: "The term 'solely' would not be construed to bar the favorable recharacterization of a discharge where only minor offenses, especially those related to or caused by drug abuse, may have been a contributing factor in the granting of an Undesirable Discharge or other than Honorable Discharge." The other services have shown an inclination to adopt this policy. Thus, if other offenses are involved, it is important to demonstrate that they are either insignificant, would not independently have caused a discharge, or that they were caused by drugs, or related to drug use; for example, a short AWOL to obtain the needed drugs or being late to duty.

On its face, then, the drug policy applies to two groups of cases: (1) those in which the military discharged the individual solely for offenses of drug use or possession for personal use and (2) those in which the individual was discharged with a record of a drug offense plus other disciplinary infractions.

There are also cases in which the veteran was discharged for nondrug offenses with a record that does not reflect the drug use that in fact caused the pattern of misconduct leading to the discharge. These cases are hard to defend, but the boards can be convinced that they do come under the drug policy. However, strong evidence is usually required. In many of these cases, servicepersons were discharged with undesirable discharges for unfitness for "frequent involvement of a discreditable nature."

There is yet a fourth category of drug-related charges that is usually covered by the Laird drug policy: civilian conviction for a drug offense. Veterans who were discharged for such convictions received undesirable discharges for "misconduct."

What is meant by "in process on July 7"?

Cases that start after July 7, 1971, do not come under the Laird policy. Therefore, in some cases, you must try to stretch the case back in time. Clearly, if an arrest or investigation occurred before that date, the vet qualifies. Sometimes it can be argued that the *addiction* causing the offense occurred before the cut-off date. There is a good chance that the policy will extend to all veterans once DOD promulgates its new discharge upgrade program. This is discussed later on in this chapter.

How should a drug case be presented to the boards?

It depends on the circumstances of the case. Individuals in the first category, pure drug abuse, who have only drug offenses on their records, or drug offenses with one or two other minor offenses, virtually have a guaranteed upgrade, provided that there is no inference of sale to be drawn from the records. In such cases, the DRBs send to an individual who has filed a DD 293 what the Army and Air Force have termed a "tender letter," and what the Navy and Marines call a "conditional." This letter contains an offer to the applicant of a general discharge (rarely an honorable discharge) based on a review of the records without a hearing. The veteran still may request a hearing if s/he wishes to press for an honorable discharge. The Army let-

83

ter, however, contains a significant warning: if the veteran requests and has a hearing, the Army reserves the option of completely withdrawing the offer of an upgrade and affirming the undesirable discharge if the evidence at the hearing warrants that action in the opinion of the board. The possibility of such a result also exists at the other boards, though no warning is given. The result is unlikely, but always consult qualified counsel before going ahead with a hearing in such a case. Do not be too concerned if you do not get a tender letter, as sometimes the various boards stop using them altogether for periods of time.

Veterans in the second category, those discharged for a combination of drug and nondrug offenses, are less likely to receive a prehearing offer of a general discharge. In many of these cases, individuals were discharged for unfitness, "frequent involvement of a discreditable nature." Therefore, the DBR will not see the case as a "drug" discharge. Further, even in those cases in which drug abuse was the reason given for the discharge, if the record shows several nondrug offenses, the DRB may now view it as a "frequent involvement" discharge.

The approach in such cases must be to convince the DRB that all the nondrug offenses were in fact drug-related (or were insignificant), and that drug abuse was the cause of the misbehavior evident in the individual's personal life. For example, short AWOLs can often be attributed to time taken to buy drugs or to the effect of drugs. Or being late for assigned duties might have been caused by being on drugs and thus unaware of time and not tuned in to responsibilities.

Veterans in the third category, those whose records do not on their face show evidence of drug use, bear a much heavier burden of proof and must corroborate the claim of drug usage. Corroboration can sometimes be made through the records by analyzing behavior patterns evident in the personnel file. For example, abrupt changes in behavior or a series of short AWOLs following a prior excellent record would lend credibility to a vet's contention that drugs were behind the disciplinary problems. Letters from family, friends, physicians, clergy who were aware of the vet's drug problem during the term of service, and before or after, should be gathered. In-service medical records may also provide corroboration. An individual may have been treated for hepatitis, for example. It is also helpful to present evidence of preservice and post-service drug use. For example, the individual may have civilian convictions of drug offenses, a high school record indicating drug use, involvement post-service in a drug-rehabilitation program, etc.

Once drug use has been established, it can be important to discuss the extent of the individual's drug habit while in the service. The more time the individual was under the influence of drugs and the heavier the dosage, the more likely it is that his/her actions were influenced by drugs and that all disciplinary infractions can be attributed to drugs.

Developing a case involving a bad conduct or dishonorable discharge for drug or drug-related offenses involves the same process as that for the undesirable discharge (except, of course, that a bad conduct discharge issued by a general court-martial or a dishonorable discharge can be recharacterized only by a BCMR).

The fourth category of individuals, those discharged for misconduct pursuant to a civilian drug conviction, is not explicitly covered by the Laird memo. However, the same principles should apply to these pre-July 7, 1971, discharges.

There appears to be a general unwritten policy of not upgrading drug discharges to honorable, but it is not hopeless. Cases involving one-time use where the record is excellent, experimental use, soft drugs, or psychiatric problems manifested by drugs appear to present opportunities for fully honorable discharges. There is usually little to lose by requesting a hearing, particularly if you really need a fully honorable discharge.

What are your chances for upgrade if your discharge was after July 7, 1971?

The drug policy discussed above applies only to those other than honorable discharges that were issued on or before July 7, 1971, or that were in process on or before that date. Since that date, the drug "amnesty" policy has been in effect, which immunizes from prosecution or undesirable discharges those who turn themselves in or those drug abusers discovered through the mandatory random urinalysis program.[1] Thus, those who did not turn themselves in or who were not discovered through the urinalysis program could be given an undesirable discharge or nonjudicial punishment, or be court-martialed for drug and drug-induced offenses and are not given special consideration by the DRBs.

In post-July 7, 1971, drug cases, then, you must demonstrate how the amnesty program failed to work for you. For instance, drugs were known to be freely available in many drug-amnesty houses on bases, so turning oneself in would in reality lead to more, not less, drug use. Many individuals simply did not believe they would not be prosecuted. And, of course, those who were addicted to heroin or who were heavily involved with other types of drugs did not have sufficient awareness of their own problems or the strength to turn themselves in. To admit drug use to the authorities may be the first step toward rehabilitation, but many are caught before they reach that step. Also, those persons discharged before March 28, 1973, qualified for consideration under the Carter special discharge review program discussed below and all veterans may qualify under the new DOD program that is also discussed below.

Is it possible to win a discharge upgrade if your bad discharge was for homosexual acts?

Yes. As Americans generally have become more tolerant and accepting of homosexuality, the military has slowly begun to reflect the changing sexual mores. Although homosexual activity is still not officially tolerated by the military and will almost always result in a discharge, in the last five years there have been more general and honorable discharges in cases of homosexual acts. Until recently, an undesirable discharge was almost automatic in cases involving homosexual acts. Thus, many of the veterans who have pre-1972 discharges for homosexual acts have undesirable discharges.[2]

The DRBs and BCMRs are beginning to reflect the more liberal current policies of the services by upgrading undesirable discharges in those cases in which the services would now award a general or honorable discharge if the cases arose today: that is, in those cases involving consensual adult behavior.

An undesirable discharge for homosexual acts will not be upgraded if the homosexual activity involved either the use of force, sexual activity with a minor or undue use of rank. In cases involving no such aggravated circumstances, an upgrade is realistic. And in many cases in which the question of force or undue influence is lingering in the background, it can be successfully refuted at the hearing and a case made for consensual adult behavior.

Cases involving homosexual activity of an officer with an enlisted person are somewhat more difficult. There is a general unwritten policy that officers should not socialize with enlisted persons. Further, an officer is supposed to command respect, display leadership, and set a "moral" example. To the military, an officer's homosexual activity with an enlisted person violates all these requirements, and creates an assumption that the officer is responsible for negatively affecting the morals of the enlisted person. Thus, sometimes the presumption of the appropriateness of an undesirable discharge is more difficult to rebut, but many upgrades occur in officer cases.

If you are gay, should you tell the DRB or BCMR?

Yes. The fact that you are gay will generally not harm your chances of getting an upgrade. Your honesty can, in fact, work in your favor.

What kind of discharge should you expect to receive?

Most DRBs are tendering general discharges without a hearing. However, some honorable discharges have been given after hearings. It is generally felt that gay people or people who engaged in homosexual acts should stand up and fight for their rights. Hence, a hearing to seek a fully honorable discharge is often desirable. If all gay people had resisted the discharges in the past, it is unlikely that there would be so many bad discharges for homosexual acts. It is also likely that the boards will begin to give fully honorable discharges in the future.[8] Those who received upgrades to general should reapply urging an upgrade under current standards.

87

If your bad discharge resulted from alcoholism, do you have a chance for an upgrade?

Yes, if you can prove that your discharge resulted from alcoholism. Although there are no available statistics to document the magnitude of the problem, alcoholism and alcohol abuse have affected large numbers of service personnel over the years. One of the results, of course, has been the issuance of less than fully honorable discharges to those who, because of their alcoholism, were unable to meet required standards of behavior.

Until approximately 10 to 15 years ago, all the services authorized the issuance of an unfitness, and thus most often an undesirable discharge, for alcoholism. That is, an individual could be given a less than honorable discharge simply for being an alcoholic even if the individual's record showed no evidence of any sort of misconduct or poor performance. It wasn't until 1959 that the military reached the understanding that alcoholism is a disease, that it should be treated rather than punished, that the unacceptable conduct of an alcoholic may be beyond his/her control, and that the product of the alcohol abuse cannot be eliminated without professional help.

In 1959, the services changed their regulations to permit an unsuitability rather than an unfitness discharge for alcoholism. Although this shift in policy eliminated the possibility of an undesirable discharge, service personnel could still be stigmatized by a general discharge for what is, in fact, a medical problem.

On March 1, 1972, Secretary of Defense Laird issued DOD Directive 1010.2, titled "Alcohol Abuse by Personnel of the Department of Defense," which was the first department-wide policy statement issued on alcoholism. The directive declared a DOD policy to prevent alcoholism with problems attributable to alcohol abuse, and to treat those who cannot be restored. The directive states DOD's recognition that alcoholism is a disease that is subject to treatment and that a member of the military should not be discharged on the basis of alcoholism unless the individual does not actively cooperate in treatment programs and then s/he "may be determined to be unsuitable for further military service and may be administratively separated."

Although the directive still permits disciplinary action to be taken to punish conduct that is the result of alcoholism and alcohol abuse, the directive does suggest that "judicious use" be made of *suspended* punishment in order that the individual be directed into a rehabiltation program. The policy was not made expressly retroactive. Thus, the review boards usually apply current standards, but are not specifically directed to do so.

Most alcoholic GIs, at least before the 1972 DOD Directive, were not discharged for alcoholism. A large number of veterans in that category were discharged undesirably either for "frequent involvement of a discreditable nature" or as a result of resignations in lieu of trial "for the good of the service" or as unsuitable, with honorable or general discharges. As in the case of drug abusers, the services generally failed to recognize or deal with the root of the individual's problem. Instead, the alcoholic individual was disciplined for his/her inevitable and uncontrollable disciplinary infractions and ultimately discharged for unacceptable performance and a bad disciplinary record.

Undesirable discharges for alcoholism, if it is clear that the alcohol abuse was the reason given by the military for separation, should be relatively easy to upgrade if all or most disciplinary infractions can be related to alcohol abuse.

The more common case, however, will be the one in which alcoholism was not the reason cited by the military for the discharge. If it can be shown that the individual was an alcoholic while in the service, and that all the problems leading to the undesirable discharge were alcohol-related, it can then be contended that the individual should have been discharged as unsuitable, for alcoholism, with a general or honorable discharge depending upon his/her record of service.

How can you show that your alcohol abuse caused your misconduct?
You can submit hospital records; statements from friends, relatives, employers, or counselors; arrest records; or anything that shows the nature of your alcohol problem. Unless there is some proof of the problem, the boards tend not to accept just the word of an applicant (and for

good reason—a person can hardly be an alcoholic without someone else knowing).

Are there any special programs that apply if you were discharged during the Vietnam era?

Yes, on March 28, 1977, the Pentagon announced a special program to review Vietnam-era discharges which occurred between August 4, 1964, and March 28, 1973.[4]

Who was eligible for this program?

Those people who (1) received general or undesirable discharges during the Vietnam era or who had their undesirable discharges changed to clemency discharges under the Ford Clemency Program or who went AWOL during the Vietnam era and returned under this program and (2) who applied to the program before it expired.

How long did the program last?

The program expired, except for the consideration of pending applications, on October 4, 1977. As this book went to press, the program had not been extended.

How did a veteran apply to the program?

By calling a toll free number: 800-325-4040 or 314-428-3500 (for Missouri, Puerto Rico, Alaska and Hawaii).

How did the program work and what were the criteria for review of discharges?

The DRBs were responsible for reviewing applications. Veterans with undesirable or clemency discharges would get an automatic upgrade, usually to general, if one of the following criterion applied to their cases:

1. Received a decoration (other than a service medal).
2. Received an honorable discharge from a previous tour of military service.
3. Was wounded in action.
4. Satisfactorily completed a tour of military service in Southeast Asia, or in the Western Pacific in support of operations in Southeast Asia.
5. Had a record of satisfactory active military service for twenty-four months prior to discharge.

6. Completed alternate service or was excused therefrom in accordance with the Ford Clemency Program.

If those criteria did not apply, an undesirable discharge could still be upgraded, usually to general after the board considered the following factors:

1. Age, general aptitude, and length of service at time of discharge.
2. Education level at time of discharge.
3. Whether entered service from a deprived background.
4. Possible personal distress which may have contributed to the acts which led to discharge.
5. Whether entered military service upon waiver of normally applicable entrance standards.
6. Whether the actions which led to discharge were alleged at the time to have been motivated by conscience.
7. Whether was discharged for abuse of drugs or alcohol and, if so, any contributing or extenuating circumstances.
8. Record of good citizenship since discharge. Boards were encouraged to give weight to this factor when a good record was shown.

If the applicant's undesirable discharge was not upgraded to general, the applicant could request a hearing with the appointment of a free lawyer.

Veterans who had general discharges could also apply for upgrading and the boards were to "consider in their deliberations the President's desire that discharges be reexamined in a spirit of compassion."

Were any Vietnam-era veterans with administrative discharges who met the automatic upgrade criteria excluded from the Program?

Yes. Undesirable and clemency discharges were not upgraded if there were "compelling reasons" to deny an upgrade. These were defined as:

1. Discharge was for desertion or absence in or from the combat zone. An individual who departed the combat zone on leave, TDY, or other authorized

absence basis and did not return was considered to have deserted in or from the combat zone. Conversely, an individual who failed to report to an embarkation point for further assignment to the combat zone was not considered to have been absent in or from the combat zone.

2. Discharge was based on an act of violence or violent crime.
3. Discharge was based on cowardice or misbehavior before the enemy.
4. Discharge was based on an act or conduct that would be subject to criminal prosecution if it had taken place in a civilian environment.

Did the boards have to tell you why they did not grant you an upgrade?

Yes, as in all discharge upgrade cases, they had to give findings and reasons and respond to any arguments you presented. However, many of the board "decisions" under this program were very short and insufficient under DRB regulations.

If you did not receive an upgrade to honorable under the Carter program, could you file another application requesting an upgrade to honorable?

Yes. You would follow the same procedures you would in any other discharge upgrade case.

What if you did not know about the Carter program until after it was over?

While it is too early to tell what would happen in such cases, it is reasonable to assume that if your case fit into the criteria of the program, and you honestly did not know about the program, that the boards would be inclined to be sympathetic to your case.

Also, on January 19, 1977, former President Ford directed that all persons who 1) applied to his clemency program (the directive does not specify if the applicant had to complete the program) and 2) who were wounded in combat or received decorations for valor in combat have their discharges upgraded to general. So if you fall in that category, your discharge may have been upgraded, or will be if you point out that you qualify.

Did Congress pass a law that affected the veterans' benefits of people who got upgrades under the Ford or Carter program?

Yes. Legislation was enacted on October 8, 1977, which affected those veterans who had their undesirable discharges upgraded under the January 19, 1977, Ford directive (not the 1974–75 clemency program) and the Carter program. This legislation removed the automatic entitlement to veterans' benefits that normally accompanied a discharge upgrade; however, the discharge upgrade itself was not affected.

(Procedures were being implemented as this book went to press to notify all those persons so affected.)

The DRB concerned will review all of the cases to see whether the person would normally have received an upgrade. The reviews will be conducted as follows:

1. If a veteran is receiving benefits, the DRB will make an expedited determination. Benefits will not be terminated before the earlier date of (i) 90 days since the initial determination, or (ii) 180 days after enactment of the legislation. Benefits already received do not have to be repaid even if the determination is adverse.

2. Those applying for benefits will go through a similar determination by the DRB.

3. All other cases are to be reviewed by the DRBs within one year of enactment of the legislation.

4. Cases upgraded under the Carter program before any new program is established (*discussed below*) will have the eligibility determination made by the DRB at the same time an upgrade is granted.

Will you have a chance to contest the DRB decision?

Yes, in all cases where the DRB determination is adverse, the veteran will be given notice and an opportunity to appear at a hearing with counsel.

If you have moved since an upgrade or since an application was made, be sure to give the DRB your new address. You can write or telephone them at:

Army	Army DRB—Room 1E479 Department of the Army Pentagon Washington, DC 20310 (202) 69-54682/73166
Air Force	Air Force DRB 1300 Wilson Boulevard Commonwealth Building— Room 903 Arlington, VA 22209 (202) 69-45249/45074
Navy and Marines	Navy DRB 801 North Randolph—Suite 905 Arlington, VA 22203 (202) 69-24628
Coast Guard	Coast Guard DRB 400 7th St., NW Washington, DC 20590 (202) 426-0884

Does the legislation deny benefits to other veterans who receive upgrades?

Yes. A new bar to benefits—which applies to those upgraded under the Ford January 19 program or the Carter program, or to those who apply to the DRB in the future—is added to 38 U.S.C. § 3103(a). That is, those persons undesirably discharged for being absent from duty for more than 180 days are barred from receiving VA benefits unless the VA determines there were "compelling reasons" for the absence. The VA presumably will promulgate regulations defining this term. Since the President said that this provision was probably unconstitutional, it is logical to assume that "compelling reasons" will be broadly interpreted. The discussion of the law of AWOL in Chapter I will be useful if the VA determines a defense in law is a "compelling reason." *See* Chapters X through XVII for a thorough discussion of VA claims procedures. Also, upgrades by the DRBs of any future cases are no longer binding on the VA (upgrades—or some action; the legislation is un-

94

clear—by BCMRs are), which must now review some cases to see if the bars to benefits contained in 38 U.S.C. §3103(a) are present. *See* Chapter X.

Will there be a special program like the Carter program for all veterans?

Yes and no. The same legislation discussed above required the DOD to promulgate "published uniform standards [and procedures] which shall be historically consistent with criteria for determining honorable service and shall not include any criterion for automatically granting or denying" a change in discharge. The legislation requires that after the promulgation of the new standards the new program must be opened for a year for all veterans who received other than honorable administrative discharges. Thus, once the program begins, the normal 15-year statute of limitations will be waived for a year. It also would seem that, even if a person has applied in the past, s/he may apply under the new program. Veterans with court-martial-ordered discharges or with general discharges will not be eligible for the new program. However, it would seem that the BCMRs, and the DRBs in the case of less than 15-year-old general discharges, would consider many of these cases using their normal rule of generally applying "current standards," that is, the standards set up by the new program.

The establishment of a new program with articulated standards will likely result in some liberalizing of standards, simply because consistent adherence to rules will be necessary and also because a lawsuit to force compliance with what are perceived to be constitutionally required standards (such as a showing that the conduct at issue actually affected the character of military service) will likely be filed.

Hopefully, President Carter will not permit any new program to be eroded by Congress, as he allowed with his Special Program by not actively working against the legislation or not vetoing it.

Under the new program, will the DRBs be required to state their reasons for granting or denying an upgrade?

Yes, the DRBs (and, to a lesser extent, the BCMRs) were, in effect, required to comply with the Administrative Procedure Act pursuant to the out-of-court settlement in the case of *Urban Law Institute* v. *Secretary*, Civil Action No. 76-0503 (D.D.C., January 31, 1977). This settlement became effective on April 1, 1977, and is fully discussed at 4MLR 6001 and 4MLR 6038-6042.

If you carefully set forth the reasons why your discharge should be upgraded, the Board must explain why it rejected your contention. If it does not, it is in violation of the *Urban Law* agreement; and you may be able to get another hearing—or at least a better statement of why you were denied the full relief you requested.

Remember, the Board cannot use general conclusiary language such as "over-all service record" (without setting it forth), "the claim is invalid," or "proper procedures were followed" if you make very specific claims.

NOTES

1. In *U.S.* v. *Ruiz*, 23 USCMA 181, 48 CMR 797 (1974), the Court of Military Appeals ruled that it was proper to refuse an order to give a urine sample if a general discharge could result therefrom. The military suspended the urinalysis program until January 1975. Thereafter, fully honorable discharges were required if evidence of drug use flowed from involuntary urinalysis testing. It would seem, therefore, that people who received general discharges before *Ruiz* should receive the benefit of that decision. However, it is not likely that DOD will agree until a lawsuit is brought. *Giles* v. *Secretary*, Civil Action No. 77-0904 (D.D.C.) raises this issue.
2. *The Rights of Gay People*, another in this series of handbooks, has an extensive discussion of the problems gay people face in the armed forces.
3. In a federal court lawsuit we filed on behalf of a gay veteran with a general discharge, the Secretary of the Navy ordered that he be given a fully honorable discharge. *Pittman* v. *Secretary*, Civil Action No. 76-0948 (D.D.C.). This it was said was a result of a contemplated change in policy.
4. A detailed discussion of this program appears at 4 MLR 6017.

VIII

Employment Problems

Your status as a former member of the armed forces can be important when you seek civilian employment. That status is useful for competitive civil service positions (with an honorable or general discharge) and for reemployment rights. Sometimes that status can be harmful. It is not the purpose of this section to list all possible employment advantages that flow from your status as a veteran. This section is intended to assist you in pursuing the appropriate legal remedies should you be denied your rights or be discriminated against.

What are a veteran's reemployment rights?

You may have a legal right to your old job or to one like it.[1] This right also includes any pay increases or promotions you would have received in the job had you been there all along. This is true whether you were inducted, volunteered, or were appointed into the military service. Federal laws on the reemployment rights of veterans apply to most jobs in private industry and in the federal government except for temporary ones. State, county, and city jobs came under federal law on December 3, 1974. Many states also have their own laws on behalf of veterans. If you do have reemployment rights, all the time you spent in service must be counted toward seniority. Sometimes this can automatically move you into a higher wage bracket.

What makes you eligible for these reemployment rights, and what if your former employer disputes your entitlement to them?

You must be leaving the service with 4 years or less of active service, unless you have been involuntarily extended, and you must have an honorable or general discharge. Most veterans have 90 days after separation from active service (or hospitalization of 1 year or less) to apply for the last job held before active service. Reservists and National Guard members with initial periods of 3 to 6 months of active duty for training must apply within 31 days. At the time of separation, you should have completed the reemployment rights form (OVRR-2) given to you.

Since there are many variables in reemployment cases due to the changing nature of many jobs, union contracts, and the like, there are many disputes as to entitlement. If it "reasonably appears [that you are] entitled to the benefits in dispute,"[2] the local U.S. Attorney's Office must represent you at no charge.

If you have problems with reemployment or feel you are entitled to more benefits, do not delay in seeking relief, for you may lose your claim to your rights.[3]

For assistance with private employment, contact the nearest regional office of the Labor-Management Services Administration, Department of Labor. These offices are listed in large-city telephone directories. The nearest state employment bureau can also help you find the office. You also can write to the national office of the Labor-Management Services Administration, Department of Labor, Washington, DC 20210.

For assistance with federal employment, contact the Civil Service Commission, at one of its offices around the country or in Washington, DC 20006.

Can a new employer require the release of your service records as a pre-condition to giving you a job?

Generally, yes. Of course, you can refuse and take your chances. In some places, such an inquiry is improper, so you will have to check your state or local fair employment regulations.[4]

Will a less than fully honorable discharge affect your ability to find a civilian job?

Yes. Veterans who do not have a fully honorable discharge do encounter serious discrimination in employment. There are many employers who simply will not even consider hiring a vet whose discharge is not fully honorable. Often, the fact of bad discharge ends the interview. The most serious discrimination appears to be encountered by those with undesirable discharges even though the reason for discharge usually bears no relationship to qualifications for civilian employment.

Is there anything you can do if you are refused a job because of the character of your discharge?

In the majority of instances of job discrimination, there is no remedy. There are, however, a few states and cities that prohibit such discrimination. The Human Rights Commission in the state of Washington has made it an unfair labor practice for an employer to discriminate on the basis of character of military discharge.[5] The same is true in San Francisco for employers who are city contractors or suppliers. Such regulations will probably be promulgated in other places, so you should check with your local or state Human Rights or Civil Rights Commission to determine if using military discharge as a criterion for employment has been prohibited.

What about employers working on government contracts?

While they have not yet been interpreted, the Department of Labor (DOL) regulations implementing the Vietnam Era Veterans Readjustment Assistance Act of 1974 require that a government contractor working on a government contract of a value of over $10,000 "consider only that portion of the [applicant's] military record, including discharge papers, relevant to the specific job qualifications for which the veteran is being considered."[6] This is part of the program requiring affirmative action by the DOL in providing employment for disabled and Vietnam-era veterans. It would seem that a bad discharge alone cannot disqualify you. The reason for the discharge must relate reasonably to the job for which you applied in order for such an employer to discriminate against you. If you feel your rights were violated by a covered employer, you should file a complaint with the Veterans Employment Service of the Department of Labor through your state Employment Services office. If you are already an employee, you must first file a complaint in accordance with your employer's internal review procedure if one exists. DOL has several ways in which your rights can be vindicated.

Is discrimination against veterans with bad discharges unconstitutional?

State or local governments and federal regulations that automatically exclude from government employment those with less than fully honorable discharges may be acting unconstitutionally under the Fifth or the Fourteenth Amendment. One federal appeals court[7] has so held in the case of such an ordinance enacted by a small town in Louisiana. If you find that such a law exists, and is being applied to you, you should check with your local American Civil Liberties Union office or other such organization for advice on the possibility of challenging the law in a court action.

Would discrimination against minority veterans with bad discharges constitute illegal racial discrimination?

Yes. In 1972, the Department of Defense Task Force on the Administration of Military Justice in the Armed Forces found that black members of the armed forces received bad discharges for all reasons disproportionately to whites with similar IQ's and educational backgrounds. This caused the Equal Employment Opportunities Commission (EEOC) to rule that the failure to hire a veteran just because of his or her bad discharge can be viewed as racial discrimination, in the case of a black veteran, in violation of Title VII of the Civil Rights Act of 1964.[8] It is possible that this same rationale can apply to Spanish-surnamed veterans. If you are black or Spanish-surnamed and were denied employment or job-related benefits due to your less than fully honorable discharge, contact the EEOC. This federal agency has the job of enforcing the 1964 Civil Rights Act, which prohibits job discrimination

related to race, color, religion, sex, or national origin. Job
discrimination in every aspect of employment—hiring, fir-
ing, training, promotion, wages, fringe benefits, etc.—is
illegal. The law covers private employers, state and local
government agencies, public and private educational institutions, labor unions, apprenticeship programs, and public
and private employment agencies. Federal employment is
covered by an Executive Order enforced by the U.S. Civil
Service Commission.

There are 32 district EEOC offices located across the
country. The addresses and telephone numbers are listed
in the telephone directory under "U.S. Government."
Should an EEOC office not be listed in the telephone
directory for your area, write to EEOC Headquarters, 2401
E Street, N.W., Washington, DC 20506, ATTN: Compliance Office. You must file a "charge" with the EEOC
within 180 days of the alleged discrimination and allege
that the employer's policy of not hiring veterans with bad
discharges has a "discriminatory impact" on racial minorities.

Such a bootstrap use of the 1974 Task Force report
does not help white vets. It could be argued that once the
rule is adopted for racial minorities, whites are discriminated against. Some people within the EEOC buy this approach, but it generally has not been followed.

**Is there any way the National Labor Relations Board can
deal with this problem?**

An untested possibility for all veterans may be the Labor Management Relations Act (LMRA), which prohibits
unions from discriminating against employees whom it
represents and prohibits "unfair employment practices" by
unions or businesses. Many combinations of union and
business practices have been found to be "unfair"; so if a
combination of rules or a rule of a union or business
keeps a vet with a bad discharge from obtaining employment, the LMRA *may* provide a remedy.[9] In order to pursue this untried remedy, the vet would have to file an
unfair labor practice charge, within 180 days of the denial
of employment, with the regional office of the National
Labor Relations Board (NLRB). The Regional Director,
or the General Counsel of the NLRB if the Regional Direc-

101

tor's decision is appealed, is the person who decides if a "charge" should be filed. If your complaint is rejected and no charge is filed, there is no remedy in the courts. Remember, this is an untested route.

Can you minimize the impact that the bad discharge may have on a prospective employer?

Any veteran with a bad discharge who is going to inform a prospective employer about a bad discharge should volunteer the reasons behind the discharge if they will serve to explain it. At least, this may help you keep your foot in the door.

What is an exemplary rehabilitation certificate?

This is a certificate issued by the Department of Labor (DOL) that indicates that a person with a less than honorable discharge has been "rehabilitated," but it does not affect the character of the original discharge or one's entitlement to VA benefits. It might help with some employers. It can't hurt.

An application cannot be made until 3 years after discharge. Write to Manpower Administration, U.S. Department of Labor, Washington, DC 20210, ATTN: METR. If an application is filed, DOL representatives conduct a work, character, and police review of the applicant's "record."

NOTES

1. 50 U.S.C. App. § 459.
2. 50 U.S.C. App. § 459 (d).
3. *Churma* v. *United States Steel Corp.*, 514 F.2d 589 (3rd Cir. 1975).
4. Washington State Human Rights Commission Employment Regulation, WAC 162-12-140(3)i, makes a request for discharge papers an unfair pre-employment inquiry.
5. *Ibid.*
6. 41 C.F.R. § 60-250.6(b). See also footnote seven.
7. *Thompson* v. *Gallagher*, 489 F.2d 443 (5th Cir. 1973). The Court also interpreted the language "other than dishonorable discharges" contained in the Emergency Employment Act of 1971, which provides funds for local governments to hire veterans, not to include the undesirable discharge.

That act is no longer in effect. The programs that were administered under that act are now covered by the Comprehensive Employment Act, and the Office of Federal Contract Compliance considers an undesirable discharge to be an "other than dishonorable" discharge, which is a qualifying discharge. Letters to David Addlestone from Lawrence Z. Lorber, Deputy Assistant Secretary, Director, OFCCP, and Diane Graham, Acting Director, OFCCP. In part, the latter letter said:

> The term "other than dishonorable discharge" appears in 41 CFR 60-250.2 of the regulations implementing Section 402 of the Vietnam Era Veterans Readjustment Assistance Act of 1974. These regulations were published in the Federal Register on June 25, 1976. The definition states:
>
>> "Veteran of the Vietnam era"—means a person (1) who (i) served on active duty for a period of more than 180 days, any part of which occurred between August 5, 1964 and May 7, 1975, and was discharged or released therefrom with other than a dishonorable discharge, or (ii) was discharged or released from active duty for a service-connected disability, if any part of such active duty was performed between August 5, 1964 and May 7, 1975; and (2) who was so discharged or released within 48 months preceding the alleged violation of the Act, the affirmative action clause, and/or the regulations issued pursuant to the Act."
>
> OFCCP has adopted a literal interpretation of this definition. "Other than dishonorable discharge," as far as OFCCP is concerned, includes all types of military discharges, except those specifically designated as "dishonorable."
>
> We have been informed that veterans eligible for benefits under Comprehensive Employment Training Act (CETA) legislation are those with "other than dishonorable discharges." Thus, there is no conflict in the language defining veterans covered under the CETA, and Section 402 of the Vietnam Era Readjustment Assistance Act of 1974.

8. EEOC Decision No. 74-25 (Sept. 10, 1973). One court has followed this ruling, *Dozier* v. *Chupka*, 395 F. Supp.

836 (S.D. Ohio 1975). This is similar to the notion that since blacks are arrested without an ultimate conviction more than whites, it is illegal discrimination to reject black applicants solely because of arrest records. *Gregory* v. *Litton Systems, Inc.*, 316 F. Supp. 401 (C.D. Calif. 1970), *modified*, 472 F.2d 631 (9th Cir. 1972). However, recent Supreme Court decisions indicate a trend to require actual discriminatory intent as opposed to policies that discriminate in effect.

9. However, the Supreme Court has ruled that it is not hostile discrimination for a union to give vets seniority preference over nonvets. *Ford Motor Co.* v. *Huffman*, 345 U.S. 330 (1953). It is unlikely that one branch of the government (the NLRB) will not permit actions of another branch (the military) to be accorded their intended weight, at least in the context of interpreting what is an "unfair labor practice." But it wouldn't hurt to try.

IX

Back-Pay Claims

If you feel that the military owes you money due to an underpayment of your salary or allowances and you are now a civilian, can you still make a claim?

Yes. You have 6 years from the date the claim accrued to present a claim for arrears in pay.[1] If your claim arose as a result of the decision of a discharge or correction board or a court, the 6 years run from the date of that action. Complete DD Form 827, which can be obtained from any VA office, or provide your name, address, former service, period of time for which you are making a claim, the last place you entered active duty, the place of discharge, and the facts or documents that support your claim, and send all to:

ARMY
Finance Center
U.S. Army Finance Support Agency, FINCS-A
Indianapolis, IN 46249

AIR FORCE
Air Force Accounting and Finance Center, AFC
3800 York Street
Denver, CO 80205

COAST GUARD
Commandant
Headquarters
U.S. Coast Guard, G-FPS-2/71

Settlements and Records Section
Personnel Support Division
Washington, DC 20590

NAVY
Finance Center
U.S. Navy, Cellebrezze Building
Cleveland, OH 44199

MARINE CORPS
Finance Center
Examination Division
Kansas City, MO 64197

If you have your bad discharge changed, are you entitled to back pay or damages?

You are not entitled to damages; however, you are entitled to any mustering-out pay, accrued leave, or dependent's travel expenses forfeited as a result of an undesirable, bad conduct or dishonorable discharge. You are not entitled to interest on this money. Apply to the appropriate finance center listed above, and the 6-year limitation begins from the date of recharacterization of your discharge. However, if the appropriate pay records have been destroyed in accordance with the law, you will have to produce documents showing that you were not paid at the time of your discharge. Sometimes the service automatically forwards your file to the appropriate finance center. If this is done, your notice of discharge recharacterization will so state.

What if you were overpaid while on active duty and the military now says you owe them money?

Generally, you must repay this money even if you did not know that you were overpaid. Claims of this nature frequently occur when a person being involuntarily discharged under other than honorable conditions is erroneously paid for accrued leave or when a person has accepted a reenlistment bonus but is discharged before that enlistment is completed. The government, however, is not likely to sue you for a small claim. With some exceptions, the government must sue you within 6 years or the claim is barred by statute. However, if you make a partial payment or acknowledge the claim in writing, the 6 years will begin to run again.[2]

There is authority[3] for the military to waive this indebtedness up to $500. To obtain a waiver, you must apply within 3 years of discovery of the error. Normally, a waiver will be granted if there is no indication of a lack of good faith or fraud on your part. If you have already paid the claim, you can request a waiver and then apply within 2 years of the waiver for a refund. Apply to the appropriate finance center listed above.

If you were AWOL and returned after your normal date of separation, were you entitled to pay?

Only if you were "assigned useful and productive duties which are considered by [your] commander to be consistent with [your] grade and years of service."[4] In other words, if you performed essentially full duties and were not in jail, you were entitled to full pay and allowances.

You were an officer who was discharged involuntarily due to pregnancy; were you entitled to severance pay?

Under pertinent military regulations, female officers honorably discharged involuntarily due to pregnancy were denied severance pay. This policy prevailed even though male and female officers with more than 3 years of service discharged honorably but involuntarily for any other reason were entitled to severance pay of up to $14,000. Suit for severance pay, challenging the regulations, was brought in the Court of Claims on behalf of a female Naval officer honorably discharged involuntarily for pregnancy, *Norcross* v. *U.S.*, Ct. Cl. No. 84-74. The government agreed to a substantial monetary settlement rather than defend the suit. Thus, any officer discharged involuntarily due to pregnancy who files suit for severance pay in the Court of Claims is likely to prevail without protracted litigation. Such a suit must be filed within 6 years of the date of discharge.

You were a female member of the armed forces who was denied allowances and benefits for your nonmilitary husband; are you entitled to any back pay?

Yes. In 1973, the Supreme Court[5] ruled that the armed

forces could not make a woman member prove that her husband was actually dependent on her before qualifying the family for dependents' allowance and benefits (for example, medical) while at the same time not placing such a burden on married male servicemembers. If this occurred to you, you can claim back pay, medical expenses, etc., that would have been covered, by writing to the appropriate finance center listed above.

Was there a retroactive pay raise for GIs that some did not receive because they were already discharged?

Yes, nearly a million veterans who served between October 1, 1972, and January 1, 1973, benefit from a court ruling[6] that President Nixon illegally withheld a pay raise from government workers.

What if the military refuses to honor your back-pay claim?

You can file suit in U.S. District Court for up to $9999.99 or in the Court of Claims for any amount. You have 6 years[7] to bring your claim but should bring it as soon as possible to avoid the government's defense of "laches" (discussed below).

What can you do if you feel that not only are you entitled to back pay but you were also wrongfully discharged?

Such a claim can be presented to the Boards for Correction of Military or Naval Records (BCMR). These boards are discussed in Chapter VI. If the board refuses to grant the requested relief including reinstatement into the service, suit can be filed in the U.S. District Court or the Court of Claims. (In 1972, the Court of Claims was given power to grant relief incidental to granting a money claim.) The district courts require that you go to the BCMR first, while the Court of Claims does not. Also, the district court can only award $9,999.99 in damages in cases like this.[8] The Court of Claims, located in Washington, D.C., is a good forum for back-pay claims, particularly for wrongful discharge.[9] One problem with the Court of Claims is that it strictly applies the rule of "laches."[10] This rule means that if your delay in filing suit prejudices the government by way of having to fill your job with another person or through the loss of evidence or inability of witnesses to recall the events, then your claim is prohibited. This rule means that suit should be filed in the Court of Claims very soon after discharge. *To be safe you should not wait for the BCMR if you plan to sue in the Court of Claims.* If laches does not bar your claim, the statute of limitations can. You have 6 years from the date of discharge to file suit in the Court of Claims.

There are many other technical legal rules applicable to such cases, and a complete discussion is beyond the scope of this book. If you feel you have such a claim, consult an attorney knowledgeable about such cases.

NOTES

1. 31 U.S.C. § 71a. This went into effect July 1, 1975, and changed the 10-year statute of limitations that was in effect before that time.
2. 28 U.S.C. § 2415(d).
3. 10 U.S.C. § 2774. SECNAVINST 7220.38B (Navy).
4. Decisions of the Comptroller General, B-180768, April 15, 1975, interpreting 10 U.S.C. § 972.
5. *Frontiero* v. *Richardson*, 411 U.S. 677 (1973).
6. *National Treasury Employees Union* v. *Nixon*, 492 F.2d 587 (9174).
7. 28 U.S.C. § 1346(a) (2).
8. *Ibid.*
9. Jeffrey M. Glosser and Keith A. Rosenberg, *Military Correction Boards: Administrative Process and Review by the U.S. Court of Claims*, 23 Am. U.L. Rev. 391 (1973).
10. *Brundage* v. *U.S.*, 504 F.2d 1382, 205 Ct. Cl. 502 (1974). If your claim is based purely on a legal error and the government is not prejudiced by your delay, laches does not apply, *Rifkin* v. *U.S.*, 209 Ct. Cl. 566 (1976); *Carter* v. *U.S.*, 213 Ct. Cl. — (No. 360-75, March 4, 1977), 5 MLR 2056.

X

Eligibility for Veterans' Benefits

Throughout its history, the government has provided former servicemembers with various special services, allowances, payments, and privileges. Combined, they constitute veterans' benefits. These benefits have been justified as gifts to thank those who served and survived; as delayed compensation for service or as continuing compensation for injury or illness; and as aids in the transition back into civilian life. They have also been called inducements to enlist in the military—and inducements to retire from the military; a means to stimulate certain sectors of the economy; and a special interest group's raid on the national treasury. There is at least a grain of truth in each of these claims. But to most veterans, the important question is not "Why should there be veterans' benefits?" The important questions are "What benefits can I get, how do I get them, and how do I deal with the bureaucratic and often unsympathetic Veterans Administration?"

The information that follows should help you to answer these important questions. Although there is not enough space to describe every benefit and every procedure, an attempt is made to answer many of your questions, or to at least direct you to the right answer. The laws governing the Veterans Administration (VA) are contained in Title 38 of the United States Code. The VA also has a set of regulations, which contains procedures and clarifications for putting the laws into operation. The VA regulations are contained in Title 38 of the Code of Federal Regulations (C.F.R.), which can be found in many libraries, but the same text may be renumbered and called VA Regulations. Any VA office must maintain a copy of VA regulations available for public inspection.

Because certain kinds of claims are often disputed by the VA, most of the material in these chapters focuses on these claims. However, the methods we describe should be helpful even if your particular problem is not specifically discussed here.

At the outset, we must caution that what we have written is based in part on our own interpretation of often vague, conflicting, and incomplete statutes, regulations, and policies; the VA's interpretations may be less sympathetic to the ex-servicemember's rights. Since the decisions of the VA cannot normally be reviewed by the courts, there is no way to force a frequently arbitrary bureaucracy to adhere to its own governing laws and regulations. Thus, your fate may turn on whether your case is in the hands of the right bureaucrat. Since many VA employees seem to be unaware of many VA regulations, be armed with those referred to in this book and have a good counsel to represent you. *Read everything that follows with this caution in mind.*

Where do you get veterans' benefits?

Where you go depends upon the type of benefit you want. Most people, when they talk about veterans' benefits, are referring to those that are administered by the VA. The VA is a federal agency that administers a broad range of benefits, including disability compensation, pensions, education and rehabilitation programs, insurance, housing and business loans, medical treatment, and even burial expenses. All of these benefits, and more, are created by acts of Congress.[1]

In addition, and not nearly so well known, all states and many cities, towns, and counties provide veterans with special benefits. These may include anything from free drivers' licenses and civil service preference to credits against real-estate taxes. The types of state and local benefits granted are unique to each state and municipality. A summary of state veterans' benefits is published by the Veterans Affairs Committee of the U.S. House of Representatives.[2] It consists of about 300 pages of fine print, but does not include locally sponsored benefits. This summary is available through the House Veterans Affairs Committee. You can probably get a complete list of benefits available in your state and locality from the nearest VA office (*see* Appendix III), from local counseling agencies, or from local politicians.

Who can get veterans' benefits?

Although it would be nice simply to answer "any veteran," that answer would be very wrong. Many veterans cannot get veterans' benefits; many nonveterans can get them. It all depends on many factors.

One of the things it depends on is the sponsor of the benefits program. Each state-sponsored program has its own eligibility requirements. Some states require that you lived there before you went on active duty; others are content if you live there when you are a veteran. Some states demand an honorable discharge for eligibility for all benefits; others have less restrictive requirements. The most important benefits, however, are sponsored by the federal government. To receive these benefits, there is a two-step determination. First, it must be shown that the veteran is *eligible* for VA-administered benefits in general. Then it must be shown that the applicant is *entitled* to receive the particular benefit sought.

The VA uses the terms "eligibility" and "entitlement" somewhat differently from normal usage. For purposes of clarity, throughout this book the terms will always be used as follows: "eligibility" relates to *general qualification* of a veteran for benefits; "entitlement" relates to *particular benefits* claimed by a person on the basis of some veteran's eligibility. There is also a fine distinction between "veteran" and "applicant" (or "claimant"). Certain benefits are granted to dependents or survivors of eligible veterans. In such cases, the veteran or servicemember through whom benefits are claimed must have been *eligible* in general, or else the claimant will not be *entitled* to receive the particular benefits for which s/he has applied. Unless otherwise specified, the rest of this discussion will relate solely to federally sponsored benefits, and for purposes of clarity, it will be assumed that the veteran personally claims the benefit.

Who is an "eligible" veteran?

For the vast majority of veterans, eligibility presents no problem. With one exception, the receipt of an honorable or general discharge traditionally established eligibility for all federally sponsored benefits.

The exception is the early discharge for purposes of immediate reenlistment or commissioning as an officer. So far as the VA has been concerned, the early discharge to re-up was not a final discharge; therefore, it did not automatically lock in future benefit eligibility.[3] Recent legislation reversed this policy.[4] Any veteran who in fact completed an initial period of obligated service (even after an early reenlistment took effect) has permanently locked in benefits based upon that period of service, regardless of the type of discharge he received for a later period of service. If you were made eligible by this change in law, you should immediately apply to the VA to establish benefit eligibility.

It is unlikely that affected veterans will be reimbursed for expenses incurred before the change in the VA law. However, the changed law makes a whole range of benefits available to the affected veterans, even though the time limits for those benefits seemed to have expired. Examples include dental treatment and G.I. educational benefits.

Until October 8, 1977, a discharge under honorable conditions permanently establishes eligibility for VA benefits based upon the honorable period of service.[5] Moreover, veterans who received upgrades of undesirable discharges under the 1977 "Special" programs must undergo a "second determination" by a DRB to determine whether they would receive an upgrade under "normal" standards. *See* discussion in Chapter VII.

Those who had their less than honorable discharges based on AWOL's of more than 180 days will face a DRB and VA review. This is discussed in more detail below.

After that date, honorably discharged veterans and other veterans who had not already had their eligibility established by a DRB, Board for Correction of Military Records (BCMR), or the VA (through a "character of discharge determination"), could be denied benefits if they were statutorily banned from benefits. *See* discussion below.[6]

Are there any exceptions to the general rule that entitlement to particular benefits must be based on the veteran's general eligibility?

There is one exception, which was created by the 1977 amendment to the basic VA law. A veteran who developed or aggravated a disability while in the "line of duty" is entitled to disability compensation and related benefits even if the veteran is otherwise not entitled for benefits because the period of service resulted in an undesirable discharge that the VA deems disqualifying. *See* Chapter XV.

What is a character of discharge determination?

The laws under which the VA and some other agencies grant benefits make certain veterans ineligible. However, in every category of ineligibility, there is at least one recognized exception. If your discharge is neither honorable nor general, the VA must make an individualized determination of your eligibility. To use the VA's language, they must decide whether your discharge was issued "under conditions other than dishonorable" (not to be confused with a "dishonorable discharge").[7] If it was, you are eligible for benefits. The VA's decision is called a "character of discharge determination."

This determination will be made in all cases where a veteran who was discharged "under other than honorable conditions" applies for benefits or where someone claims entitlement to benefits based on such a veteran's eligibility, or where another government agency—usually a state veterans' benefits agency, an unemployment compensation office, or the Civil Service Commission—requests such a determination. In addition, it will be made in cases where an enlistment has been voided and no discharge certificate has been awarded. In such cases, benefits will be denied only where the recruit acted fraudulently.[8]

What are your rights when the VA is going to make a character of discharge determination?

Under recent changes in its regulations,[9] the VA must notify a veteran that it will make a character of discharge determination. It must allow the vet 30 days to add information to the records received from the armed forces. It must inform the vet of his or her right to a hearing, at which the vet can present witnesses, documentary evidence, personal testimony, and argument. It must advise the vet of the right to counsel at this hearing. It must let the vet or counsel examine the military records to prepare for the hearing. In short, the VA must inform the vet that a determination is about to be made, and that the vet is entitled to be heard before any decision is made. It must also tell the vet how to appeal an adverse decision. However, the VA does not always adhere to its own regulations, so you may have to remind the VA that these regulations must be followed.

Until these due process rights had been recognized by the VA, almost every character of discharge determination was made without any hearing. Some official would simply inform the vet that eligibility had been denied. The vet wouldn't know who decided it, why, or how to appeal. Sometimes, even the VA had no record of the decision, because when the vet walked in the door, some clerk said the discharge was "bad," disqualifying the vet from benefits, and the vet turned around and walked out.

If you were told you were ineligible, by anyone, at any time, orally or in writing, and you were not told of your right to a hearing and/or your right to appeal from an adverse determination, you can now return to the VA and reapply for benefits. If they turn you down on the basis of a prior ineligibility determination, consider appealing on the grounds that (1) you were denied due process in the prior determination and (2) the prior determination was erroneous. The method for appealing is discussed in Chapter XII.

What disqualifies a veteran and what are the exceptions to the rules?

There are a number of congressionally mandated bases for ineligibility and a number of exceptions to the rules ("bars").

Up until October 8, 1977, a discharge upgrade removed any such bar.[10] So anyone who had an upgrade prior to that date or who had a favorable VA character of service determination has their eligibility "fixed." However, in addition to those veterans who receive upgrades after October

8, 1977, those who received upgrades under the 1977 "special" programs must undergo a "second determination" by a DRB. The same 1977 legislation provided that "action" by a Board for Correction of Military (10 U.S.C. 1552) would bind the VA. It is not clear if "action" means a discharge upgrade or an upgrade accompanied by a *change of reason* for discharge, or simply a change in reason for the discharge without an upgrade. This confusion is typical of this legislation that went through several hasty changes to meet the need for political compromise. The legislation did make clear that a veteran could apply to the VA, DRB, and BCMR at the same time. If that is done, be sure to inform each agency so records can be found. *See* Chapters VI and VII for DRB and BCMR procedures.

No mention is made about the veteran who gains an upgrade of a punitive discharge by the secretary of the service concerned pursuant to Article 74(b), UCMJ, 10 U.S.C. 74(b).

Also, it is unclear if in the rare case of a person discharged under honorable conditions, for one of the reasons listed as bar, whether that person can be denied benefits.[11]

General Court-Martial. One basis for denying benefits is that the veteran was discharged as part of the sentence of a *general* court-martial.[12] If you have a dishonorable discharge (in the case of an officer, a dismissal) or received a bad conduct discharge from a *general*, not a special, court-martial, you are not entitled to VA benefits under any circumstances, unless you were insane at the time you committed the offense for which you were convicted.[13] The general exception for insanity is discussed below.

Conscientious Objectors. Benefits are denied to veterans who were "conscientious objectors" only if they refused military duty, refused to wear the uniform, or refused to obey lawful orders.[14] In practice, veterans *administratively discharged* by reason of conscientious objection have been granted VA eligibility. This is because many of those who refused to wear the uniform or obey orders were court-martialed and received punitive, not administrative, discharges; and because a Department of Defense Directive requires that an administrative discharge for conscientious objection be under honorable conditions[15]—and the military's finding of honorable conditions normally binds the VA.[16]

Deserters. The law denies benefits to those discharged for "desertion."[17] In practice, if a court-martial did not convict you of desertion (AWOL is not the same as desertion; *see* Chapter I), you are not disqualified for this reason. It does not matter that you were administratively declared a "deserter" or that you were tried for desertion. It seems that you must have been convicted of desertion in order to be disqualified from receiving benefits. However, the VA regulation is not totally clear.[18] The 1977 legislation adds a bar (which seems to define some "deserters") for those discharged "under conditions other than honorable" for an AWOL of more than 180 continuous days absent "compelling reasons" to explain the absence. (It is unclear if this provision applies if some of the 180 days fell after normal dates of separation. Logically it should not.) This provision applies retroactively to those persons who were upgraded under the 1977 special programs and to those who by October 8, 1977, had not had a discharge upgrade under a "normal" review or who had not been made eligible for VA or a BCMR. The constitutionality of this was questioned by President Carter; nevertheless, he signed the bill, and asked the Justice Department to advise him on how to administer this aspect of the provision.

The VA has not promulgated regulations interpeting this provision but President Carter instructed the Administrator to be "compassionate." Chapter I discusses legal defenses to AWOL, a factor which certainly should be a "compelling reason." Be sure to seek assistance if you fall within this bar, for you may face a DRB "second determination" (Chapter VII) *and* a VA character of service determination. Also, the issue can be quite complex.[19]

Aliens. The law also denies benefits to aliens who, during a time of hostilities, voluntarily requested discharge because they were aliens.[20] However, if the VA finds that the alien was asked by his or her superiors to request discharge, there is no bar to benefits. And unless the military records clearly show that the alien initiated the discharge request, the VA policy is to find the vet eligible.[21]

Officers Who Resign. A more difficult situation is the officer who resigns "for the good of the service," usually to escape trial by general court-martial.[22] If the resignation resulted in an undesirable discharge (called "other than honorable" for officers) the vet is ineligible. The only exception is the one that covers all cases: insanity, which is discussed in more detail below. Despite the actual wording of the statutory exclusion, a discharge upgrade or a person with a discharge under honorable conditions is entitled to benefits. Do not accept information to the contrary. Many officers resigned to escape trial by general court-martial when charged with homosexuality. These discharges are now easy to change. *See* Chapter VII.

Discharges Not Under Honorable Conditions ("Dishonorable Conditions"). If you have an undesirable discharge, or got a bad conduct discharge as part of the sentence of a *special* court-martial, the eligibility determination becomes more complex. An upgrade to honorable or general automatically created eligibility prior to the 1977 legislation. Since that legislation (although it is not entirely clear if it meant to stop the VA from relying on upgrades in cases that did not fall within the 38 U.S.C. 3103[a] bars), i.e., the general "dishonorable conditions" requirement of 38 U.S.C. 101 (11), the VA must look at the facts that led to your discharge. Unless you provide added information, the VA will base its decision solely on the military records and normally will determine that you are not eligible for benefits if you have not had a discharge upgrade. The VA is not likely to find many cases of "dishonorable conditions" when the veteran was discharged, not for reasons specified as 38 U.S.C. 3103(a) bars, but with a less than honorable discharge that has been upgraded. Still, it is quite possible, as new regulations have not been written. The vet should be prepared to show that the DRBs upgrade meant that the discharge was improper or consider resort to the BCMR.[24]

Although Congress seems to have wanted the VA to give benefits to those who couldn't serve honorably (despite their best efforts) and to deny benefits to those who could, but would not, serve honorably, the VA has developed its own rules for classifying undesirable and special-court bad conduct discharges.

What at first seems to be a disqualifying condition, on second glance may not apply. Each of these rules must be analyzed separately. You will probably have to convince the

VA at your character of service hearing that you are technically an exception to its rule. You must persuade the VA that because of the exception, you were discharged under "other than dishonorable" conditions.[25] Each of the following are categories of cases that the VA has classified as being under "dishonorable conditions."

Acceptance of an undesirable discharge to avoid trial by a general court-martial is considered to be under "dishonorable conditions."[26] Tens of thousands of Vietnam-era GIs took "Chapter 10s," as they were called in the Army. By whatever name, this was a form of plea bargaining designed to avoid trial by court-martial (*see* Chapter I). In most cases, it is absolutely impossible to tell from military records whether the vet was avoiding trial by a general court-martial or by a *special* court-martial. The VA should resolve any real doubts about the situation in your favor, under its "reasonable doubt" doctrine.[27] What you must do is show the VA that you were not going to be tried by a *general* court. Your first line of defense—which is almost always available—is that the charges were never "referred" to a general court or that a general court-martial was never "convened." Your second line of defense, if it applies, is that there was never an Article 32 recommendation[28] for trial by a general court, or, better, that there was never an Article 32 hearing, or, best, that there was never an appointment of an Article 32 investigation officer. And if somewhere in the file you find a recommendation that you be tried by a summary or special court-martial, you are probably home free. Often the charge sheets will indicate that the case was actually referred to a special court. The important thing to remember is that although you took a discharge in lieu of trial, it was not clear whether you would have been tried by a general or a special court-martial. And unless it is virtually certain—as recorded in your military records, and not merely as you remember the actual scene—that you would have been tried by a *general* court-martial, the VA should not find you ineligible under this criterion.

In addition to contending that you were merely avoiding trial by a *special* court-martial, you might be able to convince the VA that your discharge was erroneously given. For example, the proper authority may not have approved it; you may not have been afforded qualified counsel; or you may have been coerced. If you can prove that the administrative discharge was illegal, the VA should not deny your eligibility. However, applying for an upgrade in your discharge may in practice be the only way to obtain VA eligibility.

Mutineers and spies are few and far between, but those who were discharged for these designations are considered to have been discharged under "dishonorable conditions."[29] Those who are caught almost invariably get tried by general court-martial. If they are convicted, they invariably receive punitive discharges as part of their sentences (assuming they are not executed). Under these circumstances, they are ineligible under the law, and not merely under the VA's interpretation. If you got by with a special-court bad conduct discharge for mutiny or spying, you're ahead of the game already. If, however, it's only an undesirable discharge, make the argument that you were discharged for *suspicion* of mutiny or spying; only a court-martial conviction can brand you so infamously for life. Anyway, that's the argument.[30]

If you were discharged for an *offense involving moral turpitude*, the VA considers your character of discharge to be under "dishonorable conditions."[31] The rule of thumb the VA most likely will use is whether your offenses could have resulted in lengthy *civilian* imprisonment. Armed robbery probably involves moral turpitude under this standard; willful disobedience of an order probably does not. Here, too, the disqualification should not apply to you if you received only an undesirable discharge (unless your undesirable discharge was the result of a civilian felony conviction), since only a *conviction* by court-martial should be proof that you were guilty. This should be your argument, although the VA is likely to rule against you if you were acquitted on a technicality, and then administratively discharged with an undesirable discharge on the basis of the same conduct. In any event, the only regulatory clarification is: "This includes, generally, conviction of a felony."

Although the VA usually disqualifies you from benefits if you have a *discharge by reason of homosexual acts*,[32] it should recognize the difference between acts and attitudes or preference. In many cases, there is not enough evidence in the military records to prove that you committed homosexual acts. In that event, this regulation does not make you ineligible. Chapter VII discusses discharge upgrading for homosexual acts. Upgrading would automatically remove this disqualification.

Discharge for *willful and persistent misconduct* is considered to be under "dishonorable conditions."[33] Conduct is not persistent if it only occurs once. Probably two occurances, or even three, would not be enough to support a finding of persistence. But where the line is drawn will probably depend in part on the length of time over which the misconduct occurred. Willful misconduct must create a likelihood of serious injury. It is not excused by voluntary intoxication.[34] The requirement of willfulness is not met in cases of accidental misconduct. For example, automobile accidents, oversleeping, and disease-induced misconduct, even if persistent, are probably not willful. In any event, if you were thrown out of the military for once tripping the sergeant, whether it was an accident or a practical joke doesn't matter. It was not willful *and* persistent misconduct. The regulation states "a discharge for minor offense will not, however, be considered willful and persistent misconduct if service was otherwise honest, faithful and meritorious." It is not clear if a long AWOL after a clean service record is a bar, but it certainly should not be considered to be "persistent," since it only occurred once. It surely does not create a likelihood of serious injury. But don't count on much sympathy if your AWOL led to your bad discharge.

Is insanity an exception to the above rules?

Insanity at the time of the offense causing the bad discharge creates an exception to *all* bars from eligibility for benefits,[35] except that an enlistment contract signed while insane does not result in eligibility based on that enlistment.[36]

The question of insanity is for the VA to determine, even if the military made its own determination. As a practical matter, the VA will usually follow the military's ruling, but you are entitled to a VA hearing on the question of insanity. You are entitled to present *new* post-discharge evidence—such as recent psychiatric diagnoses, or proof of psychiatric hospitalization after discharge—for a new determination by the VA. You can also appeal from an adverse decision. However, the VA often will not bother to inform you of your right to claim eligibility by reason of insanity. The VA usually places the burden on you to raise this claim and normally will not consider it unless you ask them to.[37]

You are unlikely to win in these cases unless you can produce some evidence that is not in the military records. But occasionally your own explanation of what happened, perhaps backed up by the testimony of others, might convince the VA to grant you eligibility on the insanity exception. Many VA personnel feel that the military's determination that a troublemaker was sane is typically the result of an inadequate psychiatric examination and evaluation, made under pressure from the command, and approved by nonexperts sitting as a court-martial or discharge board. If you can convince them that this happened to you, your chances are improved for being ruled eligible by reason of insanity at the time of the acts that resulted in your bad discharge.

All of that information about character of discharge determinations is complicated. Can it be summarized?

If your eligibility is questioned on any ground other than conviction by general court-martial, the VA should inform you of your right to a hearing whether or not you request one. At that hearing, you stand a much better chance of winning if you attend, give testimony and/or present other evidence (including some designed to arouse sympathy), and offer arguments—either personally or through a representative—demonstrating that under a strict construction of the regulations, you are not disqualified. It will also be helpful to ask at the hearing that the disqualification under consideration be identified, because "under conditions other than dishonorable" can mean almost anything, but desertion and homosexual acts, for example, are very specific terms. It is easier to refute a specific basis than a general basis for denying eligibility. If you do not take advantage of your due process rights, in almost every case the VA will probably find you ineligible.[38]

Although discharge upgrading and correction of military records (discussed in Chapters VI and VII) are not VA activities, they affect VA eligibility and entitlement. Don't rely on just one technique—use every resource available to you. If you think you should get veterans' benefits, challenge any adverse determination within the VA, and at the same time apply for upgrading or records correction if this would help.

Should you lose at the VA, but later have a discharge upgraded or have your records corrected, you can obtain reconsideration of the previous VA determination of ineligibility. If your discharge is upgraded to honorable or general, the VA has little alternative but to grant you eligibilty, unless your upgrade was based solely upon the automatic special programs of 1977 or occurred after October 8, 1977.[39]

How does upgrading affect the time limits on entitlement to benefits?

When upgrading removes a disqualification from eligibility, the VA treats the date of upgrade application or correction as the date of discharge for most purposes. For example, your right to one full VA dental examination and treatment is available during the year following discharge upgrading; your GI Bill educational program must be completed within 10 years of the date of upgrading.

One of the problems in determining the date of entitlement for benefits, when eligibility is based on upgrading, is that the VA might take the position that even without upgrading, they would have made a favorable character of discharge determination. That would mean that the time limits for applying for some benefits had already passed before the upgrade led you to apply to the VA. To prevent this from happening, you should apply for VA benefits, and go through a character of discharge determination— and an appeal—even if you are certain you will not be found eligible. At some future date you might get an upgrade—or even a full and complete presidential pardon.

And if that happens, you want to give the VA no legal choice except to agree that your eligibility was first created by the upgrade or the pardon.

If you were turned down by the VA and later got a discharge upgrade, can you get back payments?

If you had previously applied to the VA for disability compensation or pension, and were rejected because of your bad discharge, upgrading of that discharge would bring you only limited back benefits. The VA rules on retroactivity of benefits are very complex. In no case based upon upgrading or correction of records will the benefits date back to more than 1 year from the time you reapplied to the VA.[40] Benefits will not be paid for the period before the date of your initial application, unless it was filed within 1 year of separation of service.

Your best strategy for dealing with this complex set of rules is probably to file for VA benefits *and* upgrading at the same time. Then, if the VA initially finds you ineligible, try to slow down the VA processing until your upgrading application has been resolved. Among the techniques for slowing down the VA are the following: ask for personal hearings at the regional office and at the Board of Veteran Appeals; don't file your Notice of Disagreement with the VA's decision and your Substantive Appeal until the time permitted to do so has almost expired; ask that your hearing, or consideration of your appeal, be delayed until you get final word from the military on your upgrading application. (When you ask for a delay, point out that upgrading would produce "new and material evidence.") The technical terms just used are discussed in Chapter XII. By delaying the final VA decision until you are most likely to be found eligible, you preserve the date of your original VA application (rather than a reapplication) as the date from which benefits are first granted.

Are you eligible for benefits with a clemency discharge?

Shortly after pardoning former President Nixon, President Ford set up a "clemency program" for Vietnam-era draft resisters and veterans who had bad discharges as a result of absence-related offenses. Chapters I and

V discuss this program in more detail. One result of the program was that many veterans received a new type of discharge called a "clemency discharge." The presidential proclamation setting up the clemency program clearly stated that the clemency discharge did not make its recipient eligible for VA benefits. It is a bit early to tell what this means, as the proclamation was intentionally ambiguous. It might mean the vet is disqualified; it might mean that a character of discharge determination must be made in each case. However, the clemency discharge probably does not automatically make a person ineligible for benefits. The Department of Defense considers the clemency discharge to be just another undesirable discharge. Therefore, the VA should adjudicate any claims of eligibility on this basis. However, where a clemency discharge and a pardon replaced a punitive discharge issued by a general court-martial, receipt of benefits is unlikely without a further discharge upgrade or a finding of insanity.[41] If, however, the pardon was a "full and complete" one, a Supreme Court decision suggests that no government agency can continue to penalize you for the pardoned offense.[42]

Although you are not technically a veteran, you were forced to do alternative service for your country as a recognized conscientious objector; are you eligible for VA benefits?

In 1974, the Supreme Court ruled that the Consitution permits Congress to deny veterans' benefits to men forced into alternative civilian service because they were exempted from military service as conscientious objectors.[43] Unless Congress changes the law (which is not very likely), or the Supreme Court changes its ruling (even less likely), you are not eligible for VA benefits.

NOTES

1. These acts are codified in Title 38 of the United States Code (U.S.C.). The regulations implementing these statutes are contained in Title 38 of the Code of Federal Regulations (C.F.R.) Adjudication procedures are described in many VA manuals, the most important one

being M21-1 (VA Benefits Manual, Adjudication Procedure, July 30, 1975). You have the right to inspect all of these at any VA regional office.

2. *State Veterans' Laws—Digests of State Laws Regarding Rights, Benefits, and Privileges of Veterans and Their Dependents* (Rev. to January 1, 1976). House Comm. Pr. No. 66, 94th Congress, 2d Session.

3. 38 C.F.R. § 3.13. Under the VA's interpretation, which has never been challenged in the courts, if you enlist for 3 years, and then, after serving 2 years honorably, extend your enlistment to 6 years, it is all one 6-year enlistment. But if you completed the 3 years, received your discharge, and then immediately re-upped for another 3, the VA would view it as two separate enlistments. Either way, you enlisted twice for a total of 6 years and received an honorable discharge for your first period of service. A bad discharge from your second enlistment in the first situation would leave you with no eligibility; in the other you would be eligible for benefits locked in during the first full enlistment. A 1977 amendment to the VA law rejects the VA's interpretation. Public Law 95-126 (Oct. 8, 1977).

4. Public Law 95-126 (Oct. 8, 1977).

5. 38 C.F.R. § 3.14 (d).

6. Public Law 95-126 (Oct. 8, 1977).

7. 38 U.S.C. § 101(2). The debates in Congress during World War II suggest that Congress wanted the VA to give benefits to vets who were unable through no fault of their own to serve honorably, but to deny benefits to those who were able but unwilling to serve honorably. Neither the law as it was actually written nor the regulations adopted by the VA conform to the apparent desire of Congress. And in any event, the inconsistent manner in which the military imposes discipline—the same conduct can result in a reprimand, a general discharge, an undesirable discharge, or a punitive discharge—results in a haphazard or random distribution of eligibility when measured against the intent of Congress.

8. 38 C.F.R. § 3.14 (a), (b), and (c). These regulations specifically exclude vets who were barred from enlisting by an act of Congress, except those who were underage. In addition to these circumstances, the military voids enlistments when a court-martial determines that there is no jurisdiction over an accused because of recruiter fraud or illegal activities. When this happens, no certificate of discharge is issued (*see* discussion of this defense in Chapter I), *U.S. v. Catlow*, 23 USCMA 142, 48 CMR 758 (1974). Even though Catlow's DD 214 showed zero days of service, the

VA granted him benefits based upon the period of time he was actually in military control.

9. 38 C.F.R. § 3.13; M21-1 ¶ 14.02. These changes were apparently prompted by a series of court and agency decisions in which the VA's negative determination was not followed because the VA had denied the veteran a fair hearing on the issue of character of service. For example, in an unreported decision, unemployment compensation was granted to a New York vet who had just received an undesirable discharge even though the VA said he was ineligible. New York officials ruled that the VA determination was unconstitutionally made and therefore not binding on them.

10. 38 C.F.R. § 3.12(f); M21-1 ¶ 14.01f; VA Administrative Decision 980.

11. Public Law 95-126 (Oct. 8, 1977).

12. 38 U.S.C. § 3103(a).

13. 38 U.S.C. § 3103(b). On its face, 38 C.F.R. 3.12(f), which was promulgated to make clear that a discharge upgrade removed such bars to eligibility, appears to preclude benefits to one who got an upgrade from a general-court discharge. This is not the case. The regulation means one is barred only if a discharge review board upgrades such a discharge, because that is not within the board's authority. Only the BCMR can upgrade such a discharge. The regulation is poorly worded and may confuse some claims adjudicators. See *Federal Register,* Vol. 41, No. 60, p. 12656, 3/31/76, where the intent of the change is explained.

14. 38 U.S.C. § 3103(a); 38 C.F.R. 3.12(c) (1). The Board of Veterans Appeals in Docket No. 75-00489, May 21, 1975, ruled that two AWOL periods were not a "refus[al] to perform military duties" by an honorably discharged conscientious objector. This implies that one with an honorable discharge could be barred from benefits by 38 U.S.C. 3103(a).

15. DOD Directive 1332.14. But see Public Law 95-126 (Oct. 8, 1977).

16. 38 C.F.R. § 3.12(a). A clearer statement of the meaning of this section appears at *Federal Register,* Vol. 41, No. 60, p. 12656, 3/26/76.

17. 38 U.S.C. § 3103(a); 38 C.F.R.(c) (4).

18. 38 C.F.R. § 3.12(c) (4). It merely denies eligibility if the vet was discharged "as a deserter."

19. Public Law 95-126 (Oct. 8, 1977).

20. 38 U.S.C. § 3103(a).

21. 38 C.F.R. § 3.12(c) (5); M21-1 ¶ 14.01C (3).

22. 38 C.F.R. § 3.12(c) (3).

24. Public Law 95-126 (Oct. 8, 1977).
25. 38 U.S.C. 101(2).
26. 38 U.S.C. § 3103(a).
27. 38 C.F.R. § 3.102.
28. Article 32 of the UCMJ, 10 U.S.C. § 832, requires that before there can be a general court-martial, there must be an investigation and report by a specially appointed officer. Without an Article 32 investigation and report, the most severe court-martial possible is a special court-martial.
29. 38 C.F.R. § 3.12(D) (2).
30. The VA will probably redetermine the facts on its own, based on a preponderance of the evidence. *Cf.* M21-1 ¶ 14.11 (acquittal on homicide charges not binding on VA).
31. 38 C.F.R. § 3.12(D) (3).
32. 38 C.F.R. § 3.12(D) (5) reads: "Generally, homosexual acts" with no further guidance despite the services' recent liberalizing trend in this area.
33. 38 C.F.R. 3.12(D) (4).
34. M21-1 ¶ 14.04.
35. 38 U.S.C. § 3103(b).
36. 38 C.F.R. § 3.14(G).
37. M21-1 ¶ 14.05.
38. Until recently, fewer than one in ten character of service determinations was favorable to the veteran. The newly adopted regulations seem to have increased the percentage of cases in which benefits are given to those with bad discharges. Now that the right of appeal is known and therefore used, some consistency of interpretation can be expected. However, consistency is not the hallmark of VA adjudications.
39. Public Law 95-126 (Oct. 8, 1977).
40. 38 U.S.C. § 3010 establishes the effective dates for benefits. Subsection 3010(i) governs reopened claims based on a discharge upgrade or a records correction.
41. M21-1 ¶ 14.01e states that "a Clemency Discharge *does not* entitle or reinstate benefits." But it goes on to provide for "development," that is, examining the underlying facts —presumably so as to make an individualized determination of eligibility.
42. *Schick* v. *Reed*, 419 U.C. 256 (1974). *But see* VA Administrative Decision 78; *also see* 27 Ops. Atty. Gen. 178.
43. *Johnson* v. *Robison*, 415 U.S. 361 (1974).

XI

Entitlement to, and Applying for, Veterans' Benefits

If you are eligible for veterans' benefits, you also must be "entitled" to them. Entitlement is one of the most complex aspects of VA proceedings. In each case, the answer can only be given after some or all of the following questions, among others, have been answered:

1. What benefits do you want?
2. When do you want them?
3. What benefits have you already received?
4. When did you serve in the armed forces or allied agencies (such as Public Health Service)?
5. How long did you serve?
6. Do you have a service-connected disability?
7. What disability rating have you received?
8. Are you employed?
9. Are others financially dependent on you?
10. What insurance coverage do you have?

In the case of benefits given to *dependents* of eligible veterans or *survivors* of those killed or injured in service, most of these questions would apply to the eligible veteran through whom they claim benefits. In addition, their relationship to the eligible veteran, the time and manner in which the veteran became disabled or died, and the presence of others who claim that the entitlement desired is theirs are all factors that might affect the availability of benefits. Fortunately, in most cases, if the relevant information is known, the answer to the question of entitlement is obvious.

Does length of service affect entitlement to benefits?

Rarely is there a dispute as to how long someone served in the military. Many benefits are allowed only if service exceeded 180 days, exclusive of Reservist active duty for training. However, length of "continuous" service, although not invariably a requirement of the law, is always treated by the VA as the test for initial entitlement. Thus, if you were a National Guard pilot who flew combat in Vietnam for 3 consecutive years, you will be shocked to learn that every 179 days you had been deactivated for 24 hours—thereby never completing the requirement of 181 days of continuous service.[1] If you frequently went AWOL and got discharged after 200 days of "good" time scattered over 10 months, the VA will probably deny you entitlement to most benefits because you did not have sufficient days of consecutive service. If this happens to you, look at the language of the act of Congress that states the entitlement requirements for the particular benefit you claim. If Congress did not demand that your "good" time be consecutive, the VA violates the letter of the law when it creates an additional requirement.[2] You might be able to convince the VA, but you will probably have to get either Congress or the courts to side with you—an all but impossible task.

Length of service is of special importance under the GI Bill. The number of months for which you are entitled to educational benefits is based primarily upon your total length of service.

Does the nature of a dependent's relationship affect eligibility?

Sometimes. For certain benefits, the social or legal relationship to its father of an illegitimate child must be established. Likewise, determining who is a vet's spouse is not always easy. The validity of a divorce might be questioned; or the presence of a "common law" marriage—in states that recognize it—may not be certain. Thus, state law or particular facts can be important in resolving questions such as these. The law denies widow's or widower's benefits to a veteran's surviving spouse if they lived separately, unless the *separation* was solely the fault of the veteran.[3] The VA frequently extends this bar erroneously to cases where the failure to *reconcile* was partially the fault of the surviving spouse. Usually, however, the basis for your claimed status as a survivor or dependent of an eligible vet is clear. Once it is determined, your entitlement to particular benefits will probably be a straightforward matter.

Is it difficult to obtain VA benefits if you are eligible and entitled to them?

In almost all cases, once the benefit is identified, a glance at the records will leave no doubt about eligibility and entitlement. Usually, getting VA benefits will be automatic. You apply, your application is processed, and within a few months you get any benefit to which you feel you are reasonably entitled. In fact, almost 19 out of 20 VA decisions are not appealed. Although in some cases, the applicant might not know how to appeal, or might no longer want the benefit, undoubtedly most of the time the VA gets things right the first time around. Usually, all you've got to do is get the VA started.

Getting the VA started is a simple process. Almost every federally sponsored benefit is administered by the VA.[4] So the nearest VA office (listed in the telephone book under "U.S. Government, Veterans Administration"; *see* also Appendix III) is the place to obtain specific information, to establish eligibility for VA benefits, and to apply on the form you receive from them.

To whom do you speak at the VA when you first go there?

On your first trip to the VA, you will be sent for an interview with a "veterans' counselor" or "contact representative." These are civil service employees who are supposed to review your service history. To speed things up, bring with you your discharge certificate and DD Form 214 (separation document). The VA will later double-check your copy of the DD 214 against the copy sent to them by the Personnel Records Center.

If you appear to be eligible for benefits, they will review for you the types of benefits to which you may be entitled. Ideally, they will give you sound advice as to the conditions of entitlement for each benefit, any changes in your plans or activities that might affect your entitlement to particular benefits, and the type of proof, if any, that you will have to give the VA before benefits you desire will be granted.

If there is a question as to your eligibility, this official should *not* do anything more than tell you that you might not be eligible, tell you the conditions for eligibility, and inform you of the procedures for determining eligibility, including your "due process" rights (described in Chapter X). It is *not* this person's job to send you away. At the very minimum, this person should offer to assist you in filling out forms necessary for an official determination of eligibility. And this person should advise you of your right to have counsel assist you in completing these forms before you submit them. There is a discussion on your right to counsel in Chapter XII.

Some contact representatives may give you the impression that they make the decisions. They don't. If they tell you otherwise, demand that they tell you how to appeal their determination. Or ask to speak to their superior. On the other hand, some are very knowledgeable and helpful. If you like the contact representative to whom you are sent, make a note of that person's name. The VA permits contact representatives to act as counsel at hearings, and some of them prepare for hearings much more carefully than many of the service-organization representatives who usually serve as counsel. So consider asking your contact representative to be your counsel at any hearing that may occur. Chapter XIII discusses hearings and counsel in more detail.

When should you apply for benefits?

In general, you should apply for benefits as soon as you think you can use them. For some benefits, there is a time limit for applying, and today might be the last day. Therefore, you should at least make an inquiry at the VA and find out if you're missing out.

Among the most frequently overlooked benefits are

those granted by state governments. Some of the states give "bonuses"—one-time payments, sometimes as much as $300 for veterans and $1000 for their survivors. But these bonuses must be received before a set date. States that give tax credits give them only to eligible vets who apply. Because these credits may be allowed only for a few years, you should find out from local sources what is available, and what the deadline is.

Reemployment Rights. If you were on active duty for more than 90 days but less than 4 years, or initial active duty for National Guard or Reserve training, you have *90 days* to apply for work with your preservice employer (extended for up to 1 year for time in the hospital). *See* Chapter VIII for a discussion about enforcing these rights.

Unemployment Compensation. If you can't get work after your release from active duty, you are probably entitled to unemployment compensation. These benefits are administered by the individual states and territories, not by the VA. But your eligibility, which depends in part on your being discharged "under conditions other than dishonorable," will be determined by the VA upon direct request from the state unemployment agency. The amount of benefits, and the period for which they are granted, may vary. But they are available only after you *apply* for them. If you don't make application, benefits do not accumulate just because you're unemployed.

Life Insurance. Your Servicemen's Group Life Insurance coverage expires *120 days after discharge*. During that time period (or for a year after discharge if you are totally disabled), you can convert your coverage into an individual policy with a private company. Before you do so, you should make sure that you need this type of life insurance, and that the premiums are not higher than those charged for similar insurance from other companies.

If the VA grants you a service-connected disability rating of 10% or more, you have *1 year* from the date of the rating to purchase up to $10,000 life-insurance coverage from the VA. This insurance costs less than private policies, and your right to purchase it at low cost is not affected by your disabling condition. Should you become totally disabled while covered by VA insurance, the VA will either provide you with annuity payments, or waive collection of life-insurance premiums, depending upon the type of insurance you have. (Over the years, the VA life-insurance program has seen frequent changes in terms of entitlement, cost, and type of coverage.) These provisions become applicable after the VA is notified of your total disability.

Dental Treatment. If you apply during the *1-year* period following discharge, you are entitled to VA treatment of all existing dental problems on a one-time-only basis. Treatment must be completed within *14 months* of discharge, unless any delay is not caused by you.

Disability Compensation. If you apply within *1 year* of discharge for disability compensation, any benefits for service-connected injury or aggravation of prior injury will date back to the day after your discharge. If you do not apply within 1 year, benefits will start to run from the day you make application. Chapter XV discusses disability-benefit claims.

Education Benefits. Benefits under the GI Bill (which are not the same as those for rehabilitation of the disabled) for assistance in college, vocational training, or an apprenticeship are available if your education program *will be completed within 10 years of discharge.* If your eligibility was first obtained after a discharge upgrade, the 10 years start to run on the date of upgrading, but you can receive up to 1 year's back benefits if you applied both to the VA and for upgrading prior to the back date from which payment is sought.

Burial Allowances. The VA will provide a burial allowance, usually $250, and an allowance of up to $150 for purchasing cemetery space, if application is made within *2 years* of permanent burial or cremation. In addition, upon request, the next of kin will be given an American flag for use at the funeral.

Other Benefits. For most other benefits, such as mortgage guarantees, medical treatment, and vocational rehabilitation, there is no time limit within which you must apply. However, if you delay, you may find that later on you can't use a particular veterans' benefit; or you may find that Congress has changed the law, and the program that interested you has been closed down. So unless you have a good reason for not doing so, apply for benefits as soon as you think you can use them.

Can you appeal from a denial of these benefits?

Yes. If you apply for a benefit and you are initially rejected or receive only part of what you claim, there are strictly enforced time limits for appealing the rejection. Although in most cases *1 year* is allowed, in some situations only *60 days* or less are allowed. With the rejection notice, you should receive a paper telling you how to appeal, *and* how long you can take. *These are strict time limits that must be observed.* If you don't appeal on time, the adverse decision will become final, and you might never be able to get reconsideration. Chapter XII discusses appeals in more detail.

What's in your VA file, and how can you get to see it?

Virtually every communication received or sent by the VA that relates to you will be placed in your Claims File as a permanent record. Included are your military medical records (if you claim a disability) and copies of any congressional inquiries. The only exception applies to nuisance letters. If VA employees consider your letter to have nothing to do with your right to benefits, there is a procedure under which they are authorized to destroy the letter.

In addition to your Claims File, you are likely to have two separate medical files—one for in-patient treatment, which contains medical records of your VA hospitalization, the other for out-patient treatment, which contains medical records of your examinations in VA clinics and of any prescriptions you were given by the VA while not hospitalized. These medical records are *not* part of your Claims File, although they usually are important for adjudicating disability claims. The Claims File contains only a *summary* of medical examinations or treatment obtained in VA facilities, and it is often important that you examine the treatment files, as well as the Claims File, when preparing for hearings or appeals.

Both the Privacy Act of 1974[5] and a section of the Veterans Benefits laws[6] make your VA records privileged and confidential. Access to the records, or any portion of them, is granted only to the following: (1) VA employees who have a need to see them in the course of their official duties (2) you and your representative—except that in cases of mental disorders, information that the VA believes might aggravate the disorder can be withheld from you (and from your representative, if the VA expects your representative to pass it on to you; *see* the section on mental disabilities in Chapter XVI), (3) courts of law, (4) approved research programs. In addition, VA personnel are authorized to provide information concerning cases of certain communicable diseases to appropriate state and federal public health officials.[7] Names and addresses of present or former members of the armed services may also be given to nonprofit organizations solely for use in programs related to VA benefit claims. Although one law[8] also permits the VA with the approval of the President to release information contained in any claims file, and authorizes the VA to publish the amount of any pension, compensation, or dependency allowance received by any person from the VA, the Privacy Act probably prevents any such release of your claims data without your personal consent.

Does the Privacy Act apply to VA records in the same manner as it applies to military records?

Yes (*see* Chapter IV). Under the Privacy Act, if you desire to see your VA records—whether or not your representative is with you—you need only make a request to do so at your regional VA office. The only basis you are likely to encounter for denying that request is that the records are temporarily out of the office (in which case they should be recalled for your inspection without substantial delay) or that examination of the records would aggravate your mental disorder. Regardless of the reason given, you have a right under the Privacy Act to appeal any denial of your access to the records, and the VA has a duty to tell you how to do so. They must give you the name and business address of the officer who will rule on your appeal and the time limits within which you can appeal. If your appeal is unsuccessful, the VA must inform you of your right to sue in federal court. If you do sue and if the court determines that the VA has violated the Privacy Act, it should order that you promptly be permitted to inspect and copy your records. It should also award you reasonable attorneys' fees and the other costs of bringing suit.

NOTES

1. 38 C.F.R. § 21.1040.
2. Cf. 38 U.S.C. § 1652(a) (1) with 38 C.F.R. § 21.1040.
3. 38 U.S.C. § 101(3).
4. The major exceptions and the places to get information or to apply are:

Reemployment Rights: U.S. Department of Labor, Labor-Management Services Administration field offices; and Manpower Training Programs. *See* Chapter VIII.

Unemployment Compensation: State employment service, local office.

Civil Service Preference: Federal Job Information Centers.

Naturalization Preference: Immigration and Naturalization Service offices.

Burial flags: Can be obtained either from VA offices or from most post offices; information concerning burial in a *national cemetery* or obtaining a headstone or grave marker can be obtained from the VA.

5. 5 U.S.C. § 552a.
6. 38 U.S.C. § 3301.
7. 1976 Amendments to 38 U.S.C. § 3301.
8. 38 U.S.C. § 3301(6).

XII

VA Claims Adjudication and Appeals

Can you get a lawyer to assist you in presenting your claim?

The VA recognizes that you have a right to the assistance of counsel, but most of what they recognize with their right hand they take away with their left. The law has been written to make it almost impossible to get a lawyer to represent you in VA proceedings, other than in cases of insurance claims and loan disputes. In claims for benefits, a lawyer, by statute and under penalty of criminal punishment, may not charge more than $10 for representing you, plus any approved out-of-pocket expenses.[1] And s/he may not charge you anything unless you win your claim. Because lawyers can make much more money doing other things, they generally won't agree to represent vets at VA hearings.

Legislation has been proposed that would alter these limits on attorneys' fees. At the time this book was printed this proposal had not been enacted into law.

If you can't get a lawyer, who will represent you?

Nonlawyers are permitted to represent vets, if they charge no fees. Most of the nonlawyers who provide representation work for one of the "service organizations": American Legion, Disabled American Vets, Veterans of Foreign Wars, Red Cross, and a handful of other national organizations. These organizations are given free office space in VA facilities and will represent you even if you don't belong to them.

The quality of their services, however, is highly variable. Only the VFW has a centralized training program. The other organizations train representatives locally, if at all. The VA has no official involvement in the certification of representatives of the national service organizations. The VA "recognizes" the organization, and the organization decides whom to certify, and what training to require.[2] Although the VA is authorized to certify individual claims representatives,[3] it does not do so. Nor will it certify new organizations, except those that are official agencies of a state government.[4]

However, there is a provision in the regulations that permits virtually anyone to be recognized as a representative for one particular claim.[5] Under this provision, members of local counseling organizations and students at law schools have acted as representatives on a case-by-case basis. Before the VA will approve them, they are usually required to sign a statement that they will not accept any fee or other remuneration, and some VA offices have arbitrarily refused to permit such case-by-case representation. Thus, some aggressive veterans' counseling organizations that try to represent younger veterans are prevented from representing vets.[6] If you are not permitted to have the person of your choice represent you, you should contact your congressperson, one of the counseling groups listed in Appendix I, and the General Counsel of the VA, who is located in the Central office at 810 Vermont Avenue, N.W., Washington, DC 20005.

In addition to service-organization and individual representatives, the VA permits its contact representatives or "veterans benefit counselors" to assist vets at hearings.[7] Fifteen years ago, contacts frequently acted as representatives, but today this practice is quite rare. Nonetheless, it is still permitted, and if you were impressed by your contact representative—if s/he was particularly helpful in advising you about problems you might encounter, and the kind of proof you would need—you would be well advised to return to that person and find out if s/he is willing to act as your representative at any hearing.

Should you try to represent yourself?

The VA is operated—at least in theory—under a complex collection of laws, regulations, and policies. After the VA has initially notified you that it will not grant your claim for benefits, you should at least consult with someone who has experience in dealing with the technicalities of procedure. Even if you don't want anyone to represent you, you might be saved from making a bad mistake by having your case file reviewed by an expert, and by having that expert read and criticize any letter or statement you want to send to the VA before you submit it.

Can you change representatives?

You can change your representative at any time by notifying the VA (and, as a courtesy, the old representative) that you have obtained a new representative or will represent yourself.

How does the VA process applications for benefits?

The VA is a vast bureaucracy that has its own way of doing things. Because of this, the list of steps in the processing of an application is likely to seem terribly complex. From the applicant's position, however, there are very few steps to be taken—although you may have to take them over and over again.

When you initially apply for benefits, you fill out a form. This form—it varies with the benefit you seek—constitutes a *"formal claim."* An "informal claim" is any written request for information or for benefits that names the specific benefit you desire. When an informal claim is received—whether from the applicant or some other person acting on behalf of the applicant—the VA will send out the proper form on which to make a "formal claim." If time limits are involved, the date on which an informal application is received will be the date from which benefits run, *if* you were eligible and entitled on that date *and* if the formal application is received within 1 year of receipt of the informal claim.[8]

When the application form is received, you are given a "C" number, which is simply your VA identification. Some, but not all, veterans have identical "C" and Social Security numbers. *Use that number on all correspondence with the VA.* Make sure you get the number right. One vet mixed it up, and his application for compensation for a nervous disorder was rejected because there was "no evidence of tonsillitis during military service."

What happens after you file your formal claim?

Formal claims are examined by VA employees to determine whether the claim is justified. To do this, they first look at the application and review the military and VA records that they have on file. If eligibility and entitlement are obvious, routine approval from an adjudicator follows. Similarly, if it is clear that you should not at this time receive the benefit you seek, an adjudicator will immediately reject your application. Often, however, there is some doubt as to the facts. For example, if you want educational benefits, the VA records will not usually contain information about the fact of your enrollment in school; or if you want disability compensation, the available records may not indicate the extent of your disability.

When there are questions of fact that cannot be easily determined from examination of the file, the VA attempts to gather more information. The gathering of information related to a claim for benefits is called "development." Development can be done in many different ways. Sometimes, the VA will send you additional forms to complete or ask you to bring in statements from witnesses. Sometimes it will send forms to other agencies, such as schools, for them to complete. On occasion, the VA will ask you to come to its office for an interview, or to come to a clinic or hospital for an examination. Although the VA is responsible for attempting to complete development of every claim, it requires your cooperation. And since the benefit will be yours, it makes sense for you to do all you can to assist the VA. Indeed, if you are uncooperative, the VA may treat your conduct as the abandonment of your claim.[9] In that event, all processing will cease, and your claim will be treated as finally rejected.

Once the VA determines that is has all the facts it needs, or all the facts it can get, development is complete. At that point, your file goes to the adjudication section, where an employee decides whether the facts reflected in the file entitle you to the benefit you want. If s/he rules in your favor, that normally ends the matter. If s/he rules against you, you will be sent a "Notice of Decision," together with forms that explain to you what you must do, and how soon you must do it, if you are not satisfied with the VA's decision.

"Adjudication" is the first official action that grants or denies a claim for benefits. Because it is *your* responsibility to learn about an adverse adjudication (the VA considers *mailing* your notice the end of its responsibility), you should call the VA office and check up on the status of your claim if 3 or 4 months go by without any word from the VA.

What if you are dissatisfied with the adjudication?

Normally, all that you must do initially if you are dissatisfied with the VA decision is write the VA a letter saying so. A postcard that simply says, "I am not satisfied with your decision of [date]," followed by your signature and your "C" number is good enough. It is not necessary, but it won't hurt, to tell them why. Such a letter is called a "Notice of Disagreement." It must be *received* by the VA within 1 year of the date of their adverse decision.[10] In contested claims, where two or more persons dispute who is entitled to a benefit, a 60-day time limit may apply.[11] If more than 1 month passes from the time you send a Notice of Disagreement, and you hear nothing from the VA, send them another letter referring to the date of your first letter, or call them to make sure they received your first letter. It is your responsibility to see that the mail gets to them, since it is the receiving, not the sending, of your letter that protects your rights. *Send important letters by certified mail and keep copies of all correspondence for your own file.*

What happens after you file a Notice of Disagreement?

After receiving a Notice of Disagreement, the VA reviews your file. If it is obvious to them that they made a mistake, they send you a new Notice of Decision, approving your claim. In most cases, however, they next prepare a "Statement of the Case." This document is supposed to be a detailed analysis of your claim. It should include your dates of military service, the date of your application for the benefit that was denied, a summary of the evidence, a listing of the rules and regulations that determine eligibility and entitlement, a discussion of the evidence in your case, and an explanation of why the benefit was denied. The Statement of the Case is supposed to assist you in identifying the reason for the VA's refusal to grant your claim.[12]

Occasionally, a Statement of the Case will be of no real assistance to you, because it doesn't point out the important facts. For example, if it merely says that the file contains a "Report of Medical Examination, June 17, 1974," you have learned nothing about what the report contains. Or if it concludes with a statement such as "The veteran was discharged with an undesirable discharge, which was not under conditions other than dishonorable," you have no way of knowing whether you were denied eligibility because of willful and persistent misconduct, or because you accepted the discharge to avoid trial by a general court-martial. Techniques for learning the particular reason, or the important facts, when they are camouflaged with that kind of general and vague language—or when camouflaged under boilerplate phrases such as "unsubstantiated" or "the evidence was merely cumulative"—are discussed later.

What do you do after you receive a Statement of the Case?

You normally will be given at least 60 days from the date the VA mails your Statement of the Case in which to respond to it.[13] Your response is called a "Substantive Appeal." That's just fancy language for the reason why you feel your claim should be granted. But preparing the Substantive Appeal is not easy. For the most part, it takes the same kind of care and effort that goes into preparing for a hearing as described in Chapter XIII.

A Substantive Appeal is a written document that you or your representative submits to the VA. It contains your factual and legal arguments. It is your response to the Statement of the Case. Anything in the Statement of the Case that you do not challenge will be taken as true.[14] This rule applies even though the VA promotes an image of informality, insisting that it bends over backward to give every vet the benefit of all reasonable doubt. Because every unchallenged fact listed in the Statement of the Case will be treated as beyond dispute, you must carefully review the Statement of the Case, line by line and sentence by sentence. If anything is false, or unclear, or misleading, or incomplete, you must point out the truth as you understand it. As a final protection, at the end of your Substantive Appeal, write the sentence: "I dispute every item in the Statement of the Case that is not fully consistent with the facts and argument set forth in this substantive appeal."

Should you let your representative file the Substantive Appeal without your seeing it first?

No. In most cases, the Substantive Appeal will be written and submitted by a representative. But in all cases, the claim is the veteran's, not the representative's. Consequently, you should make clear to your representative that s/he is to work *with* you, not just *for* you. At the very minimum, you should insist that your representative let you see your Substantive Appeal before it gets filed. You should correct any errors that you find in the document. You should make sure that the representative is asking for the same benefits you want—all too often, s/he decides to ask for something less, without letting the vet know, and without explaining to the vet why the claim should be partially abandoned. You should make sure that you understand what your representative has written—and you should insist that your representative explain to you anything that you don't understand.

Most important, make sure that the Substantive Appeal states *why the VA was wrong*, and not just why you are right. If you don't convince them that they were wrong, they won't care how justified you may feel in claiming the benefit they have withheld.

How carefully should the Substantive Appeal be worded?

Very. You or your representative will have to write out a statement explaining why you think you should get the benefits that you were denied. This is the text of your Substantive Appeal. In this statement, you should be as precise and specific as possible. If you know the date when something happened, include the date. If you know the name of the doctor who treated you, or the sergeant who mistreated you, include the name. If you feel that the VA has not followed its own regulations, state the number and text of the regulation that would help your case.

Do you have a right to a hearing?

The sequence of processing that has been described—filing of Formal Claim, Development, Adjudication, Notice of Disagreement, Statement of the Case, Substantive Appeal—applies, with minor variations, to almost every claim for benefits (all of this takes place at a VA regional office). At almost any point, the sequence may include a hearing.[15] A hearing must be held if you request one. A discussion of hearing strategy appears in the next chapter. At VA offices, hearings are conducted by a panel of three VA employees with training in specialties related to your claim. After they make a determination, they will send you a notice of their decision. You will then have at least 60 days to file a Notice of Disagreement, and the processing sequence is repeated.

At some point your appeal will be removed from the jurisdiction of a Regional Office and will be submitted to the Board of Veterans Appeals (BVA). This will happen when the Regional Office, after reviewing your Substantive Appeal and any newly submitted evidence, determines that it will stick by its decision as being procedurally and factually valid. At that point your appeal is "certified" to the BVA for determination. You are entitled to a personal hearing at the BVA, whether or not you had one at the VA Regional Office.

What is the Board of Veterans Appeals, and how does it work?

The BVA is the supreme court of the VA. The BVA consists of up to 50 members appointed by the President, who normally sit in panels of three. Some members are lawyers, some are physicians, some have other special training. Almost all used to be employed in other VA positions. BVA panels hold hearings in Washington, D.C., and from time to time a "traveling panel" will hold a hearing at regional offices. When you appeal to the BVA and you want a hearing, you should specify whether you want to have it in Washington, D.C. or before a traveling panel, or whether you are content to have it before three Regional

Office employees who will thereafter send the transcript of your hearing, together with your file, to Washington for a decision by a BVA panel.[16] Since it is impossible for the BVA panel members to ask you questions they might have unless you meet them face to face, in most cases you should request to appear before the next traveling panel that comes to your area, or make the trip to Washington. The VA will not pay for your transportation to the site of a hearing or any other expenses that you incur.

How does the BVA process cases?

At the BVA, files are processed by staff personnel who are usually called "legal consultants." They prepare an outline of the case for the panel members. If a hearing is held, one might be present; and prior to the hearing, one might, if asked, indicate to your representative what questions are considered the most important or the most difficult.

Ultimately, the legal consultant will draft a proposed decision for the panel. Usually, the panel members will vote to accept that recommendation and will issue the proposed decision as their own. But the panel members will often disagree with some or all of the proposed decision, in which case they will either write their own decision or tell the "legal consultant" to rewrite his or her proposed decision. On rare occasions, one member of a panel will dissent from a decision. When this happens, the Chairperson of the BVA reviews the case. If s/he agrees with the dissent, the case is reconsidered by a six-member or larger panel.[17]

Because of the immense number of appeals that go to the BVA, each member of the BVA is generally responsible for voting on more than 1,500 cases a year. Obviously, it is impossible for each BVA member to read each file. This means, as a practical matter, that almost every case is decided in fact by a legal consultant, subject to the occasional disapproval of a panel. However, after you leave your hearing, the panel members will often tell the legal consultant which way to decide the case. Thus, if you ask for a hearing, you probably increase your chances of winning, since the BVA panel may immediately vote in your favor, or the legal consultant, acting on his or her own, may later conclude that you should win. You also increase your chances because the panel members have an opportunity to hear you answer their questions. Thus, they need not guess at the answer. Your going to the trouble of appearing increases the possibility that others will become convinced that you firmly believe in your cause.

A further increase in your chances might come from selecting a national service organization to represent you at a BVA hearing, whether or not you are able to attend it. This is because the BVA offices of some national service organizations are staffed with lawyers and physicians (for disability cases) who are likely to be much more capable than the representatives at local offices.

How does the BVA decide cases?

In deciding a case, the BVA looks at the whole file, but decides only issues certified by the Regional Office. The BVA decision can take a number of forms. It can deny the appeal, in which case you lose. It can return the case to the Regional Office ("remand to the agency of original jurisdiction" is their phrase) either for further development or for consideration of additional evidence that was incorporated in your Substantive Appeal or presented at a hearing. Or it can grant your appeal, in which case you win.[18]

Roughly two out of three BVA appeals are denied. More than half of the remainder are returned for further development and reconsideration. Only about one in eight appeals is won. However, one-half of the cases where Notices of Disagreement are filed never reach the BVA. Of these, about one in three wins in the Regional Office, and most of the others fail to submit a Substantive Appeal.[19]

If your case is returned, the BVA retains jurisdiction over the appeal in the event you are dissatisfied with the results after the Regional Office reconsiders the case. Regional employees often view returns as a slap on the wrist, and a demand by the BVA that the original decision-makers correct their errors. Consequently, your chances of winning after a return or remand are good.

Will the BVA reconsider cases?

If the BVA denies the appeal, this decision will be final, with four exceptions. The first exception is your right to a *rehearing.* If you make a *request for reconsideration* within 1 year of the BVA's decision, and specify the error that you believe they made (for example, failure to give due consideration to a particular fact; failure to abide by a particular law or regulation), the BVA will routinely review your case even if it is clearly frivolous. If you so request, they will give you an opportunity to appear again, at a full hearing, limited to the errors specified in your reconsideration request.[20] Very often, if you ask for a full hearing on reconsideration, the case will be heard by an "augmented" panel, consisting of six members. Otherwise, reconsideration by the BVA is processed in much the same way as the original consideration.

The second exception to the finality rule is the adoption of a new VA law or policy, called a *liberalizing issue.* Occasionally Congress decides that VA treatment of certain facts, although technically lawful, is unfair. Or the VA may reach that conclusion on its own. The liberalizing issue changes the outcome in cases presenting those facts. The new policy permits old claims to be treated as new ones, without any new evidence or proof of past error by the VA.[21]

The third exception to the finality rule is the presentation of *new and material evidence.*[22] Where your claim was denied because you were unable to prove a necessary fact, you may subsequently find some evidence that might have resulted in your claim being granted. For example, if you were unable to prove that an incident in service happened in a particular way, you might later run into somebody who was a witness to the incident. A sworn statement from that person might constitute new and material evidence. Any time you present new and material evidence, the VA will reopen your file and process your claim from the start, whether or not a prior decision was final. But if the prior decision was final, benefits will be granted retroactively (back-dated) *only* if the new evidence came from official military agencies, such as the BCMR or the Surgeon General, or the VA admits, as it rarely does, that it made a "clear and unmistakable error," and not just an error in judgment or an error based on inadequate evidence.[23] Otherwise, the new information is treated as a new formal claim which can, however, be rejected solely because the information is not important or duplicates data already considered.

A finding of "clear and unmistakable error" in its prior decision is the fourth exception to the rule that BVA decisions—or unappealed Regional Office decisions—are final.

Would it be wise to withhold some of your evidence, so you can get a rehearing if you lose?

Because of the finality policy, it would be foolish to hold some useful evidence in reserve, expecting to get a second chance to win your claim if you should lose the first time. The VA has its own version of Catch-22, which consists of two boilerplate phrases: "unsubstantiated" and "merely cumulative." Quite frequently, a claim will be rejected initially because the vet's version of the facts is declared to be "unsubstantiated." That means they decided you didn't have enough supporting evidence to back up your claim. It doesn't really matter that the VA is supposed to take your word for the truth, unless and until it has hard evidence to the contrary.[24] In fact, very frequently you will not be believed—and even your physician will not be believed—because some petty bureaucrat chooses not to believe you. But once your version of the facts has been declared "unsubstantiated," the subsequent presentation of new and material evidence—evidence that substantiates your version—will frequently result in a determination that the new evidence was "merely cumulative" (that is, "just more of the same") and therefore not a basis for overturning the prior decision. Even if you do win on the second try, the benefits will probably not be granted retroactively. So, if you have additional evidence, even if it merely duplicates your testimony, use it now to "substantiate" your version of the facts. Don't keep it in reserve. *Present the best case possible the first time.*

If you lose all your VA appeals, can you sue the VA for benefits?

Almost never. The VA is the only federal agency that is exempted by Congress from the requirement that it defend its decisions in court. Except for insurance and loan disputes, and suits that do not relate to decisions to grant or deny benefits, no court has jurisdiction to review the VA's findings of fact or application of the law in a particular case. So the failure of the VA to find you eligible, or its determination that your disability is not service-connected, becomes final (subject to the exceptions listed above) once you have lost—or failed to make—your appeal to the BVA.[25]

There are some minor exceptions, and there is room for an enterprising attorney to test the limits of the law, but there have been almost no successful suits against the VA based upon a claim for benefits.[26] The Supreme Court has ruled that the act of Congress that forbids such suits does not apply to interpretations of the Constitution; so if you claim that your constitutional rights were violated by the VA, a federal court might look into the matter.

There is also a provision in the Privacy Act of 1974[27] that guarantees to every person a day in court if s/he contends that any federal agency, including the VA, maintains false, misleading, incomplete, or inaccurate records affecting him/her. At the time this book went to press, there were no reported court decisions applying the Privacy Act to VA claims for benefits. It is possible, however, that the Privacy Act would permit judicial review of a VA claim that was denied solely on the basis of a clearly false document or solely on the basis of a statement about the history or origin of a disability signed by a veteran while on active duty that cannot be used as evidence (*see* Chapter XIV). The courts are not likely to be enthusiastic about the Privacy Act requirement that they make their own, independent determination of the accuracy and completeness of your VA file.[28]

It is also possible that a court would order the VA to conduct an examination, or grant a hearing, in a case where the VA wrongly refused to do so.[29] But in such cases, the court would not dictate the outcome of the examination or hearing; that would be the exclusive right of the VA.

Legislation has been proposed that would allow the courts to review VA benefit determinations. At the time this book was printed, the proposals had not been passed by either house of Congress. In the event they are enacted, these proposals would permit suits for benefits to be filed against the VA within six years of the time the BVA denied the claim. Those who did not appeal to the BVA might not be allowed to bring suit.

Is there anywhere else you can go if you lose at the BVA?

Although you cannot sue the VA for benefits, there are two situations in which the Administrator of Veterans Affairs will review cases after the usual VA procedures—application followed by appeal to the BVA—have proved futile. The most important of these provisions permits payment equivalent to the denied benefits in cases where they were denied "by reason of administrative error on the part of the federal government or any of its employees."[30] This provision might benefit some disabled veterans who were denied treatment or compensation until they obtained eligibility through the upgrading of a bad discharge. In such cases, the law permits only 1 year of retroactive payments, but the veteran might have lost 5, 10, or 20 years' benefits. If upgrading was required because of an error made while the vet was in service and was not the result of a more liberal attitude toward the same facts that resulted in a bad discharge, this special provision should be applicable. An example of this would be where a Discharge Review Board or a Board for Correction of Military Records found that had the discharge regulations been properly followed, the veteran would not have received a bad discharge, or where a court-martial conviction was later invalidated by a court.[31] *See* Chapter III for a discussion of this last possibility.

The second special provision applies to cases in which an erroneous VA determination induced a person to act in a manner that resulted in financial loss.[32] In such situations, the Administrator will grant a payment equal to the loss. One example where this provision was invoked successfully involved a veteran who was attending college under the GI Bill. He wrote to the VA indicating that he wanted to transfer to another college because the one he attended did not offer the major he desired to take. He asked the VA if he would still get educational benefits if he transferred. The VA wrote back and informed him that the transfer would not result in any loss of entitlement. He transferred, and a few months later got another letter from the VA. In the second letter, the VA declared that it had made a mistake because the college he transferred to had not been approved for veterans; consequently, the vet could not receive the benefits he was counting on. The vet then invoked this special provision, and asked the Administrator to grant him benefits for his new program of study. The Administrator found in his favor, and granted him a single payment equal to the amount he had lost when, in the good faith belief that he would continue to get benefits, he transferred to the nonapproved college.

If you win benefits, can the VA appeal its own decision and take away the benefits?

There are provisions in the law for the VA to appeal to the BVA from its own decision.[33] Such an action is called an "administrative appeal." Administrative appeals are very rarely taken by the VA. In most cases, they are based on a dissent by one member of the three on a hearing panel. When such appeals are taken, you are entitled to an opportunity to be heard in much the same manner as though you were appealing. You will, however, have two advantages. First, you are certain to know exactly why the administrative appeal was filed—so you won't have to guess about the other side's position. Second, you will get two chances to win, because you have the option of taking your own appeal *after* the BVA rules on the administrative appeal.[34] This means that you can argue against the administrative appeal, and if you lose it, you can appeal from that loss afterward. Your appeal will be heard by a different panel of the BVA from the one that heard the administrative appeal.

In addition to the administrative appeal, there are procedures by which the VA can reopen your case and reduce or withdraw your benefits on the grounds that you obtained them fraudulently or that you are no longer entitled to receive them. Also, *failure to answer a routine questionnaire or to report for an exam can result in withholding of benefits.*[35]

If you have received benefits by accident or fraudulently, the VA has procedures for determining whether or not you should be forced to pay back the money you should not have received.[36] According to an act of Congress, the Administrator of Veterans Affairs, who is the highest VA official, should not attempt to recoup on accidental overpayments, or on loan defaults, if to do so "would be against equity and good conscience."[87] If, however, you obtained the overpayments or defaulted on the loan through conduct that was fraudulent, misleading, or not done in good faith—in other words, if the fault was largely yours—the VA must attempt to recover the overpayments or collect on the loan. In practice, the VA almost always tries to get back any money it paid you in error if it determines that you knew an error was being made.[88] This might be accomplished by reducing future benefit payments below the proper level until the reductions total the amount paid in error. You are entitled to notification that this method will be adopted, *before* any benefit check is reduced. If you object to the reduction, you are entitled to a full and fair hearing, and to an appeal from that hearing to the BVA, *before* any payments are reduced. You must, of course, make a prompt demand for a hearing when you are notified of the planned reduction.[39]

Why do we present such a gloomy picture of VA procedures?

We do it to alert you to the worst possible things that can happen, so you will not casually or sloppily file your claim. Be thorough, be diligent, ask questions, check the regulations, present your best case. It's your life and your money at stake. Don't let a bureaucracy trip you up.

NOTES

1. 38 U.S.C. §§ 3404(c), 3405. The constitutionality of these sections was summarily upheld in *Gendron* v. *Levi*, 423 U.S. 802 (1975).
2. 38 C.F.R. § 14.627.
3. 38 C.F.R. § 14.629(a).
4. 38 C.F.R. § 14.626.
5. 38 U.S.C. § 3403; 38 C.F.R. § 19.131; Board of Veterans Appeals Rule 19; 38 C.F.R. § 14.639.
6. One such organization has filed a lawsuit to compel the VA to let it represent veterans, in the U.S. District Court

for the Northern District of California, *Swords to Plow-shares* v. *Roudebush*.

7. A contact representative meets the requirements of the authorities cited in note 5 above.

8. 38 C.F.R. § 3.155.

9. 38 C.F.R. § 3.158.

10. 38 U.S.C. § 4005(b) (2); 38 C.F.R. § 19.118; Board of Veterans Appeals Rule 18.

11. *Ibid.*

12. 38 C.F.R. § 19.115.

13. 38 U.S.C. § 4005(d)(3); 38 C.F.R. § 19.118(b); Board of Veterans Appeals Rule 18(b). Only 30 days are allowed when two claimants each seek the same dependents' or survivors' benefit. The 30- or 60-day period, however, never expires before the final day upon which a Notice of Disagreement could have been filed.

14. 38 U.S.C. § 4005(d) (4); 38 C.F.R. § 19.115(c) (2) (iii); Board of Veterans Appeals Rule 15(c) (2) (iii).

15. 38 C.F.R. § 3.103(c).

16. 38 C.F.R. § 19.138; Board of Veterans Appeals Rule 38.

17. 38 C.F.R. § 19.145(e); Board of Veterans Appeals Rule 45(a).

18. New evidence can be presented to the BVA. The BVA may consider it and reach a decision or return the case to the Regional Office; 38 C.F.R. § 19.145, 19.146; Board of Veterans Appeals Rules 45 and 46.

19. Annual Report of the Administrator of Veterans Affairs.

20. 38 C.F.R. § 19.148 *et seq.*

21. 38 C.F.R. §§ 3.105 and 3.114(a).

22. 38 C.F.R. § 3.156.

23. 38 U.S.C. § 4004(b); 38 C.F.R. §§ 3.104, 19.155; Board of Veterans Appeals Rule 55. Upgrading and correction of military records is treated as "new and material evidence" that may have retroactive effect. Other evidence that does not come from official military sources merely permits a claim to be reprocessed as though it were a new claim, without retroactivity of benefits, unless the VA finds that its initial rejection constituted "clear and unmistakable error"—38 C.F.R. § 3.105(a).

24. 38 C.F.R. § 3.102 provides that all reasonable doubts as to the facts are to be resolved in favor of the vet, and states in pertinent part, "Mere suspicion or doubt as to the truth of any statements submitted, as distinguished from impeachment or contradiction by evidence or known facts, is not a justifiable basis for denying the application of the reasonable doubt doctrine. . . ."

25. 38 U.S.C. § 211(a) declares "the decisions of the Adminis-

trator on any question of law or fact under any law administered by the Veterans' Administration providing benefits for veterans and their dependents or survivors shall be final and conclusive and no other official or any court of the United States shall have power or jurisdiction to review any such decision by an action in the nature of mandamus or otherwise." Proposals to repeal these provisions were being considered by Congress when this book was printed.

26. The only recent successful suit is *Plato* v. *Roudebush*, 397 F. Supp. 1295 (D. Md. 1975).

27. 5 U.S.C. § 552a(g); *see also* the *Congressional Findings and Statement of Purpose*, Pub. L. 93-579, Section 2(b).

28. 5 U.S.C. § 552a(g)(2)(A).

29. Although 38 U.S.C. (a) precludes review of VA decisions by mandamus (*see* 28 U.S.C. § 1361), it is not clear whether mandamus lies to compel procedurally proper processing of a claim. It is arguable that the statutory reference to "decisions" relates only to final rulings on the merits of claims, and not to procedures adopted in violation of the Constitution, the law, or the VA's own regulations. In particular, it is possible that a court would require the VA to give consideration to a particular statute, e.g., 38 U.S.C. § 311 (presumption of sound condition), where the VA decision does not speak to a claimant's invocation of the statute. But, clearly, the court is without jurisdiction to compel a particular outcome.

30. 38 U.S.C. § 210(c)(2).

31. Other examples: this provision might apply if your bad discharge was the result of a court-martial where you were denied effective assistance of counsel, since the denial of counsel makes the findings of the court unreliable. On the other hand, if upgrading resulted from liberalized attitudes toward homosexual acts or drug offenses, this provision probably would not be applicable.

32. 38 U.S.C. § 210(c)(3)(A).

33. 38 C.F.R. § 19.123 *et seq.*; Board of Veterans Appeals Rules 23 *et seq.*

34. 38 C.F.R. § 19.127; Board of Veterans Appeals Rule 27.

35. 38 C.F.R. §§ 3.158, 3.655, 3.656, 3.500 *et seq.*, and 3.900 *et seq.*

36. 38 U.S.C. § 3101(b).

37. 38 U.S.C. § 3102.

38. *See* 38 U.S.C. § 3012(b) (9, 10).

39. DVB Circular 20-75-83 (Revised Nov. 19, 1975) implementing *Plato* v. *Roudebush*, 397 F. Supp. 1295 (D. Md. 1975), a class-action suit upholding the right to pretermination notice and hearing in VA pension cases.

XIII

VA Hearings

Often the best way to obtain benefits to which you feel you are entitled is to present your case orally to the bureaucracy responsible for issuing the benefits. The VA has a policy of granting a hearing almost any time a veteran requests one after his or her claim has been questioned.[1] In other words if you have a bad discharge and know it will be an issue, you might request a hearing before "adjudication." Sometimes this could be a very good tactic. In most cases, however, hearings are requested after an adverse determination is first made.

At a hearing, the vet or his or her representative can present documentary evidence, offer testimony—from the vet and from any witnesses the vet brings along—and present argument designed to prove the vet's entitlement to the benefit s/he seeks. However, the VA will not pay the expenses of witnesses.

Hearings are normally conducted before a panel of three VA employees with training in specialties related to your claim. They will later decide by majority vote whether or not to grant the benefit you desire. Hearings are recorded on tape, and thereafter a transcript of the tape is typed up. You and your representative can get free copies if a request is made before or at the hearing.

Should you always request a hearing?

Not necessarily. Scheduling of hearings, transcribing of tapes, and related activities take time. Whenever you ask for a hearing, you are likely to find that it delays any decision by 3 or 4 months, or even a year. So you should only ask for a hearing when you believe it might help you win the benefits you seek.

A hearing is not likely to help you if you don't know *why* your claim was rejected. A hearing is not likely to help you if you cannot emphasize some facts or some legal requirement that the VA has overlooked. A hearing is also not likely to help you if you don't carefully prepare for it. So first you need to know why your claim was rejected.

How can you force the VA to tell you why your claim was rejected, so you can decide whether you need a hearing?

The VA is required to give you an explanation of its decision to reject your claim.[2] The VA need not give you this information until you have filed a "Notice of Disagreement."

Unfortunately, all too often the information contained in the "Statement of the Case"—which is the VA's official reason for rejecting your claim—is vague or merely states a conclusion, without clearly pointing out how it was reached. Occasionally, the official reason will not even be the real reason—because the real reason, which might have a basis in common sense, is not permissible under the VA's rules and regulations.

What is important from your perspective is finding out exactly why you were denied the benefit you seek. A number of techniques have been developed by veterans' representatives for pinning down the VA to a precise explanation. Although none of them is guaranteed to work, you should discuss using any or all of them with your representative if you cannot figure out precisely why your claim was turned down.

Should you write to the VA?

One technique is to write a *short* letter to the VA, politely requesting a more detailed explanation. The letter must be short, because the bureaucratic mind often does not like to deal with long letters—and it responds by ignoring what a long letter says. Your short letter should also be courteous. It will become a permanent part of your

157

file, and can be read by those who later decide your case. Your letter should simply state who you are, what the VA did to you, that you don't understand why they did it, and you would appreciate receiving a more detailed explanation. A sample of the type of letter we suggest is the following:

Dear Adjudication Officer:

I have just received your letter declaring that I am not eligible for VA benefits because my discharge was not issued "under conditions other than dishonorable." I did not receive a dishonorable discharge; I received an undesirable discharge solely because I once cursed back at a foul-mouthed Sergeant. Would you please explain to me precisely why that disqualifies me from benefits.

Thank you.

Sincerely,

[signed]
Victor Veteran
(VA Claim Number)

In response to a letter such as this one, the VA will probably do one of two things. It might send back a letter specifying the basis on which eligibility was denied. For example, "Your undesirable discharge was accepted in order to avoid trial by general court-martial. This disqualifies you from benefits under 38 C.F.R. § 3.12(d)(1)." Or the VA might issue you what they call a "Supplemental Statement of the Case," containing a similar explanation in more formal language. The important thing, however, is that you have received a precise reason. You now know that the VA does not contend that you were guilty of "willful and persistent misconduct," which would be disqualifying under another provision of the regulations. This information is important, because it will guide you in preparing your case. As in the case of Victor Veteran, you will know that you must go to your military records, and try to demonstrate that you would have been tried by a *special*, not a *general*, court-martial. You will know that you don't have to try to explain away every indication of misconduct that appears in your military records, such as Article 15 punishments.

What about using a congressional inquiry?

A second technique for pinning down the VA to a single explanation, but one that is used too often, and not used well at that, is the congressional inquiry. The VA tries to keep members of the Congress happy, because Congress votes on VA appropriations, can create or destroy VA programs (jobs for VA bureaucrats), and could permit veterans to sue the VA, thereby putting the courts in a position to enforce the provisions of the law that the VA administers. And members of Congress try to keep their seats in Congress. So there is a great deal of correspondence by members of Congress on behalf of vets who believe that the VA has given them a raw deal. All of this correspondence becomes part of the veteran's VA claim file. Most of this correspondence, unfortunately, is routine nonsense, which does nothing except waste the taxpayers' money and slow the processing of claims. If you want congressional assistance, do it the right way, by understanding how a congressional inquiry is processed.

When your member of Congress gets a letter complaining about the VA, the letter is photocopied. A copy is sent to the VA's congressional liaison office, together with a covering note that usually says, "I am concerned about this veteran's rights. [signed] John Doe, Member of Congress." If the letter to the member of Congress is not *very specific* about the vet's complaint, the VA sends back a form letter, which says something like this:

Dear Congressperson Doe:

We have carefully and compassionately reviewed the claim file of Victor Veteran, C-0000000. On [date or dates], after a thorough and complete evaluation, the Regional Office determined that he was not eligible for benefits because his discharge was not issued under conditions other than dishonorable. Mr. Veteran is entitled to appeal that decision to the Board of Veterans Appeals if he so desires. He has already been sent information explaining how to do so. For your convenience, we enclose a copy of the

159

communication previously sent him concerning the
way to appeal to the Board of Veterans Appeals. We
hope the foregoing information will be of help.
Thank you for your inquiry.

Sincerely,

Bennie Bureaucrat

A response such as the foregoing is photocopied in the
office of the Congressperson, and the original is sent to
you together with a note, containing a facsimile of the
member's signature, telling you that "it has been a
pleasure assisting you. Please feel free to call upon me for
further assistance."

Face up to it. Assistance of this sort won't get you the
benefits you have claimed. Only use a congressional inquiry if you can state, in two or three sentences, exactly
what you want to find out. A letter such as the following
might produce a truly helpful response—one that pins the
VA down to a single and precise explanation.

Dear Congressperson Doe:

The VA has ruled me ineligible for benefits because my discharge was not issued "under conditions
other than dishonorable." They have not told me *why*
my undesirable discharge, which I was given because
I once cursed back at a foul-mouthed Sergeant, is
treated as though it were a dishonorable discharge.
Do you know why?

Sincerely,

[signed]
Victor Veteran
(VA Claim Number)

Similarly, if the VA had told Victor Vet that his discharge was for "willful and persistent misconduct," the
following letter to a member of Congress might get back a
meaningful response.

Dear Congressperson Doe:

I once shot my mouth off at a foul-mouthed Sergeant who deserved worse. Now the VA has denied me benefits, declaring that I engaged in "willful and persistent misconduct." I admit that I acted willfully, but can you find out how one string of obscenities can be declared "persistent"?

Sincerely,

[signed]
Victor Veteran
(VA Claim Number)

("Willful and persistent misconduct" is discussed in Chapter X.)

Getting more technical for the moment—and it is often good to phrase your letter to a member of Congress in technical terms—your claim for disability benefits might have been denied on the grounds that your disability existed before you entered service. If the VA has no clear evidence that your condition developed before you entered on active duty, you might write the following letter.

Dear Congressperson Doe:

I developed high blood pressure while serving honorably in the Marine Corps. My condition prevents me from being employed, but the VA has denied me disability compensation on the false assertion that I always had high blood pressure. My enlistment physical shows that I had normal blood pressure at that time. Why has the VA not honored the act of Congress (38 U.S.C. § 311) that establishes a *presumption of sound condition*?

Sincerely,

[signed]
Victor Veteran
(VA Claim Number)

(Disability compensation and the presumption of sound condition are discussed in Chapter XV.)

Letters that are as short, precise, and clear as the samples presented above—and that *ask only simple questions*—are the only ones that are likely to receive a useful response from the VA. No guarantee, of course. Even these might be answered with bureaucratic gobbledygook. But the long-winded letter, which asks complex questions, is all but certain to receive a long-winded response that answers nothing. So only write to your senator or representative if you have simple, precise questions you want answered. If you must ask two questions, first ask one; then, if you get a meaningful response, send another letter, asking your second question.

Can you find out why your claim was denied by using a formal VA process?

Sort of. A third technique for forcing the VA to give you a precise explanation is to include in your Substantive Appeal a complaint that the Statement of the Case was too vague to be of value to you. Congress knew that when a bureaucrat says "No" an appeal would be useless, *unless* you know *why* you were denied benefits. Thus, a statute requires the Statement of the Case to be reasonably specific. The VA's own regulations also contain that requirement. And the form letter that comes with the Statement of the Case declares that the Statement of the Case is *not* a decision; it is only an explanation of the reasons your claim was rejected, which is supposed to help you in preparing an effective appeal.[3]

If the Statement of the Case you receive is so vague that you can't figure out exactly what facts or regulations were in the mind of the adjudicator when your claim was denied, then it does not meet the requirements of the law. For example, if your claim for medical disability was disallowed because "examination failed to reveal the claimed condition," and the only other reference to an examination merely stated that it was "held on June 15, 1974," you really don't know what the examination did or did not reveal. Therefore, the Statement of the Case is of no assistance in making your appeal. If a letter to the VA doesn't get you more specific information—who examined you, what that physician's specialty was, what examination procedures were attempted, exactly what the examination revealed—your Substantive Appeal cannot be written effectively. You are in no position to go to an expert and find out whether the techniques used by the VA physician were the best ones—or the only ones—for diagnosing your disabling condition. In other words, if you had more information, you might be able to show that the VA doctor who examined you did not do so carefully—or, as occasionally happens, was not even looking for the ailment you claim. And until you get more information, you cannot make your right to appeal meaningful.

In these types of situations, appeal to the BVA on the grounds that your right to appeal has been watered down by an inadequate Statement of the Case. Also state in your appeal that you have the condition you claim; include any statements from witnesses—whether medical specialists or merely family and friends—that might substantiate your claim. The BVA is in no hurry to remand for reprocessing a claim that appears to have absolutely no supporting evidence. But if your claim *might* be valid, the BVA usually won't tolerate a Regional Office decision based on inadequate development.

What about using the Freedom of Information Act?

Although the Notice of Decision sent to you by the VA does not explain the reason for rejecting (or granting) a claim, there will be a useful, but highly technical, document in the VA files, on which their Statement of the Case will later be based. That document summarizes the evidence and the applicable law. The file document is called a "rating decision" in disability cases, an "administrative decision" in other cases. If you make a Freedom of Information Act (FOIA) request for a copy of that document, the VA will provide it to you (except in some mental health cases—see Chapter XVII).

The easiest way to do this is to ask the VA for VA Form 07-3288. Fill out that form and file it with the VA. This will constitute a FOIA request.

These techniques, and others that you might think of, can sometimes help you pin down the VA. Unless you can pin them down, and get them to say exactly why they are rejecting your claim, it will be very difficult to prepare an effective Substantive Appeal, or a winning hearing presentation.

Now, you need to know something about how VA hearings are conducted.

The VA says that hearings are "nonadversary" proceedings. What does that mean?

Everyone knows that there are at least two sides to every disagreement. When two sides face one another, and attempt to settle their disagreement—whether in combat or in court or at an administrative hearing—they are engaged in "adversary proceedings." Each side is adverse, or opposed, to the other.

Most disagreements about legal rights can be settled in adversary proceedings, typically in a courtroom. In theory, things work as follows. In a court setting, each side gets to know the other side's position before any decision is made; each side gets to present its evidence and the testimony of its witnesses (uncooperative witnesses can be forced to testify); each side gets a chance to question the other's witnesses, hoping to belittle their testimony. After each side has had its turn, an unbiased fact-finder—either a jury or a judge—will determine what actually happened, and the judgment of the court will declare the legal significance of the facts.

Nothing like this happens at the VA because the VA pretends that there are no disagreements; there are no opposed, or adverse, parties. You are supposed to believe that the whole VA bureaucracy is doing its best to help you, and is cutting through the procedural rigmarole of adversary proceedings by holding informal hearings where your side is the *only* side that has an opportunity to present evidence and the evidence is not limited to highly technical rules—all of which is just fine if they grant you the benefits you claim. But if they deny your claim, the "nonadversary" system will prevent you from questioning the other side in order to expose its weaknesses. While Congress wrote laws that allow for fair hearings, it has in reality left matters in the hands of the VA, and not the courts, to enforce the laws. With rare exceptions, decisions by the VA are *not* reviewable by *any* court.[4]

Nonadversary proceedings are usually justified on the grounds that they are inexpensive and flexible.[5] The problem is that they generally tend to become shams. Facts are

164

found before the proceeding starts, and the fact-finders are able to conceal their biases and their errors with bureaucratic jargon. Thus, good intentions often do not suffice when legal rights are disputed.

Whenever you disagree with a VA decision, you would do well to remember that the bureaucrats at the VA are as "friendly" as were your neighbors on your draft board, and as "impartial" as the officer who conducted summary courts-martial in boot camp. You will probably be treated with more courtesy at the VA, and your chances of winning might be a good deal better, but don't forget that the hearing panel you encounter has already looked into the file. It knows the other side's position, and tends to assume that the other side—the VA—is right.

If you are going to win, you will probably have to first find out the other side's position. That, as we have indicated, can be very difficult. Perhaps because the VA tries so hard to promote its image of being every vet's best friend, it hesitates to tell you what you don't like to hear. If you have found out the VA's position, you are going to have to convince the hearing panel that the VA has made a mistake. Only *after* you demonstrate that the VA is wrong will the hearing panel pay attention when you tell them that you are right. That is the key to success in "nonadversary" proceedings. Try to convince them first that the VA is wrong, and then that you are right. To do this, you will have to plan for your hearing with great care.

How should you prepare for your hearing?

There are five steps you should take in preparing for a VA hearing: (1) Choose your represenative. (2) Analyze your strong and weak points. (3) Assemble evidence and outline testimony that is available. (4) Hold a dress rehearsal, a "pretend" hearing. (5) Make a checklist of facts and arguments you want to emphasize at the hearing. Let's look at these five steps in greater detail.

1. *Choose your representative.* Earlier in this chapter we indicated who could act as your representative. Here, we are worried about bad representation. All too often, representatives don't look at a veteran's file until the morning that a hearing will be held. Then they meet with the

vet half an hour before the hearing. With that kind of preparation, there is little the representative can do except tell the vet to tell his or her story, and then present a 2-minute speech that says little more than "Why don't you give this vet a break?" Not all representatives act that way, but more than a few do.

You don't need that kind of representation. You would never dream of going to court with a lawyer like that. You need a representative who will work with you, preparing well in advance for your hearing.

If the representative you selected won't sit down with you to review your file well in advance of your hearing, you need another representative. Changing representation is easily done. You can either go to the VA contact officers, and tell them you want to withdraw the power of attorney you previously filed, or you can pick a new representative, and have that person help you fill out the required forms for changing representatives. If, because of the change in representatives, you need more time to prepare for your hearing, the VA will always grant your request for a short postponement.

The reason you need to review your file long before the hearing is that documentary evidence cannot be obtained instantaneously. If you need a hospital record, or a statement from your high school guidance counselor, or a medical examination by a private physician, it will often take you weeks, or even months, to get it. If you need a letter from a buddy whom you haven't seen since the day you were discharged, which would confirm that a particular incident occurred—or if you need a copy of the record of a board hearing or a court-martial—you can't get it in one day. Your representative can help you prove that the VA made a mistake only by determining as soon as possible what evidence you will need. Any representative that doesn't want to take the trouble to prepare ahead isn't worth having as your representative.

2. *Analyze your strong and weak points.* You disagree with the VA. Probably there is information in the file that seems to support your position, and also some that supports the VA's (access to this file is discussed below). Your goal is to make little of the information that sup-

ports the VA, while reemphasizing the data that help your side.

Make a list of your strengths and weaknesses. Then try to figure out what sort of evidence or explanation will put your apparent weaknesses into a better light. For example, in an eligibility hearing, you might be able to show that a string of minor infractions—which resulted in your being discharged for "frequent involvement"—was really your response to a drug or alcohol problem, or to racial discrimination. Letters from other troops, records of arrests for drunk and disorderly conduct, or records of medical treatment for drug addiction are likely to put your service record into a different perspective—one that evokes sympathy instead of contempt. If you claim disability from an injury sustained while in service, but the VA insists that you are not disabled to a compensable degree, letters from treating physicians, family, or employers that describe your suffering might help convince the VA that you really are disabled by your injury.

By analyzing the information that is available to the VA, you and your representative should be able to figure out what kind of additional information will convince the VA that it is wrong to deny your claim, and what added evidence will substantiate your version of the facts.

3. *Assemble the evidence.* Once you know what you will need, it may take a lot of leg work getting everything. But if you are going to go to the trouble of preparing carefully for a hearing—and thereby increase your chances of winning[6]—you ought to know before the hearing what you will do at the hearing. You should know what items already in your VA file you intend to call to the panel's attention. You should know what is in the documents you will submit at the hearing. You ought to know what testimony you and your witnesses will give—and what answers you don't want given. You are under no obligation to tell the VA facts that would hurt you, so long as you don't stray from the truth in the information you do give them. Any good lawyer tries to know well in advance everything that is going to come out in court.

4. *Hold a dress rehearsal.* One of the most effective techniques for preparing your presentation is to hold a dress rehearsal, a "pretend" hearing. The purpose of this is

167

not to help you learn your lines—you already know what happened to you. The purpose is to get a critical reaction to your presentation, to know how a hard-nosed bureaucrat is likely to view your claim.

Have your smartest friend, or better yet your representative, make believe that he or she is the hearing panel. Present your testimony. Present or summarize the testimony of any other witnesses you intend to call. State what is in the documents you will submit. Let your friend interrupt you with questions, hard questions.

If you can, tape-record this rehearsal. If you can't do that, have your friend write down all the questions that were asked of you. Afterward, when you listen to the tape or review the questions, you may develop a better feel for the VA's attitude—and therefore be better able to convince the VA that it was wrong.

Such dress rehearsals are used by all good lawyers who prepare their clients for testifying. There is nothing wrong with being prepared to tell your story in its best light.

5. *Make a checklist.* Hearings don't progress along a straight line. An occasional question can distract you or your representative from a line of thought. Nervousness can result in omission of an important fact or argument.

Before you go into the hearing room, you and your representative should each have a copy of a checklist. On that list should be every fact and every regulation that you want to call to the panel's attention. As the hearing progresses, you and your representative should *each* be placing a check mark next to each item as soon as it is covered. (You should each do this because the activities of testifying or presenting argument may sometimes prevent one or the other of you from checking off an item that has been covered.) When you think you are ready to conclude the hearing, ask the panel for a moment to consult with your representative. During that time, compare notes, and see if anything important has been overlooked. If it has been, you still have a chance to cover it.

These five steps should help you make the most of your hearing. Of course, we can't guarantee that you'll win by using them. If all the facts line up against you, and the law as applied to those facts leads logically to the rejection of your claim, the most thorough preparation with the aid of the finest representative will probably not win you benefits. But if yours is a close case, which could reasonably go either way, combining careful preparation with an emphasis on demonstrating that the VA was wrong is the best way to win you benefits.

Where are VA hearings held?

VA hearings are held at Regional Offices and in Washington, D.C., at the BVA. If you request a local hearing, it will normally be held at the Regional Office that has jurisdiction over your claim. If, however, you live far from that office, but close to another, it is possible to have your hearing held at the closer office.[7] A transfer to that office will cause additional delay in deciding your claim. BVA hearings are held in Washington, D.C., or before traveling panels at Regional Offices.

What are VA hearings like?

About four out of five hearings are concerned with claims for disability compensation or pension. When those are the benefits desired, the hearing is held before a Regional Office "Rating Board" or a BVA panel consisting of a physician, a lawyer, and a third member who is either a lawyer or an occupational specialist (a person trained in judging the impact of a physical disability on your opportunities for employment). In most other cases, the hearing will be held before three lawyers.

When are hearings held?

The VA has a very liberal policy of granting requests for hearings. If you request one at any time concerning any claim for benefits, a hearing will be set up.[8] You will normally receive notice of the time and place a week or two before the hearing is held. Your notice will include a telephone number to call in order to arrange for a postponement if the time scheduled is inconvenient.

You should try to arrive early for your hearing. This will give you an opportunity to review your planned presentation with your representative, if you have one. It will also give you a final opportunity to review your file—although VA personnel will often resist your request to do so because prior to enactment of the Freedom of Information and Privacy Acts the VA would only permit your representative, not you, to examine the file. In mental disorder cases, they still will usually refuse to let the claimant see the file (*see* Chapter XVII). You should never wait until the last minute to see your file. Review it when you begin to plan your presentation. *See* Chapter IV for information on obtaining your service records.

Who attends VA hearings?

Once you or your representative informs the VA receptionist that you are ready for your hearing, you will be ushered into a room in which there will probably be a long table. Three VA panel members will sit along one side of the table, and you and your representative will sit on the other side, facing them. Sometimes you and the panel will sit at separate tables. There will be microphones in front of every seat, and there will be another small table at which a VA employee, operating a tape recorder, will record the whole hearing. Make sure you request that you and your representative be given free copies of the transcript that is made from the tape.

The only persons permitted to be present are VA employees and anyone whom you invite. There are no regulations that limit the number or type of people you invite. The only reason the hearing is not public is to protect your right to privacy. You are free to waive that right.

Will your VA file be available during the hearing?

Yes. If your claims file is not already on the table when you enter, one of the panel members will probably be carrying it when the panel arrives. During the hearing, don't be surprised to see members of the panel leafing through your file, examining its contents. Sometimes they do this because they came to the hearing unprepared and want to quickly familiarize themselves with the details of your claim. Other times, they are looking for a particular document that they believe relates to the testimony and argument being presented. Rarely will the members stop the hearing while they examine your file. You might consider requesting a recess if they appear to be missing important testimony while they read the file.

How much gets said, and who says it?

The scope and duration of the hearing will be determined primarily by you. The panel will ask very few questions and make almost no comments. Occasionally, as they are required by regulation to do, they will bring your attention to a particular regulation or document that is helpful to your claim. Otherwise, aside from listening (if they do), all the panel will do is make formal opening and closing statements and administer oaths to witnesses. The standard opening statement includes a recitation of the date, the location, the names of the panel members, the name of the claimant and any representative, and the benefits being claimed. Typically, you will be asked if the information given in the opening remarks was correct. If it was, you and any witnesses will be sworn in, and the show is turned over to you.

You or your representative can now make an opening statement or begin the presentation of evidence. A statement of what you intend to prove is often helpful. Evidence can be in the form of documents or testimony. Documents should be official or business records with signed cover letters certifying their accuracy, or else statements made under oath and notarized. Statements not made under oath need not be given any weight.[9] (It is a federal crime to intentionally introduce false statements at VA or any other federally conducted hearings.) Testimony can be from anyone willing to testify voluntarily.[10] The costs of attending the hearing, however, must be met by you. The VA will not cover your expenses or the expenses of witnesses.

Will the VA present testimony or evidence at your hearing?

The VA will introduce no evidence whatsoever. Their evidence—the evidence against you—is supposed to be in the file ever since your claim went through "Development." However, if your hearing is before a rating panel, you have the right to be visually examined by the physician member of the panel during the hearing.[11] (A visual examination normally will not require the physician to physically touch you or to use any special instruments.) You are then entitled to have the physician testify as to

171

the medical impressions obtained from that examination, and you or your representative may question the physician.[12] This is the only situation in which you can compel a witness to testify at a VA hearing, and it is the only time that a witness at a VA hearing is subject to cross-examination by anyone.

At most hearings, the members of the panel will not interrupt your presentation to ask questions. There are at least two reasons for this. First, the tape-recording system is not very sophisticated; so that if two people are talking at once, it will later be all but impossible to prepare an accurate transcript. Second, the panel members must not give you the impression of being hostile. Any questions they ask are supposed to be friendly and helpful and must not be cross-examination designed to refute your case or your witnesses' integrity.[13] In order to avoid complaints that the conduct of the hearing was unfair or that you weren't given an opportunity to tell your side of the story, the panel members tend to keep quiet.

After you have presented all of your evidence, you or your representative is permitted to make a closing argument. When you have finished, you would be well advised to ask the members of the panel if they have any questions or if there is any additional evidence you might provide that would assist them in reaching a fair ruling. At that point, the Chairperson of the panel, usually a lawyer, may ask some questions or may ask the other members if they have any questions. There probably will not be more than one or two. When these have been answered, the Chairperson will make the formal closing remarks. They consist of a question to you and your representative as to whether you have completed your presentation and whether you feel that you have been given a full and fair opportunity to present your case. When you declare that you are satisfied with the content and conduct of the hearing, the Chairperson will state the time of day and adjourn the hearing. No decision will be announced for some weeks, during which time the transcript will be typed and the file will be reviewed.

What happens if the panel wants to go "off the record" at a hearing?

There is only one additional event that is likely to occur at a hearing. That is the off-the-record discussion. Very often, at your request or on the panel's initiative, the tape recorder will be turned off, and an informal discussion will be held. This discussion may consist of a simple procedural question, for example, whether a particular witness will testify about certain events or whether a written statement you desire to include in the record could be made under oath before a notary or a VA employee. It might concern your feelings about being interrupted with questions. Other times, the discussion will give you a very good idea as to just what the panel members believe to be the important factual or legal problem in your case. This is because the rules governing the conduct of VA employees at hearings cannot be enforced when they go off the record; the friendly, helpful image can be abandoned; therefore, they are free to state the other side's case, instead of sitting silently.

When the panel tells you their main concern off the record, you have received a candid indication of the reason for the decision that will probably be made. The rest of your presentation should focus on providing a winning answer to the questions that really concern the panel members. If necessary, you should ask that the hearing be recessed for a short period, or even for a week or two, while you research the law and regulations or obtain further documentation. Such a recess will probably be granted at your request. In any event, when you go back "on the record," you may sometimes want to indicate that the problem was raised off the record, and what your response to the problem is. The off-the-record discussion will have served for you the same purpose as the three techniques we described previously for obtaining clarification of the VA's precise reason for rejecting your claim. Those techniques were based on the saying, "Forewarned is forearmed." The off-the-record discussion does the same thing: "Better late than never."

What if you can't attend your hearing?

If you can't come to your hearing, your representative may nonetheless appear on your behalf and present evidence (including any written statement you care to sub-

173

mit) and argument. But if you can attend the hearing, you definitely should. Hearing-panel members are inclined to view sympathetically a claimant who demonstrates a sincere conviction in his or her entitlement to benefits; they might be suspicious of the claim where the veteran won't even go to the trouble of attending a hearing. A personal appearance almost always gives you an important psychological advantage; so if you can't attend on the date scheduled, change the hearing date to a day when you can attend.

If you don't attend your hearing and you are represented by a "service organization" representative who has an office on the VA premises, most of your hearing will often be an off-the-record discussion between your representative and the hearing-panel members. These people see each other and discuss cases almost every day. They become personal friends, and your representative may be treated as though s/he were a fourth member of the panel. Informally, the four will review your file and perhaps negotiate what all four believe to be a fair decision. Then they will go on the record for a 5-minute formal hearing, at which time everything of importance will be briefly mentioned—and everyone present already knows the outcome. If the four have not reached any agreement on your claim, the hearing is nonetheless likely to be merely a formality because the details of the presentation were already covered informally. The panel will later make its decision (after the transcript of the formal hearing has been prepared) and your representative will be given a sneak preview of the decision.[14] At that point, there may be another round of negotiations between your representative and one or more members of the panel in which your representative again attempts to convince the VA people that their decision was wrong. Sometimes the panel will reverse itself at this point, but usually they will not. At any rate, only after they have considered your representative's response to the sneak preview will an official decision be made. When this has happened, you will be sent a Notice of Decision. together with information on how to file a Notice of Disagreement, if the panel decides against you, and thereby initiate an appeal.

Are presentations to the BVA by service-organization representatives desirable?

Presentations to the BVA by national service-organization representatives tend to be informal and limited to written memos. These representatives have easy access to your file and might indicate to the BVA's staff legal consultant—who will draft the BVA's tentative decision—the reasons why they feel your claim should be granted. But BVA members insist that, unlike local Rating Boards, they never give service-organization representatives or anyone else outside the BVA staff a sneak preview of their decision.

The fact that service-organization representatives are able to take advantage of their continuing contacts with the VA decision-makers and present claims informally is not necessarily bad. Often, it is an advantage, especially in those close cases where a decision could go either way. In addition, because the BVA presentations are sometimes made by physicians or lawyers on the Washington staff of the service organizations, they may contain expert opinions and analyses that are beyond the skills of most of the Regional Office representatives. But you should't be in too much awe of their skills. One study developed data that indicated that in cases where a disability was acknowledged but its service connection (for disability-compensation purposes) was disputed, claimants won more frequently by presenting their own claims without the aid of a representative. On the other hand, where the extent of disability was in dispute, representatives generally got better results than did unrepresented claimants.[15]

NOTES

1. 38 C.F.R. § 3.103(c).
2. 38 U.S.C. § 4005(d)(1); 38 C.F.R. § 19.115; Board of Veterans Appeals Rule 15.
3. *Ibid.*
4. 38 U.S.C. § 211(a).
5. *See,* for example, *Henry v. Middendorf,* 425 U.S. 25 (1976), where the Supreme Court overruled the Court of Military Appeals and said the military need not appoint counsel at a summary court-martial.

6. At least one unpublished research report indicates that a hearing itself does more to help you win benefits than your choice of a service-organization representative or your decision to represent yourself.
7. 38 C.F.R. § 3.103(c).
8. *Ibid.*
9. 38 C.F.R. § 3.200.
10. Although the VA has subpoena powers, it rarely exercises them. 38 C.F.R. § 2.1.
11. 38 C.F.R. § 3.103(c).
12. *Ibid.*
13. 38 C.F.R. § 3.103 (c).
14. Rabin, *Preclusion of Judicial Review in the Processing of Claims for Veterans' Benefits: A Preliminary Analysis,* 27 Stanford L. Rev. 905 (1975).
15. Popkin, *Counsel in the Welfare State,* 33 (unpublished manuscript, February 23, 1976).

XIV

Service-Connected Disabling Conditions

One of the major reasons that originally led Congress to create veterans' benefits was concern for the welfare of those who were injured in combat. Although the after effects of combat-incurred injuries continue to receive high priority among VA programs, numerous expansions of the range of veterans' benefits have occurred. For the past 40 years, injuries incurred in active service, whether or not they were suffered in combat or in the performance of noncombat military duties, have resulted in entitlement to benefits substantially the same as those granted for battle wounds. In addition, a broad range of benefits has been granted to eligible veterans whose disabilities do not derive from disease or injury during their service experiences. But the law has been written so as to draw a distinction between those who were disabled in service and all other eligible veterans. A number of VA programs are exclusively for those disabled in service; others give them larger benefits. Affected programs include disability compensation, free hospital and out-patient treatment, waiver of VA insurance premiums, eligibility for vocational rehabilitation and loans, and entitlement of dependents and survivors to VA benefits.

In addition to the VA disability-compensation program, the armed services operate their own disability retirement programs. A disabled veteran, if eligible for both the VA and armed services programs, must choose ("elect") to participate in one or the other. In addition, the VA has a pension program, which awards smaller amounts to aged or fully disabled veterans, although they were not disabled in service.

Because the range of benefits to which a veteran (or the veteran's survivors or dependents) is entitled will be based primarily on the presence or absence of a "service-connected" disability, it is important to discuss in detail the types of disability that are considered to be service-connected, before examining the different programs of benefits.

What is a "service-connected" disability?

Those who have represented veterans claiming VA benefits are in agreement that the most difficult cases to present involve disputes over service connection of a disabling condition. In such cases, there are two separate points that must be won: proving the service connection, and proving the extent of disability. *A disabling condition resulting from disease or injury is considered service-connected under any of the following circumstances.*[1]

1. It originated while *in service during time of war or national emergency.* From the day during the Great Depression when President Roosevelt proclaimed a national economic emergency, until September 14, 1976, when Congress passed the National Emergencies Act[2] (which rescinded all proclamations of national emergency), a presidential proclamation of national emergency was always in effect. Consequently, virtually all living veterans discharged "under conditions other than dishonorable" prior to September 1976 are "entitled" to a finding of service connection for any disabling condition that originated while on active duty (unless it was the result of the vet's own "willful misconduct").

2. Service connection is only granted for disabling conditions that originated in service when *not* in time of war or national emergency if the disabling condition is the *direct result of performance of military duties.*

3. A disease or injury that existed before the veteran entered service but *became worse as a result of service* (and therefore not from the normal or natural progression of the condition) is also considered to be "service-connect-

ed"—subject to the same time-of-war or national-emergency provisions as apply to service origin. However, for purposes of disability ratings (*see* Chapter XV), your rating for a preservice condition that became aggravated in service will be based on the difference between the degree of severity before you entered service and at the time of the rating, except that if your service-aggravated condition is 100% disabling, you will receive compensation at the 100% rate.

4. A disease or injury that originated as a *result of VA or military medical treatment* (or maltreatment), or during the course of VA vocational rehabilitation, will create the same entitlement to disability benefits as would be the case if that disability were service-connected. For example, if you were permanently disabled as a result of improper administration of anasthesia in a military or VA hospital, your new disability is "service-connected," even if you were being treated for a non-service-connected condition.[8]

5. A disease or injury whose origin was *caused by a service-connected condition* will also be considered service-connected. For example, if you are service-connected for a broken bone, even if it resulted in no direct disability, you will probably be granted service connection for any disabling arthritic condition that later develops at the joints surrounding the injured bone. The VA treats the hastened occurrence of arthritis as a "secondary" after effect of the primary condition—the broken bone.

Can these technical definitions be stated more simply?

Yes. As a general rule,

1. Any disability that originated or was aggravated while on active duty will be considered "service-connected" unless it resulted from the veteran's willful misconduct.

2. Any disability incurred during treatment of a veteran in a VA or military hospital will be deemed "service-connected."

3. Any new disabling condition that later develops will be considered "service connected" if it was probably caused or aggravated by another service-connected dis-

ability. *Disability compensation* is paid regardless of the basis for service connection; some *other benefits* may not be derived from these secondary disabling conditions.

Are there any special rules for determining "service connection"?

There are a number of legal "presumptions" that influence the determination of service connection. (A presumption substitutes for actual evidence in proving a fact.) The VA presumptions give the affected veteran the benefit of any doubt as to service connection, even though most medical specialists might consider service connection to be unlikely under the circumstances. These presumptions must be honored unless the VA comes up with clear proof that the presumption is false in a particular case. In essence, where there is an applicable presumption, instead of the vet having the burden of proving service connection, the VA has the burden of disproving it.

What is the "presumption of sound condition"?

The most important VA presumption is the "presumption of sound condition."[4] Under this rule, any condition that was observed by medical authorities while you were in service (including at the time of your separation physical exam) is considered service-connected, *unless* the same condition was noted at the time of your enlistment or induction examination, or the nature of the condition makes it obvious that it existed before you entered service. For example, a missing finger should have been noted before you went in, but unless your military records explain the loss of that finger, the VA will probably insist that it had been lost before you entered military service. On the other hand, if you were treated for asthma while in service, you are probably entitled to a service-connected rating, because asthma might first develop in service (although it usually shows up before then), and had it been observed before you went on active duty, you should have been rejected for enlistment, induction, or commission as an officer.

You signed a false statement, saying your disability existed prior to service, in order to speed your discharge.

Can this statement be used by the VA to deny service connection?

No. The "presumption of sound condition" cannot be overruled by the VA on the basis of any statement you signed while on active duty. At many military facilities, there was an unauthorized policy of informing servicemembers who were about to be discharged that their discharge would be delayed unless they signed statements declaring that a medical condition first observed at the separation physical had originated before they entered on active duty. Congress recognized that it would be unfair to deny disability compensation on the basis of such statements, since they were often not true. It passed a law that states that any statement signed while on active duty that declares that a disease or injury originated at a particular time, or progressed in a particular fashion, cannot be used as evidence against the servicemember who signed it. This prohibition applies to all civilian proceedings, including VA activities.[5]

What other presumptions are important?

Other presumptions that apply to VA determinations of service connection relate to specific ailments. There is a long list of chronic and tropical diseases that, if they were found to be at least 10% disabling within 1 year of separation from service (3 years for leprosy and tuberculosis; 7 years for multiple sclerosis) are considered to be service-connected.[6] For each of the chronic diseases, if there is an abatement followed by a renewed manifestation, the reoccurrence is presumed to be service-connected unless there is clear evidence of a new intervening cause. For former prisoners of war, there are a few conditions that are presumed to be service-connected if they were 10% disabling within 2 years of separation from service. For all veterans, any psychosis that becomes manifest within 2 years of separation from service is considered service-connected *for purposes of medical treatment* on an in-patient or out-patient basis, even if not considered service-connected for other purposes, such as disability compensation.[7]

How does the VA determine degrees of disability?

If you have a service-connected condition, your entitlement to a wide range of VA benefits will depend, at least in part, on the degree to which that condition is considered to be "disabling." In evaluating degrees of disability, the VA generally considers the impact of the disease or injury on the *average* person's ability to hold a full-time job. Therefore, you might receive a disability rating that does not reflect the actual degree to which you have had to change your daily activities. For example, loss of a big toe is rated at 30% disabling. Yet, for a construction worker, loss of that toe may force a complete change of occupation; for a lawyer, loss of that toe might have absolutely no adverse impact on earning ability. The VA publishes a long list ("schedule") of disabling conditions, together with the average degree of disability associated with each.[8] For conditions not included on that list, the VA attempts to award a rating on a case-by-case basis, which approximates the rating for conditions of similar severity.[9] In a few cases, where a combination of conditions produces an impact on a vet's earning ability that is far greater than the average, the VA will award a larger, "extra-schedular" disability rating.[10] We will discuss rating principles in greater detail in the next chapter, where we look at some of the individual benefits programs.

What if your medical records are inaccurate?

Service connection for a disability is usually based upon your military medical records. Where those records are incomplete or in error, you may have to obtain correction of the records from the BCMR, or through invocation of the Privacy Act of 1974, before the VA will recognize your entitlement to disability benefits. *See* Chapter VI, where correction of military records is discussed. Keep in mind that when you apply to a BCMR for a medical-records change, the BCMR will request an advisory opinion from the Surgeon General's office of the service concerned. As with all BCMR applications, request to see the advisory opinions before your case is submitted to the BCMR for a final decision. You may be able to rebut an erroneous advisory opinion.

NOTES

1. 38 U.S.C. §§ 310, 351; 38 C.F.R. §§ 3.301 *et seq*.
2. P.L. 94-412.
3. 38 U.S.C. § 351. Note that these conditions do not create entitlement to other VA benefits such as rehabilitation, specially equipped autos and housing, or dependents' educational allowances. They only create entitlement to disability compensation.
4. 38 U.S.C. § 311; 38 C.F.R. § 3.304(b).
5. 10 U.S.C. § 1219; 38 C.F.R. § 3.304(b)(3).
6. 38 U.S.C. § 312; 38 C.F.R. §§ 3.304-3.309.
7. 38 C.F.R. § 17.33.
8. 38 C.F.R. §§ 4.40 *et seq*.
9. 38 C.F.R. § 4.20.
10. 38 C.F.R. § 3.321(b); *cf*. 38 C.F.R. § 3.324 (10% rating permitted in cases of multiple 0% conditions).

XV

VA Disability Benefits and Pensions

What is the difference between disability compensation and pension?

The VA has two related programs under which an old or disabled vet receives a monthly allowance. One program is called *disability compensation*; the other is called *pension*. Compensation is granted to veterans for service-connected disabilities. It is the military's counterpart of civilian workmen's compensation. Pensions, which generally pay lower sums, are granted because an eligible veteran is unable to earn a living. They are a counterpart of public assistance. A single application form is automatically treated as a claim for *both* pension and compensation.[1] A veteran who is entitled to benefits under both programs will be paid only by the program that would give him or her the larger monthly check.[2] The two benefits cannot be combined; payment is always based on one or the other.

How do you qualify for a VA pension?

The important thing to remember about VA pensions is that they are based upon a combination of *need, age,* and *permanent disability*, regardless of when or how you become disabled.[3] Other entitlement criteria include 90 days of active-duty service during periods of war[4] (unless you were discharged for service-incurred injuries), and that your disability must not result from your own willful misconduct or "vicious habits."[5]

184

Because the standards for determining need are occasionally changed, the important thing to keep in mind is that if you have practically no income because you are unable to work, you will meet the need requirement unless you have a small fortune in assets. If you are 65 or over, the VA presumes you are unable to work; so you don't have to demonstrate any physical or emotional disability. If you are under 40, the VA will be very cautious about your case, tending to the view that you are not permanently disabled because with rehabilitation you might be able to hold a job. When you are between 40 and 65 years old, and have a large, but not total, disability, the VA makes a case-by-case determination of whether, as a practical matter, you are ever likely to hold a job.[6] Generally, the older you are, and the more severe your disabling condition(s), the more likely it is that you will be granted a pension. Finally, the nature of your condition, especially if you are under 40, must be permanently and totally disabling. This is what the VA calls "P&T." Most people who are P&T disabled would never be able to hold a regular job. To be permanently disabling, the condition must be one that is not likely to change for the better in the foreseeable future.

If you are eligible for a pension, the amount you receive will depend upon your outside income and the number of dependents you have. In addition, your pension will be increased if the VA finds that you are housebound or in need of special services.

Do pension payments end when a veteran dies?

After a veteran on VA pension dies, pension entitlement is continued for his or her surviving spouse, so long as there is need and the marriage lasted 1 year or produced children.[7] If there is no surviving spouse, entitlement is continued for surviving children upon a showing of need, regardless of how old the children are.[8] It is under these provisions that the VA is still paying benefits based upon Civil War service. In many cases, the children first become entitled to pensions in their old age. Their entitlement is not affected by the fact that for many years they did not receive a pension. Nor is it affected by the fact that the eligible veteran through whom they claim entitlement had

185

not applied for a pension, so long as s/he was entitled to either a pension or disability claim.

The amount granted for a widow's (or a widower's) and children's pension is calculated differently from a veteran's pension, and is likely to be different from the amount the veteran was receiving. These pensions are also paid to the widow and children of any vet who, at the time of death, was entitled to, or was actually receiving, VA disability compensation or armed services disability retirement pay.[9]

How do you qualify for VA disability compensation?

The VA awards monthly compensation payments for service-connected disabilities. Every veteran eligible for VA benefits who claims to suffer from a disabling condition that is service-connected will be rated for each such condition. (Some veterans who have an undesirable discharge that makes them generally ineligible for benefits do receive disability compensation under the 1977 amendments to the VA laws.) Although the VA may rely on records of other agencies, usually the rating will be based on a VA medical examination.

What is the disability rating system?

Each disability is given a rating that reflects primarily the extent to which it would interfere with the average person's ability to earn a "normal" income.[10] In addition, some conditions, while not occupationally disabling, are given an arbitrary disability rating. For example, injuries to the reproductive organs are compensable under the VA schedule, even though they don't affect employability.

Ratings are expressed in percentages, ranging from 0% to 100%. They are rounded off to the nearest 10% when computing compensation payments. Ratings are subject to reconsideration at any time, based upon a change in the severity of the disability. If your condition becomes more severe in future years, you will be entitled to an increased disability rating. You must apply for the increase before you will be given a higher rating. Conversely, if your condition becomes less severe, the VA can reduce your rating, unless you have had it for more than 20 years (and did not obtain the rating through fraud).[11]

The amount of the monthly compensation payment depends on the degree of disability, but Congress chose not to make a 40% disability payment double a 20% payment. Instead, the VA follows an arbitrary schedule of payments for each particular rating. Disabled vets *with dependents,* if their service-connected disability rating is 50% or more, receive larger compensation payments than they would get if they had no dependents.[12]

You have a 0% disability rating. What good is it?

Ratings of 0% do not result in a compensation payment, but they do establish service connection. This means that at some later date, if your condition gets worse, you would receive compensation based on the deterioration. For example, if you fell in basic training, and developed a trick knee, your trick knee may not be a major problem until years later, when severe arthritis sets in. If you went to the VA before the arthritis developed, your knee condition might well be rated as 0% disabling. Years later, it might get you a monthly check based upon a 20% or greater disability. If, however, you were shy about complaining of injuries that seemed not to have any lasting effect, when you go to the VA years later, it may be impossible for you to convince them that you ever had problems with your knee while in service. So don't be shy. Go to the VA. Tell them everything you can remember about little aches and pains, stumbles and twists, that you suffered in service. Do it while the service records still exist, and while people who might remember your minor complaints—for example, medics—can still be located.

The 0% rating you get today for a trivial condition may be the only way of winning your claim for a severely debilitating condition 10, 20, or 30 years from now.[13]

You have two disabling conditions, one rated at 60%, the other at 40%. Why is your combined rating only 80%, and not 100%?

The VA rates each disabling condition separately. In order to calculate a combined rating for more than one condition, it does not simply add each rating. If it did that, some vets would receive ratings of 150% or more. Since the rating is supposed to measure your loss of earning ability, a total loss would be equal to 100% disabled. It is logically and legally impossible to be more than 100%—i.e., totally—disabled.

If you have multiple service-connected disabilities, the VA uses a formula for combining them to get a total rating.[14] One disability rating, say the highest one, is subtracted from 100%. If your highest rating is 60%, then the remainder, after you subtract it from 100% is 40%. Your next disability rating is multiplied by that remainder. In our example, if you also have a 40% rating, it is multipled by 40% (the remainder), giving a product of 16%. If those are your only ratings, the 16% product is now added to the original 60% rating, to give you a combined rating of 76%, which is rounded off to 80%.

If you also had a 10% rating, the VA would first subtract the 76% combined rating from 100%, leaving 24%. Then it would multiply the 24% remainder by the 10% disability, giving a product of 2.4%. It would add that product to the earlier 76%, to give a total of 78.4%. Since the VA rounds off combined ratings to the nearest 10%, compensation in this case would still be based upon an 80% combined rating.

Although this formula seems complex, all it does is state in mathematical terms a simple principle, sometimes called the "whole person" formula. If you are partially disabled by one condition, any disability from a second condition only applies to the portion of your whole earning ability that remains after taking into account your first disability. Similarly, for each additional rating, the VA adds on only the degree to which it further reduces your remaining earning ability. Under this formula, no matter how many ratable disabilities you suffer from, your maximum combined rating is 100%—total disability.

If your service-connected disability gets worse, when will your benefits be increased?

The VA has fairly straightforward rules concerning the effective date for an increase of a disability rating. Changed ratings take effect on the date when you apply for an increased rating, or the date when you are entitled to it, whichever comes later.[15] Therefore, at the earliest suggestion that your disabling condition has become worse, you should request an increased rating. (Don't forget that if you apply for disability compensation within 1 year of discharge, your benefits will be granted from the day following discharge, not the date of your application, if you were disabled at that time.) You should also be aware that the date of a rejected disability application may influence the retroactive payment of disability or pension benefits, if benefits were denied solely on the grounds of ineligibility, and you subsequently became eligible through action at the DRB or the BCMR (*see* Chapter VI and VII).

What if you are denied disability payments or a pension to which you feel you are entitled?

You have the right to appeal *any* VA determination, including pension entitlement, service connection, degree of disability, and effective date of awards (*see* Chapter XII).

What is the difference between VA disability compensation and armed services disability retirement?

In addition to the VA program, there is an overlapping program run by the armed services, which also compensates for service-connected disabilities.[16] This program is fairly complex, and must be entered immediately upon separation from active duty. An eligible disabled veteran must choose ("elect") which program of benefits s/he wants, armed forces disability or VA compensation. S/he cannot get full payments from both at the same time. Usually the choice of which program will be based upon the veteran's rank at time of discharge. The VA pays the same amount to every disabled vet with the same rating, while the armed forces disability payment is based upon your basic military pay at retirement and therefore reflects your rank and the number of years you were on active duty. If you elect to receive armed forces disability retirement pay, this does not disqualify you from receiving other VA benefits; it only affects your entitlement to VA disability compensation (or pension).

Are there different military disability benefits programs?

Three types of benefits are offered by the armed services program. Under one, called "disability separation,"[17] the veteran is given a lump-sum severance payment, equal to not more than 2 years' base (monthly) pay, calculated by

189

multiplying the final base pay by twice the number of years served on active duty. Disability separation payments are made to those who served fewer than 20 years and were rated by the military at less than 30% disabled on the VA rating schedule. If you received this severance pay, and later apply for disability compensation from the VA, each VA payment to which you are entitled will be withheld until the total amount held back equals the disability separation payment you received from the military.[18]

The second type of armed forces benefit is called "permanent disability retirement" (PDR).[19] PDR pay is the larger of (1) base pay times disability rating on the VA schedule or (2) base pay times years of service divided by 40; but the maximum PDR pay is three-fourths of base pay.

PDR is available to those whose disabling condition is rated by the military at over 30% or more on the VA schedule of ratings or who have served more than 20 years. In addition to the disability pay, those on PDR enjoy all the privileges of military personnel who retired without disabilities: medical care in military hospitals, commissary privileges, etc. These additional benefits are allowed even to those who elect to receive compensation under the VA system.

In the event a person eligible for PDR is also eligible for military-retirement pay based upon 20 or more years of service, the portion of the retirement pay that would be received under the PDR program is exempt from income taxes.[20] (All VA compensation and pension payments are also exempt from income taxes.[21]) In almost every case, this makes retirement pay with a PDR tax exemption worth more than receiving straight retirement pay (fully taxable) plus VA disability compensation.

The third type is "temporary disability retirement" (TDR).[22] TDR is given whenever a serviceperson is unable to perform duties because of a qualifying condition that may be, but is not clearly, permanent. Except for the question of permanency, all of the requirements for receiving PDR must be met. If they are, the recipient is entitled to all PDR benefits. However, those on TDR have, in addition to the pay options for PDR, a third option: half of base pay. Those on TDR must report every 18 months for a physical exam, on the basis of which their disability rating, and the permanency of the disabling condition, are reconsidered. Thereafter, they may be placed on PDR, continued on TDR, or asked to accept a return to duty. But at the end of 5 years, the military must remove them from the TDR list. Then they either go on the PDR list or return to active duty.

What determines entitlement for armed forces disability benefits?

To be entitled to armed forces disability benefits, you must have a disabling condition that is not only service-connected in the VA sense, but actually *prevented you from performing* your military duties. Since September 14, 1976, when all presidential proclamations of national emergency were revoked, entitlement has been further limited to those with 8 years of active duty or who were injured or disabled as a *direct result of performing military duties*. Should war be declared or another national emergency proclaimed, the armed forces program will again apply to all service members who are prevented by their disability from performing military duties.

Denial of any military disability benefit can be "appealed" to the appropriate BCMR (*see* Chapter VI). These boards can correct any "error or injustice" in military records. For example, the BCMR has been convinced to change a Vietnam veteran's undesirable discharge to a permanent disability retirement with $7,000 in back benefits. The VA then rated the injury at a higher rate, and the vet elected to take future payments under the VA program.

Are the same rating schedules used by the VA and the military?

Although the armed forces use the same schedule of ratings as the VA does, quite often a veteran will receive different ratings from the two agencies. There are two ways this can come about. First, each agency makes its own judgment, and need not adopt the rating given by the other. Second, the VA will increase your rating whenever your condition gets worse; the armed forces won't, except for those on the temporary disability retired (TDR) list. Thus, often it is best to go to the VA after qualifying for

191

armed forces benefits to see which program offers the most.

NOTES

1. 38 C.F.R. § 3.151.
2. 38 C.F.R. §§ 3.700, 3.701.
3. 38 U.S.C. §§ 501 *et seq.*
4. The periods of war since 1900 are:
   August 4, 1964 to May 8, 1975 (Vietnam era)
   June 27, 1950 to June 31, 1955 (Korean conflict)
   December 7, 1941 to December 31, 1946 (World War II)
   April 6, 1917 to November 11, 1918 (World War I)
   April 21, 1898 to July 4, 1902 (Spanish-American War)
5. 38 U.S.C. § 521(a).
6. 38 C.F.R. § 3.342.
7. 38 U.S.C. § 541(e). Widows who do not otherwise qualify may be entitled to pension based on the date of marriage. The controlling date varies with the period of service, which is the basis for the veteran's eligibility.
8. 38 U.S.C. §§ 531 *et seq.*
9. *Ibid.*
10. 38 C.F.R. § 4.10. In cases of emotional disorders, social, as well as occupational, impact is considered. *See* 38 C.F.R. § 4.130.
11. 38 U.S.C. § 110. This "protected rating" provision also applies to determinations of permanent and total disability for pension or insurance purposes.
12. 38 U.S.C. §§ 314, 315.
13. The VFW has developed a reputation for getting 0% ratings for the nondisabled vets it represents. They don't do anything special. They simply review each new vet's complete military medical records, and ask the vet if anything happened that hurt at the time, but doesn't hurt now. Then they bring this to the attention of the VA.
14. 38 C.F.R. §§ 4.25.
15. 38 U.S.C. § 3010 *et seq.*
16. 10 U.S.C. §§ 1201-21, 1372-73, 1401-03. *See* generally Wellen, *Armed Forces Disability Benefits—A Lawyer's View*, 27 JAG JOURNAL 485 (1974).
17. 10 U.S.C. § 1203.
18. 38 C.F.R. § 3.700(a)(3).
19. 10 U.S.C. § 1204.
20. 26 U.S.C. § 104(a)(4).
21. *Ibid.*
22. 10 U.S.C. § 1202.

XVI

Medical Treatment and Hospitalization

The VA operates the largest hospital system in the nation. Included in its program are about 170 separate hospitals, with almost 100,000 beds, in which about 1 million patients each year receive treatment. More than half of the VA hospitals are medical research and training institutions, as well as treatment centers. About one-fourth are primarily neuropsychiatric facilities. In addition, the VA operates over 200 out-patient clinics and pharmacies. It also purchases medical services from state agencies and the private sector. All combined, these services cost the taxpayers 3 billion dollars a year.[1]

Can you obtain medical treatment in a VA hospital?

Admission for treatment at a VA hospital is dependent upon the availability of a bed, eligibility for benefits, and a sequence of priorities. A *special priority*[2] is given to emergency cases (whether or not otherwise eligible, if delay in admission would cause loss of life or severe physical damage) and to patients scheduled for additional treatment of a condition previously treated in the same hospital. Then there are ten priority groups.[3] The most important of the priority groups are subject to the following three preferences. First preference is given eligible vets needing hospitalization for disease or injury incurred or aggravated in service (or in subsequent treatment of such conditions), that is, for treatment of *service-connected*

193

conditions. Second preference is given those who have, or are eligible for, VA disability compensation, when needing treatment for a *non-service-connected* ailment. Third preference is given all other vets, provided that they are either over 65, or are receiving VA pension, or swear that they are *unable to pay* for needed hospitalization elsewhere.

Does hospitalization affect your disability rating?

If you are hospitalized for treatment of a service-connected condition in a VA hospital (or the VA authorizes treatment in a non-VA hospital) and your total consecutive time in the hospital and on convalescence is more than 21 days, you are entitled to a temporary 100% disability rating for your period of hospitalization, including not more than six 1-month periods of convalescence.[4]

If you go into a VA hospital, do you have any say as to the manner in which you are treated?

Yes. The VA has published a "Code of Patient Concern" (CPC), which high VA officials consider to be more effective than a patient's bill of rights. In their view, the CPC places a definite duty upon VA employees to honor the principles that would be recognized in a patient's bill of rights. The CPC is reprinted in its entirety in Appendix V.

The CPC seems to recognize that VA in-patients have important rights concerning the manner in which they are treated, both medically and personally. Included are the following rights:

1. *Diagnosis, treatment, prognosis.* You are entitled to know what medical condition is being treated, what treatment you are receiving, and what the probable result of this treatment will be (CPC ¶6).

2. *Who's in charge.* You are entitled to know which hospital employee has authority and responsibility for supervising every aspect of your treatment (CPC ¶¶ 7, 8).

3. *Requesting and refusing medical treatment.* You have the right to request, or to refuse, any particular form of treatment (CPC ¶¶ 8, 9, 12). The VA will determine whether the treatment you request is appropriate.

4. *Experimentation.* You may not be subjected to experimental (as distinct from generally accepted) forms of

treatment unless you have given approval based upon a detailed explanation of the procedures, the risks, and the alternatives (CPC ¶ 13).

5. *Patients' behavior.* You are entitled to receive a copy of any rules governing the conduct of patients. (CPC ¶ 16)

Are there exceptions written into the Code of Patient Concern?

The language of the CPC appears to permit exceptions in every instance, based upon avoiding probable harm— usually emotional in nature—to the patient. But these exceptions are actually very narrow because any determination that probable harm justifies withholding information can be made *only* by senior officials.[5] It cannot, under VA regulations, be made by orderlies, nurses, or even attending physicians. Of course, in practice, the senior officials will routinely adopt an attending physician's prediction of probable harm. But an orderly's or nurse's prediction will probably not carry much weight.

In any event, where this information is withheld from the patient, the VA must attempt to provide it, and obtain any necessary consent from, a next of kin or guardian. Consequently, in very few nonemergency situations can the VA legally conceal the fact that it is not informing and treating the patient in accordance with the CPC.

Can you be punished for exercising your right to refuse treatment?

A right is not a right if it comes only at a price. Your right to refuse treatment is not grounds for any kind of punishment or discipline. Refusal of treatment, or even violation of VA hospital rules, is *never* a legal reason for reducing or terminating your compensation or pension payments.[6]

However, exercising some of your rights may not endear you to the VA hospital staff any more than exercising your constitutional privilege against self-incrimination would endear you to a police officer. And there are obviously some subtle ways in which hospital staff can "punish" you for asserting your rights. Food might come late, cold, and off the plate. Nurses might answer your calls only after they first take a coffee break. Other forms of harassment might also be encountered. While it would be improper and unethical for such punishment to be inflicted upon you, as a practical matter all you could do about it would be to keep a written record of each incident and when the record is very long, or after you have been discharged from the hospital, send it to the VA central office in Washington, D.C., to your congressperson, and to your local newspaper. The VA is often more sensitive to adverse publicity than to anything else.

We should also point out that your purpose for being in a VA hospital is to receive treatment. If you refuse treatment just to be ornery, then there is no valid reason for keeping you in the hospital. The hospital has the right to discharge you for interfering with its proper functioning, or because it is unable to provide needed treatment, or because no treatment is needed.

What can you do if your CPC rights are violated?

If a VA medical facility violates the CPC, for example, by refusing to inform you of your diagnosis, or by forcing a particular treatment upon you against your will, you should try to straighten things out by speaking with the Chief of Medical Administration at the hospital. If that does not resolve the situation, you can sue the VA and the responsible employees in the appropriate federal court. In most instances, your suit, even if successful, would *not* get you any money. What it would get is a court order requiring the VA hospital personnel to observe the provisions of the CPC.

If you are injured as a result of malpractice in a VA hospital, can you sue the VA for damages?

Yes. A suit for damages is a suit for money; the amount of money awarded, if any, normally should equal the amount of damages or harm you have suffered.

A special federal law immunizes VA physicians from personal liability for malpractice.[7] Therefore you cannot successfully sue the doctor (unless your suit is for *intentional* wrongdoing, rather than negligent or incompetent treatment). But you can sue the United States for any harm done you, including emotional harm (pain and suffering).[8] To do so, you must comply with a complex set of procedural requirements. Among other things, you must file an administrative claim with the VA within 2 years of the time you were injured[9] (by malpractice or otherwise). The VA may settle your claim at that point. If they don't, you will then have 6 months from the time the claim is rejected (failure of the VA to act on the claim within 6 months constitutes a rejection) to file suit in federal court. Your suit will be decided by a judge, not by a jury.[10]

Obviously, the procedures involved in claiming damages from the VA (for malpractice or for any other reason not related to the grant or denial of a benefit) are so technical that the assistance of a lawyer will be necessary in almost every case. There is no serious statutory restriction[11] on attorney's fees (25%, or 20% if settled administratively) in this type of case, so you should have little difficulty in obtaining effective representation if your claim appears to be meritorious. But the VA will not warn you of the time limits within which you must act; it will not advise you to consult a lawyer. You must take that first step on your own, and you must take it without delay.

NOTES

1. See *1975 Annual Report*, Administrator of Veterans Affairs, Table 72, 196.
2. 38 C.F.R. § 17.49(a) (1), (2).
3. 38 C.F.R. § 17.49(a)(3).
4. 38 C.F.R. § 4.29.
5. 38 C.F.R. § 1.522 states: "Determination of the question when disclosure of information . . . will be prejudicial to the mental or physical health . . . will be made by the Chief Medical Director; Chief of Staff of a hospital; or the Director of an outpatient clinic."
6. 38 C.F.R. § 3.900(2)(c).
7. 38 U.S.C. § 4116.
8. *See* 28 U.S.C. §§ 2671 *et seq*.
9. 28 U.S.C. § 2401(b).
10. *Ibid.*
11. 28 U.S.C. § 2678 allows a maximum fee of 20% of the recovery for administrative settlements, and 25% for trial recoveries.

XVII

The Rights of Veterans with Emotional Disorders

Vets with emotional disorders are subject to special provisions at almost every phase of VA activities. Some of the special provisions aid them; others may not. For example, in determining character of service, if the VA finds that you were insane at the time of the misconduct that resulted in a bad discharge, you are automatically eligible for benefits[1] (unless your whole enlistment was void because, being insane at the time you enlisted, you were legally unable to enter into an enlistment contract[2]). For purposes of compensation, disability resulting from suicide attempts is presumed not to be the result of willful misconduct[3] (which would destroy entitlement); for purposes of survivors' benefits, it is presumed that suicide resulted from insanity.[4] For purposes of receiving benefit payments, a veteran will not be required to have a guardian unless s/he is clearly unable to manage his or her own finances.[5] On the other hand, the veterans' benefits laws authorize the VA to refuse to show you your whole file.[6] The Privacy Act permits "special procedures" for disclosure to an individual of his medical and psychological records, but gives no indication as to the types of procedures permitted, or the legality of refusing disclosure as the VA often does.[7]

How can you pursue a claim if you can't see your file?
Because you may be denied access to your whole file,

and therefore you cannot know the whole story when you try to appeal from an adverse VA determination, it is essential that you obtain a representative, and do not represent yourself in any proceeding in which the origin, nature, or intensity of your emotional disability is an issue. The emotional disability claim is almost as difficult to present and win as the service-connection dispute (see Chapter XV). When the issue is a service-connected disabling emotional disorder, the need for effective representation is greatest. In part, this reflects the subjective element in psychiatric diagnosis, which is much greater than in other medical specialities.

The VA invariably will refer to your condition as a "nervous disorder" in all communications to you. It will use technical terms in communications sent to your representative. It will provide your representative with a much more detailed Adjudication or Appeals Decision than you will get.[8] In short, the VA is authorized to hide from you the medical records, and the reasons for decisions based on those records, on the grounds that if they didn't conceal this information from you, your condition might get worse. But they can't hide the records from your representative, if s/he says s/he won't show them to you.

The VA is usually unsympathetic to the suggestion that the act of withholding information—or benefits—from you is likely to make your condition worse. This is one place where you cannot successfully "fight City Hall." Months of effort and anguish, during which you invoke every possible device for obtaining a glance at your own file, are not likely to prove successful.[9] Get yourself a good representative and hope that s/he carefully analyzes all the information in your file.

If you are intent upon trying to see your records, perhaps an application to the BCMR will produce your military and VA medical records for a viewing, if you claim that your VA records relate to your BCMR application. But you would then have to travel to Washington, D.C. to see your file, because that is the only place where BCMR proceedings take place. You might invoke the Freedom of Information Act and the Privacy Act, and also insist that any withholding of access to your records be made by the proper, high-ranking official.[10] Any of these techniques might work; but none is sure to get you a look at your file.

Which emotional disorders are compensable?

One of the difficulties frequently encountered in claims for compensation based upon emotional disorders is the tremendous disagreement among mental health specialists as to the origin, intensity, and classification of any "nervous condition." Numerous studies have demonstrated that two mental health specialists will express totally different opinions about the condition of one patient. The VA is aware of this.[11] The VA, however, is required by law to reach a single opinion in each case. In doing so, it might pick and choose arbitrarily among competing opinions. In one case, the BVA discounted the opinion of the veteran's treating physician as "unsubstantiated," and instead followed a military psychiatrist's opinion, which was known to be based upon false data. And because the courts cannot review benefits claims, the decision of the BVA is final, unless the vet can convince the BVA that it made a "clear and unmistakable" error.[12] Unfortunately, in the area of mental health, few mistakes are clear. (One military psychiatrist, when informed that a veteran whom he had certified as clearly sane for purposes of a court-martial had been picked up the day after his discharge walking naked through downtown Brooklyn, remarked, "I guessed wrong in that one.")

In determining service connection for emotional disorders, the VA distinguishes between *psychoses and psychoneurotic reactions*, which are compensable if they impair working ability, and *personality disorders and chronic psychoneurosis* manifested by preservice evidence of a lifelong pattern of action or behavior, which are not compensable.[13] The special regulations upon which these distinctions are drawn are so complex[14] that in most cases, the VA decision might just as well be made by flipping a coin.

The VA's reputation for arbitrary decisions in emotional-disorder claims is almost legendary among other federal agencies. In one case, the VA, after applying its "reasonable doubt" doctrine,[15] denied benefits to a man who was wholly disabled by his psychiatric condition. A few months later, Social Security officials found that this man's condition was a psychosis, and not merely a personality or character disorder (as the VA had ruled). In so deciding, Social Security had reviewed the VA's file, and based its award on the weight of the evidence (which for the claimant is a *less* favorable standard than the VA's reasonable-doubt standard). If Congress does pass proposed legislation that would permit vets to sue the VA for unfairly denying benefits, it is almost certain that most of the vets who win in court will be seeking compensation for service-connected psychiatric disabilities.

How can you prove that your "nervous condition" is service-connected?

In presenting your claim for psychiatric disability, your chances for winning will probably be improved if you can provide any of the following evidence:

1. Full diagnostic reports from mental health specialists (clinical psychologists or psychiatrists), which are as detailed and technical as possible. Remind the specialists that their reports will be read by other specialists. You should ask them to state the diagnosis and prognosis in terms of the American Psychiatric Association's *Diagnostic and Statistical Manual*.[16] Proof of bizarre behavior or treatment received during the first year after separation from service is often the key to winning. This is because service connection is presumed if a chronic psychosis was at least 10% disabling during the first year after separation from service, even when there was no in-service evidence of the disorder.[17]

2. Statements from family, friends, school and police authorities, and clergy, describing in lay terms your typical conduct and behavior *prior* to entering on active duty. These statements are essential if you are going to convince the VA that you were "normal" before you went on military duty. For these purposes, "normal" means that you were not always fighting, breaking the law, playing hookey, or otherwise acting in a way that middle-class bureaucrats would dislike or disapprove.

3. Statements from family, friends, employers, probation officers, and others who have known you *subsequent* to your discharge and that describe your acts and attitudes since leaving service.

The disability rating you get will be based in large measure upon the degree to which your mental disorder interferes with your ability to work and to get along with others.[18] Statements documenting your "social and occupational adaptation" before and after military service are likely to be the best evidence you can produce. They should describe your day-to-day conduct, and the manner in which you act and react "inappropriately," from the perspective of middle-class bureaucrats. The best of these statements are those that are written by people who knew you both before *and* after service. They should describe the difference in your behavior—a difference that should be attributed to your experiences in service.

Do any special presumptions apply to entitlement for VA benefits based on emotional illness?

If you developed an emotional disorder within 2 years of your discharge from active duty, and your service was during the time of the Vietnam war, Korean conflict, or World War II, it is presumed to be service-connected for purposes of receiving *free treatment* from the VA.[19] If you developed a psychosis (an extremely severe mental disorder, often requiring hospitalization) within 1 year of your discharge, it is presumed to be service-connected for purposes of disability compensation.[20] The rate of compensation should reflect both the potential loss of earning capacity and the social impact of your nervous condition.

Do veterans in neuropsychiatric wards have any say about the manner in which they are treated?

Mental health patients are subject to the same Code of Patient Concern as are other patients in VA facilities. Unless committed involuntarily under applicable state or federal law, the patient retains the right to come and go, and to accept or refuse treatment. However, when a voluntary patient is uncooperative with hospital procedures and personnel, any hospital, including a VA hospital, has the right to discharge the patient.[21] Unlike the voluntary patient, the involuntarily confined cannot, if they so desire, simply walk out the door. However, the other rights implicit in the VA's Code of Patient Concern (see Appendix V) would seem to apply with full force to involuntary mental health patients. Moreover, the VA has adopted a policy and practice of reviewing the status of each involuntary patient at least once every 6 months.[22] The review must be made "by a panel of professionals who are not directly involved in treating the patient." The patient is entitled to receive advance notice of the review, to participate in a hearing, and to bring "a relative, friend or an attorney." Undoubtedly, the panel would permit more than one such person to attend the hearing if there were any good reason for the person(s) to attend. The panel will make specific findings as to a need for further treatment as a voluntary or involuntary patient, and will state its specific reasons. These new procedures constitute the most enlightened approach to periodic review of the status of involuntary mental patients to be found in this country.

The findings made by the panel, and the supporting reasons, can be challenged in a habeas corpus suit. For a thorough discussion, see *The Rights of Mental Patients*, another in the series of ACLU Handbooks.

NOTES

1. 38 U.S.C. § 3103(b); 38 C.F.R. § 3.12(b).
2. 38 C.F.R. § 3.14(b).
3. 38 C.F.R. § 3.302(b)(2).
4. 38 C.F.R. § 3.302(a).
5. 38 C.F.R. § 3.353(d).
6. 38 U.S.C. § 3301(1); *cf.* 38 C.F.R. § 1.500(b).
7. 5 U.S.C. § 552a(f)(3).
8. 38 C.F.R. § 19.4.
9. The courts also generally have not been receptive to demands from former mental patients that they be given access to their treatment files. *See*, for example, *Gotkin* v. *Miller*, 514 F.2d 125 (2nd Cir. 1975).
10. 38 C.F.R. § 1.522 authorizes only a hospital Chief of Staff, the Director of an out-patient clinic, or a Chief Medical Director to refuse disclosure of your records on grounds of probable harm to you.
11. 38 C.F.R. § 4.125 states, in part, "The field of mental disorders represents the greatest possible variety of etiology, chronicity, and disabling effects, and requires differen-

tial consideration in these respects." *See also* 38 C.F.R. §§ 4.126 *et seq.*

12. 38 C.F.R. § 3.105(a).
13. 38 C.F.R. §§ 3.303(c); 412; 4.127; 4.132.
14. 38 C.F.R. §§ 4.125 *et seq.*
15. 38 C.F.R. § 3.102.
16. *Diagnostic and Statistical Manual of Mental Disorders* (19— , Rev. Ed.), American Psychiatric Association. Although 38 C.F.R. § 4. refers to the original, 1952 Edition, the BVA in fact bases its decisions on the latest edition.
17. 38 C.F.R. §§ 3.307(a) (3) and 3.309(a).
18. Although most disability ratings reflect industrial adaptability, 38 C.F.R. § 4.1, psychiatric disabilities are rated on the basis of both social and industrial adaptability—38 C.F.R. § 4.129.
19. 38 U.S.C. § 602; 38 C.F.R. § 17.33. This presumption will not apply to cases arising after May 7, 1977.
20. 38 C.F.R. §§ 3.307—3.309(a).
21. 38 C.F.R. § 17.66; *cf.* 38 C.F.R. §§ 1.218(e); 17.61.
22. VA Department of Medicine and Surgery CIRCULAR 10-76-37 (March 8, 1976; corrected copy). Although this (and every) VA circular expires after 1 year, its basic provisions will probably be continued indefinitely.

Appendix I
Counseling Groups

ORGANIZATION	In-Service Counseling	Discharge-Upgrade Counseling	Provide Lawyer Referrals	VA Counseling
ALABAMA Discharge Upgrading Project PO Box 6415 University 36486 (205) 348-6770	X	X		
ARIZONA Friends Draft & Military Counseling 303 N. Lindsay Road Mesa 85203 (602) 832-0811	X	X	X	X
Pima County Discharge Review Project 45 W. Pennington St. #407 Tucson 85701		X		
Discharge Review Project 1202 W. Thomas Road Phoenix 85013 (602) 623-7951		X		
People's Legal Services PO Box 306 Window Rock 86515 (602) 871-4151		X		

206

ARKANSAS
Legal Aid
209 W. Capitol Avenue
Little Rock
(501) 376-3423

CALIFORNIA
Office of Veteran Affairs
Cabrillo College
6500 Soquel Drive
Aptos 95003
(408) 425-6411
12–4 M–F

Military Counseling Dept.
Gay Center for Social Services
2250 B Street
San Diego 92102
(714) 232-7258
10–10 7 dys/wk

Center for Servicemen's Rights
820 5th Avenue
San Diego
(714) 239-2119

CCCO
1251 Second Avenue
San Francisco 94122
(415) 566-0500

207

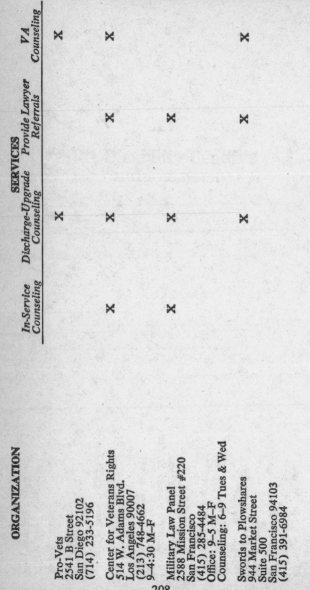

ORGANIZATION	SERVICES			
	In-Service Counseling	Discharge-Upgrade Counseling	Provide Lawyer Referrals	VA Counseling
Pro-Vets 2541 B Street San Diego 92102 (714) 233-5196		X		X
Center for Veterans Rights 514 W. Adams Blvd. Los Angeles 90007 (213) 748-4662 9–4:30 M–F	X	X	X	X
Military Law Panel 2588 Mission Street #220 San Francisco (415) 285-4484 Office: 9–5 M–F Counseling: 6–9 Tues & Wed	X	X	X	
Swords to Plowshares 944 Market Street Suite 500 San Francisco 94103 (415) 391-6984		X	X	X

L.A. County Military & Veteran Affairs 1816 So. Figueroa Street Los Angeles 90015 (213) 747-5361 8–4 M–F	X	X	X	
American G.I. Forum 1680 E. Santa Clara Street San Jose 95116			X	
Mendocino County Veterans 461-B N. State Street Ukiah 95482 (707) 468-0652			X	
Marin Military & Draft Help 404 San Anselmo Avenue San Francisco 94960 (415) 453-7613 By appointment	X	X	X	X
San Diego Discharge Review Project c/o Veterans Affairs Office San Diego State University San Diego (714) 286-5813 8–4:30 M–F	X	X	X	

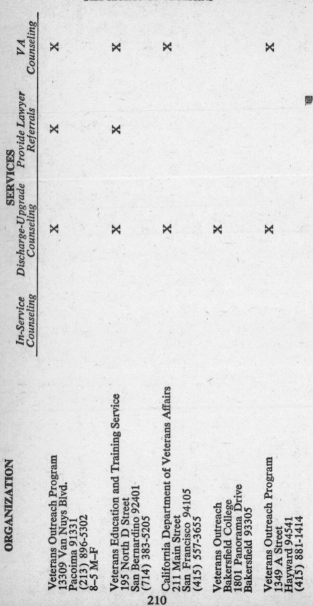

ORGANIZATION	SERVICES			
	In-Service Counseling	Discharge-Upgrade Counseling	Provide Lawyer Referrals	VA Counseling
Veterans Outreach Program 13309 Van Nuys Blvd. Pacoima 91331 (213) 896-5302 8–5 M–F		X	X	X
Veterans Education and Training Service 195 North D Street San Bernardino 92401 (714) 383-5205		X	X	X
California Department of Veterans Affairs 211 Main Street San Francisco 94105 (415) 557-3655		X		X
Veterans Outreach Bakersfield College 1801 Panorama Drive Bakersfield 93305		X		
Veterans Outreach Program 1349 A Street Hayward 94541 (415) 881-1414		X		X

New Growth 1671 Bay Road East Palo Alto (415) 323-5125	X	X
Flower of the Dragon 3947 Santa Rosa Ave. Santa Rosa 95401 (707) 527-8967	X	X
Veterans Outreach Center N. County Community Action Program 166 West Mission Avenue Escondido 92023 (714) 746-8641	X	X
Office of Veterans Affairs Long Beach City College 4901 East Carson Street Long Beach 90808 (213) 498-5436	X	X
Office of Veterans Affairs UC Santa Barbara Santa Barbara 93106 (805) 961-4193	X	

ORGANIZATION	SERVICES			
	In-Service Counseling	Discharge-Upgrade Counseling	Provide Lawyer Referrals	VA Counseling
Office of Veterans Affairs Pasadena City College 1570 E. Colorado Blvd. Pasadena 91106 (213) 578-7294		X		X
About Face Veterans Service Center 1215 Sixteenth St. Sacramento 95814 (916) 422-6283		X		X
San Diego State Discharge Upgrading Project 5402 College Avenue HA 525 San Diego 92115				
Rev. Frank Ivey, OFM St. Francis Church 1112-26th Street Sacramento 95816 (916) 443-8084 451-7256	X	X	X	

212

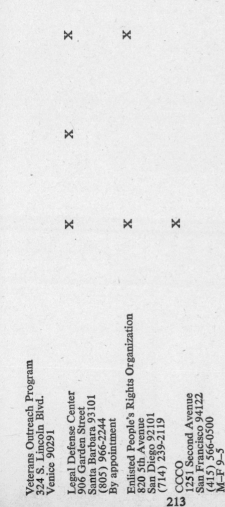

Organization			
Veterans Outreach Program 324 S. Lincoln Blvd. Venice 90291			
Legal Defense Center 906 Garden Street Santa Barbara 93101 (805) 966-2244 By appointment	X	X	X
Enlisted People's Rights Organization 820 5th Avenue San Diego 92101 (714) 239-2119		X	X
CCCO 1251 Second Avenue San Francisco 94122 (415) 566-0500 M–F 9–5		X	
COLORADO VETS 1100 Santa Fe Drive Denver 80204 (303) 534-2292	X		X
Southern Colorado Discharge Upgrading University of Southern Colorado Pueblo 81001 (303) 549-0123 ext. 2368	X		

213

ORGANIZATION	In-Service Counseling	Discharge-Upgrade Counseling	Provide Lawyer Referrals	VA Counseling
Veterans Service Coordinator Veterans Information Program 1435 Fox Street, Room 104 Denver 80204 (303) 629-2452		X	X	X
CONNECTICUT Director, VETS of HECUS 328 Park Avenue Bridgeport 06604 (203) 334-9348		X	X	X
Connecticut Concerned Veterans, Inc. 115 Blackstone Village Meriden 06450 1-203-237-1914 (night) 1-203-397-2101 ext. 434 (day)		X	X	X
Enduring Peace 107 Beach Avenue Woodmont (203) 878-4769		X		
Veterans Affairs 60 Sargent Drive New Haven		X		

Veterans Action 266 Dixwell Avenue New Haven		X	
DELAWARE Linnis Cook 120 Main Street St. Georges 19733 (302) 834-9006	X		X
DISTRICT OF COLUMBIA American Veterans Committee 1333 Conn. Avenue, N.W. Washington, D.C. 20036 (202) 293-4890 4–5	X	X	
National Interreligious Service Board for Conscientious Objectors 550 Washington Building 15 Street and NY Avenue, N.W. Washington, D.C. 20005 (202) 393-4868 8:30–5 M-F	X		X

215

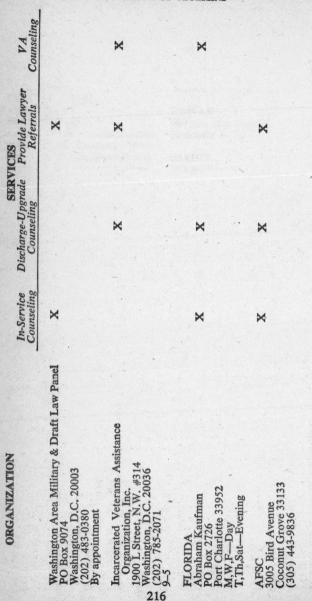

ORGANIZATION	In-Service Counseling	Discharge-Upgrade Counseling	Provide Lawyer Referrals	V.A. Counseling
Washington Area Military & Draft Law Panel PO Box 9074 Washington, D.C. 20003 (202) 483-0380 By appointment	X		X	
Incarcerated Veterans Assistance Organization, Inc. 1900 L Street, N.W. #314 Washington, D.C. 20036 (202) 785-2071 9-5		X	X	X
FLORIDA Abraham Kaufman PO Box 2726 Port Charlotte 33952 M,W,F—Day T,Th,Sat—Evening	X	X		X
AFSC 3005 Bird Avenue Coconut Grove 33133 (305) 443-9836	X	X	X	

Organization			
Jacksonville Economic Opportunity PO Box 52025 Jacksonville 32201 (904) 358-7474	X		
Florida Legal Services Prison Project 2614 S.W. 34th Street Gainsville 32606 (904) 377-4212	X		
GEORGIA Southern Center for Military and Veterans Rights 848 Peachtree Street, NE Atlanta 30308 (404) 881-6666 9–6	X	X	X
VETS EOA Office 75 Marietta Street, N.W. Atlanta 30303 (404) 542-0864	X	X	X
Project Director, VETS PO Box 8225 135 Whitaker Street Savannah 31402 (912) 232-2681	X	X	X

ORGANIZATION	SERVICES			
	In-Service Counseling	Discharge-Upgrade Counseling	Provide Lawyer Referrals	VA Counseling
HAWAII AFSC 2426 Oahu Avenue Honolulu 96822 (808) 988-6266 9–5 M–F	X	X	X	X
ILLINOIS Project Verdict College of DuPage Glen Ellyn 60137 (312) 858-2800 ext. 2204, 2205 8–5 M–F	X	X	X	X
VETS 430 Wimmer Place East St. Louis 62201 (618) 875-7033		X		
Project Director VETS Chicago Committee on Urban Opportunity 640 North LaSalle Chicago 60610 (312) 744-8118		X	X	X

218

Office of Vets Affairs
South Illinois University
Edwardville Campus
Illinois 62010
(618) 692-2707

X

Midwest Committee for Military Counseling
317 Fisher Building
343 South Dearborn
Chicago, Illinois 60604
(312) 939-3349

X X X

Veterans Service Center
321 E. Broadway
Alton 62002
(618) 465-0111

X

Veterans for Peace
542 S. Dearborn Street
Chicago 60605
(312) 922-0065

X

Legal Services Center
Chicago-Kent Law School
77 So. Wacker Drive
Chicago 60606
(312) 567-5050

X

ORGANIZATION	SERVICES			
	In-Service Counseling	Discharge-Upgrade Counseling	Provide Lawyer Referrals	VA Counseling
INDIANA Project Director VETS, CAAP 611 North Park Suite 516 Indianapolis 46204 (317) 369-9421		X	X	X
CITY OF GARY Veterans Affairs 900 Madison Street Gary 46404 (219) 882-1160		X		
IOWA AFSC 4211 Grand Avenue Des Moines 50312 (515) 274-0453 9–4:30 M–F	X	X	X	
KENTUCKY Discharge Upgrading Project 120 State Street Lexington 40503		X		

Veterans Affairs Community College
109 E. Broadway
Louisville 40202
(502) 584-0181 ext. 315

LOUISIANA
Incarcerated Vets
Louisiana State Penitentiary
Cypress #3
Angola 70712

Project Director, VETS
Community Advancement, Inc.
2147 Government Street
Box 66043
Baton Rouge 70806
(504) 387-0465

Director, Veterans Outreach
Total Community Action
1770 Tchoapitoulas Street
New Orleans 70130
(504) 523-2477

Ralph F. Navarro
PO Box 663
Metairie 70004
(504) 834-5592
(504) 837-6665

221

ORGANIZATION	In-Service Counseling	Discharge-Upgrade Counseling	Provide Lawyer Referrals	VA Counseling
MAINE Maine Civil Liberties Union 193 Middle Street Portland 04111 (207) 774-5444 9–5 M–F	X	X	X	
MARYLAND American Friends Service Committee 317 E. 25th Street Baltimore 21218 (301) 366-7200 9:30–5 M–F	X		X	
Executive Director Human Resources Development Agency 1301 Reisterstown Road Pikesville 21208		X	X	X
John C. Love 30 Office Street Bel Air (301) 838-7575 9–5 M–F	X	X	X	

VETS
1301 Keisterstown Road
Pikesville, Maryland 21208
(301) 486-0600

VETS
Human Resources Agency
530 Eastern Blvd.
Essex-Middle River 21222
(301) 687-6990

MASSACHUSETTS
Legal In-Service Project (of the Arlington
  Street Church)
355 Boylston Street
Boston 02116
(617) 262-1431
10–5:30 M–S

Comm. on Military Justice
Rm. 303 Austin Hall
Harvard Law School
Cambridge 02138
(617) 495-4820
9–5 M–F

ORGANIZATION	SERVICES			
	In-Service Counseling	Discharge-Upgrade Counseling	Provide Lawyer Referrals	VA Counseling
Veterans Affairs Room 236 Whitemore Admin. Building University of Massachusetts Amherst (413) 545-1346 8:30–5		X		X
Veterans Coalition 21 N. Market Street Northampton 01006 (413) 586-4237		X		
MICHIGAN Niles Switchboard An Information Center PO Box 744 Niles 49120 (616) 684-4495 3–9 M–F 9–12 Sat.	X	X		X

224

Draft & GI Counselling Center 621 E. William Ann Arbor 48108 (303) 769-4414 Tuesdays 7-9	X		
Project Director, VETS CERV Program City of Detroit Neighborhood Services Department 5031 Grandy Avenue, Room 112 Detroit 48211 (313) 224-6262 (313) 224-6263		X	X	X
MINNESOTA Veterans Assistance & Outreach Discharge Review Service University of Minnesota 1633 Eustis Street St. Paul 55108 (612) 376-5085		X	X	X
Room 102 Marril Hall University of Minnesota Minneapolis, Minn. 54455 (612) 376-5085 373-2144, 376-7294		X	X	X

ORGANIZATION	SERVICES			
	In-Service Counseling	Discharge-Upgrade Counseling	Provide Lawyer Referrals	VA Counseling
MISSOURI GI Assistance Project PO Box 24276 St. Louis 63130 (314) 725-2418 Weeknights & Weekends	X		X	
Military Law Project Lindell and Skinher Blvds. St. Louis 63130 (314) 863-0100		X		
NEBRASKA Veterans Office Court House Columbus 68601 (402) 564-5064		X		X
NEW HAMPSHIRE Headrest 18 Banks Street Lebanon 03755 (603) 448-4400, 448-4872	X			

226

NEW JERSEY Program Director VETS Program 53 Washington Street Newark 07102 (201) 648-5817	X	X	X	
Ass't. University Admin. Educational Opportunity Fund Office of Veterans Affairs Box 4 Winants Hall New Brunswick 08903 (201) 932-7067	X	X	X	
Office of Veteran Affairs 300 Pompton Road Wayne 07470 (201) 881-2102 or 2478	X	X	X	X
Patrick C. Miller 184 Warren Street Newark 07103 (201) 645-5103 9–5	X		X	
Friends Military Counselling 137 A Fort Dix Street PO Box 62 Wrightstown 08562 (609) 723-2250 M, Th, F 9–5 T, W 10–7		X		X

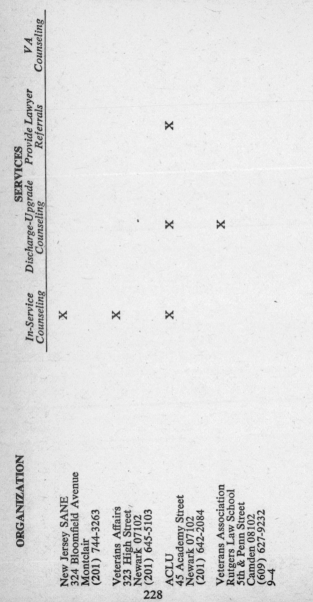

ORGANIZATION	SERVICES			
	In-Service Counseling	Discharge-Upgrade Counseling	Provide Lawyer Referrals	VA Counseling
New Jersey SANE 324 Bloomfield Avenue Montclair (201) 744-3263	X			
Veterans Affairs 323 High Street Newark 07102 (201) 645-5103	X			
ACLU 45 Academy Street Newark 07102 (201) 642-2084	X	X	X	
Veterans Association Rutgers Law School 5th & Penn Street Camden 08102 (609) 627-9232		X		

9–4

NEW YORK Charles H. Garland Gold Star 530 Canal Street New York 10013 (212) 966-6504	X		X	X
Mil. & Vets. Couns. Ctr. 462 Ninth Avenue New York 10018 T&Th 7–10, Sat. & Sun. 1–5 (212) 564-5074	X	X	X	X
Deros Vets Services 16 N. Broadway Yonkers 10701 (914) 968-0224 9–5 M–F	X		X	X
Legal Services Project Veterans Association City College 1038 S. Convent Avenue New York 10038 (212) 690-6980	X			
NY State Div. of Veterans Affairs 26 Court Street Brooklyn 11202 (212) 875-1077	X			

ORGANIZATION	SERVICES			
	In-Service Counseling	Discharge-Upgrade Counseling	Provide Lawyer Referrals	VA Counseling
American Friends Service Committee 821 Euclid Avenue Syracuse 13210 (315) 475-9469 9–5 M–F	X	X		
Military Counseling Program Religious Society of Friends 15 Rutherford Place New York 10003 (212) 533-2350 9–5 Th & F 7–9 PM Th	X		X	
Veterans Upgrade Center 84 5th Avenue New York 10011 (212) 675-2777		X		
Veterans Affairs 3445 Main Street Buffalo 14217		X		

Workers Defense League 84 5th Avenue, Rm. 402 New York 10011 (212) 691-7660	X	X	X	X
Military & Draft Counseling Center of Buffalo 100 Ivyhurst Road Buffalo 14226 (716) 836-1216 By appointment	X	X	X	X
VETS Project 75 West Monroe Avenue Rochester 14607 (716) 428-7444	X	X	X	
Veterans Outreach Program 75 West Monroe Avenue Rochester 14607 (716) 428-7445 or 325-5116	X		X	
NORTH CAROLINA Spring Lake GI Union 110 N. Main-Box 437 Spring Lake 28390 (919) 497-9048		X		X

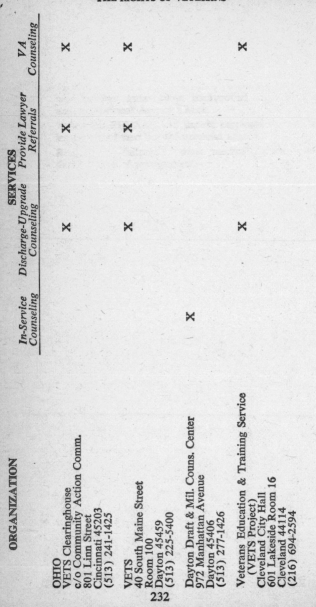

ORGANIZATION	In-Service Counseling	SERVICES Discharge-Upgrade Counseling	Provide Lawyer Referrals	VA Counseling
OHIO VETS Clearinghouse c/o Community Action Comm. 801 Linn Street Cincinnati 45203 (513) 241-1425		X	X	X
VETS 40 South Maine Street Room 100 Dayton 45459 (513) 225-5400		X	X	X
Dayton Draft & Mil. Couns. Center 972 Manhattan Avenue Dayton 45406 (513) 277-1426	X			
Veterans Education & Training Service (VETS Project) Cleveland City Hall 601 Lakeside Room 16 Cleveland 44114 (216) 694-2594		X		X

X

X

X

X

X

X

Legal Aid
3408 Lorain Avenue
Cleveland 44113
(216) 961-6630

Veterans Affairs
3304 N. Main Street
Dayton 45405
(513) 234-0801

Military and Vets Project
255 W. 5th Avenue
Columbus 43201
(614) 299-6921

ACLU
2108 Payne Avenue
Cleveland 44414
(216) 781-6276

American Friends Service Committee
475 W Market Street
Akron 44303
(216) 253-7151; 253-8281
9–5 M–F
(anytime for emergencies)

233

ORGANIZATION	SERVICES			
	In-Service Counseling	Discharge-Upgrade Counseling	Provide Lawyer Referrals	VA Counseling
KSU Military Counseling Service Room 219, Wright Hall Kent State University Kent 44242 (216) 672-2860 8-5	X	X		
OREGON Project Return 1412 S.E. 25th Street Portland 97214 (503) 234-0801		X	X	X
Office of Veterans Affairs Rogue Community College 3345 Redwood Highway Grants Pass 97526 (503) 476-9392		X		
AFSC 1501 Cheny Street Philadelphia 19120 (215) 241-7000		X		

Organization				
Portland Military and Veterans Counseling Center 633 SW Montgomery Street Portland 97201 (503) 224-9307 10–5 M–F	X		X	X
PENNSYLVANIA CCCO 2016 Walnut Street Philadelphia 19103 (215) 568-7971 9–5 M–F	X		X	X
Ted Koontz Mennonite Central Comm. Akron 17501			X	
LEPOCO 14 W. Broad Street Bethlehem 18018 (215) 691-8730			X	
RHODE ISLAND Rhode Island Veterans Action Center 742 Broad Street Providence 02907 (401) 941-1331	X	X	X	

235

ORGANIZATION	In-Service Counseling	Discharge Upgrade Counseling	Provide Lawyer Referrals	VA Counseling
Vietnam Era Veterans Ass'n 242 Prairie Avenue Providence 02907 (401) 521-6710		X		X
SOUTH CAROLINA Legal Aid Service Agency PO Box 1056 Columbia 29202 (803) 799-9668 9–5 M–F	X	X	X	
SOUTH DAKOTA Veterans Affairs Augustance College Sioux Falls 57102 (605) 336-4124		X		
TENNESSEE Legal Services Military Law Project 316 Dermon Bldg. 46 N. Third St. Memphis 38103 (901) 526-5132 9–5		X	X	X

				X
X			X	X
	X		X	X	X
X			X	

Gerard A. Vanderhaar
Dept. of Humanities
Christian Brothers College
650 East Pkwy, Sth
Memphis 38104
(901) 278-0100, ext. 218
10-3

Veterans Program
3625 Midland Avenue
Memphis 38001
(901) 323-4790

TEXAS
AFSC Peace Ed Office
704 W. 25th
Austin 78705
(512) 477-5654

Director, VETS
1716 E. Yandell Avenue
El Paso 79902
(915) 533-2456

G.I. Forum
1713 Castroville Road
San Antonio 78237
(512) 434-0677

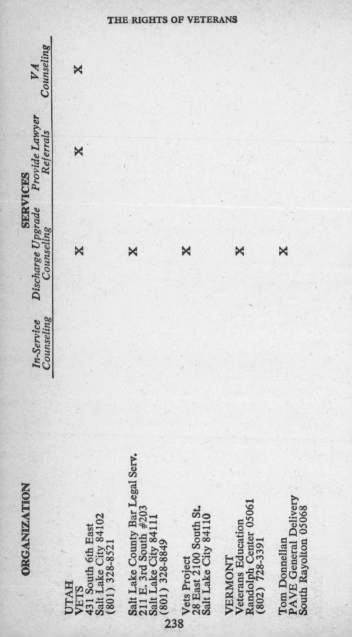

THE RIGHTS OF VETERANS

ORGANIZATION	In-Service Counseling	Discharge Upgrade Counseling	Provide Lawyer Referrals	VA Counseling
UTAH				
VETS 431 South 6th East Salt Lake City 84102 (801) 328-8521		X	X	X
Salt Lake County Bar Legal Serv. 211 E. 3rd South #203 Salt Lake City 84111 (801) 328-8849		X		
Vets Project 28 East 2100 South St. Salt Lake City 84110		X		
VERMONT				
Veterans Education Randolph Center 05061 (802) 728-3391		X		
Tom Donnellan PAVE General Delivery South Rayolton 05068		X		

Listing				
VIRGINIA Clyde Carter Box 85 Daleville 24083 (703) 992-2042 9–12	X	X		X
Project Director, VETS 904 Granby Street Norfolk 23510 (804) 622-1361		X	X	X
VETS Outreach c/o STOP 415 St. Paul Blvd. Norfolk 23510 (804) 627-3541		X		
WASHINGTON Seattle Veterans Action Center (SEA-VAC) 1300 Madison Street Seattle 98104 (206) 625-4656 8–5 M–F		X	X	X
Discharge Upgrade Project 303 NE Northlake Way Seattle 98105 (206) 633-0155 9–5	X	X	X	X

ORGANIZATION	In-Service Counseling	Discharge Upgrade Counseling	Provide Lawyer Referrals	VA Counseling
WEST VIRGINIA Dr. Frank L. Horton 802 17th Street Huntington 25703 (304) 529-3086 By appointment only		X		X
WISCONSIN Vets House 1102 S. Park Street Madison 53715 (608) 255-8387 9–5	X	X	X	X
Vets Coordination Project 4240 W. Fond Dulac Avenue Milwaukee 53216 (414) 442-6110 8:30–4:30 M–F	X	X	X	
Pre-Enlistment Counseling Program 2272 Winnebago Madison 53704 (608) 241-4767 Evenings	X		X	

SERVICES

X

X

X

X

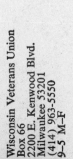

Wisconsin Veterans Union
Box 66
2200 E. Kenwood Blvd.
Milwaukee 53201
(414) 963-5550
9–5 M–F

Appendix II

Procedures For
Article 69 Appeals
(AFM 111-1)

Article 69 of the UCMJ (10 U.S.C. § 869) permits
Judge Advocate General to vacate or to modify, in whole
or in part, the findings or sentence or both in a court-
martial case that has been finally reviewed, but that has
not been reviewed by the Court of Military Review (See
Manual for Courts-Martial [1969, Rev. Ed.], ¶ 110A).
An application for action under Article 69 will be made in
writing, will be under oath or affirmation, and will be
signed by the accused or his/her legal representative. The
application will contain:

1. The name, Social Security number, and present mailing address of the accused.
2. The date and place of trial and kind of court.
3. The sentence of the court as approved or affirmed
   and any subsequent reduction by clemency or otherwise.
4. A statement of the specific grounds on which relief
   is requested and the specific relief requested.
5. Any documentary or other evidence that the applicant believes pertinent to the facts asserted under the
   specific grounds alleged, including copies of court-
   martial orders, if available.

Applications will be submitted to the general court-martial authority when the case was tried by summary court-
martial or by a special court-martial where the approved
sentence did not include a bad conduct discharge and the
applicant is still in the command in which the case was
tried. All other applications will be forwarded directly to

HQ USAF/JAJ. When an application is received by an officer exercising general court-martial jurisdiction, the officer will forward the application, together with the original record of trial and copies of all relevant orders and other documents, to HQ USAF/JAJ. In forwarding an application, neither the officer exercising general court-martial jurisdiction nor his/her staff judge advocate is required to make any recommendation as to the disposition of the case; however, either is permitted to include such comments or recommendations as may be appropriate in the particular case.

Navy (Manual of the Judge Advocate General of the Navy)

Applications for relief may be submitted by letter to the Judge Advocate General. All applications for relief shall contain:

1. Full name of the applicant.
2. Service number and branch of service, if any.
3. Social Security number.
4. Present grade if on active duty or retired, or "civilian" or "deceased," as applicable.
5. Address at time the application is mailed.
6. Date of trial.
7. Place of trial.
8. Command title of the organization at which the court-martial was convened (convening authority).
9. Command title of the officer exercising general court-martial jurisdiction over the applicant at the time of trial (supervisory authority).
10. Type of court-martial that convicted the applicant.
11. General grounds for relief, which must be one or more of the following:
    a. Newly discovered evidence.
    b. Fraud on the court.
    c. Lack of jurisdiction over the accused or the offense.
    d. Error prejudicial to the substantial rights of the accused.
12. An elaboration of the specific prejudice resulting

244

from any error cited. (Legal authorities to support the applicant's contentions may be included, and the format used may take the form of a legal brief, if the applicant so desires.

13. Any other matter that the applicant desires to submit.

14. Relief requested.

The applicant's copy of the record of trial will *not* be forwarded with the application for relief, unless specifically requested by the Judge Advocate General.

Signatures on Applications. Unless incapable of making application, the applicant shall personally sign his/her application under oath before an official authorized to administer oaths. If the applicant is incapable of making application, the application may be signed under oath and submitted by applicant's spouse, next of kin, executor, guardian, or other person with a proper interest in the matter.

Army (AR 27-10)

The application must be signed by the individual convicted by court-martial. In those cases where the individual is deceased, incapable of making application himself, or where his whereabouts are unknown, the Judge Advocate General may permit application to be made by such person as he shall determine to be competent and suitable, and to have a proper interest therein, including, but not limited to, a spouse, parent, or relative of the person convicted by court-martial substantially affected as a result of the findings or sentence, or both, that the applicant maintains should be vacated or modified. If the application is not signed by the individual convicted, full explanation should be included.

The application must be submitted under oath or affirmation executed before an official authorized to administer oaths.

The applicant should describe the error(s) on which the request for relief is based. Relevant facts that support the applicant's contentions should be included. Legal authorities may be presented in this section, or may be attached in the form of a legal brief, if the applicant desires. Other matters tending to support the applicant's allegations of error or impropriety, including, but not limited to, sworn affidavits, official records, and other documents, may be attached, and should be listed. The applicant bears the burden of establishing an alleged impropriety. Unsupported allegations of matters outside the record of trial will seldom be sufficient to warrant relief.

A copy of the court-martial order promulgating the findings, sentence, and action of the convening authority in the case, and a copy of any later modifying order(s), if available to the applicant, should be submitted with the application.

A copy of the record of trial should be submitted in connection with the application for relief from a summary court-martial tried more than 1 year before application is made, or a special court-martial tried more than 10 years before application, if available. The applicant's copy of the record in other cases, including those tried by general court, should *not* be submitted.

Also include:

1. Name.
2. Service number.
3. Social Security number.
4. Date of trial.
5. Place of trial.
6. Command convening court-martial.
7. Type of court-martial.
8. Offenses charged.
9. Findings of court, sentence adjudged, and later modifications, if any.
10. Relief requested.
11. Name and address of counsel, if any.

Appendix III

U.S. Veterans' Assistance Centers

ALABAMA
474 S. Court St.
Montgomery 36104
Local call also from Birmingham, Huntsville, and Mobile.

ALASKA
429 D St., Suite 214
Anchorage 99501

709 W. Ninth St.
Juneau 99802
Except within local dialing areas of Anchorage and Juneau, dial Zenith 2500 to reach either Anchorage or Juneau office.

ARIZONA
3225 N. Central Ave.
Phoenix 85012
Local call also from Tucson.

ARKANSAS
700 W. Capitol Ave.
Little Rock 72201
Local call also from Fort Smith, Pine Bluff, and Texarkana. WATS number for other areas.

CALIFORNIA[1]
101 S. Willowbrook Ave.
Compton 90220

11000 Wilshire Blvd.
Los Angeles 90024

929 N. Bonnie Beach Pl.
East Los Angeles 90063
Local call also to Los Angeles from Inglewood, La Crescenta, San Pedro, Santa Monica, Sierra Madre, Van Nuys, Whittier, Anaheim, Bakersfield, Huntington Beach, Ontario, Oxnard, San Bernardino, Santa Ana, and Santa Barbara. WATS number for other areas to Los Angeles.

1250 Sixth Ave.
San Diego 92101
Local call also to San Diego from Riverside. WATS number for other areas to San Diego.

211 Main St.
San Francisco 94105
Local call also to San Francisco from Fremont, Fresno, Modesto, Monterey, Oakland, Palo Alto, Sacramento, Salinas, San Jose, Santa Rosa, Stockton, and Vallejo. WATS number for other areas to San Francisco.

COLORADO
Denver Federal Center
Denver 80225
Local call also from Colorado Springs and Pueblo. WATS number for other areas.

CONNECTICUT
450 Main St.
Hartford 06103
Local call also from Bridgeport, Bristol, Danbury, Meriden, New Britain, New Haven, New London, Norwalk, Stamford, and Waterbury. WATS number for other areas.

DELAWARE
1601 Kirkwood Hwy.
Wilmington 19805

DISTRICT OF COLUMBIA
25 K St., N. E.
Washington, DC 20002

FLORIDA
Post Office and Courthouse Bldg.
Jacksonville 32201

51 S. W. First Ave.
Miami 33130

144 First Ave. South
St. Petersburg 33731
Local call to St. Petersburg from Cocoa/Cocoa Beach, Daytona Beach, Fort Lauderdale/Hollywood, Fort Myers, Gainesville, Jacksonville, Lakeland/Winter Haven, Melbourne, Miami, Orlando, Pensacola, Sarasota, Tallahassee, Tampa, and West Palm Beach. WATS number for other areas to St. Petersburg.

GEORGIA
730 Peachtree St., N. E.
Atlanta 30308
Local call from Albany, Athens, Augusta, Columbus, Macon, and Savannah. WATS number for other areas.

HAWAII
680 Ala Moana Blvd.
Honolulu 96801

IDAHO
550 W. Fort St.
Boise 83707

ILLINOIS[2]
2030 W. Taylor St.
Chicago 60612
Local call also from Bloomington/Normal, Carbondale, Champaign/Urbana, Decatur, East St. Louis, Peoria, Rockford, and Springfield. WATS number for other areas.

INDIANA[3]
575 N. Pennsylvania St.
Indianapolis 46204
Local call also from Anderson/Muncie, Evansville, Fort Wayne, Lafayette/West Lafayette, South Bend, and Terre Haute. WATS number for other areas.

IOWA
210 Walnut St.
Des Moines 50309
Local call also from Cedar Rapids, Davenport, Sioux City, and Waterloo. WATS number for other areas.

KANSAS
5500 E. Kellogg
Wichita 67218

Local call also from Kansas City and Topeka.

KENTUCKY
600 Federal Pl.
Louisville 40202
Local call also from Lexington. WATS number for other areas.

LOUISIANA
701 Loyola Ave.
New Orleans 70113
Local call also from Baton Rouge and Shreveport.

MAINE
Togus 04330
Local call also from Portland.

MARYLAND[4]
31 Hopkins Plaza
Baltimore 21201
WATS number for all other areas.

MASSACHUSETTS[5]
John F. Kennedy Federal Bldg.
Boston 02203
Local call also from Brockton, Fitchburg/Leominster, Haverhill, Lawrence, Lowell, Pittsfield, Springfield, and Worcester. WATS number for all other areas.

MICHIGAN
801 W. Baltimore St.
Detroit 48232
Local call also from Ann Arbor, Battle Creek, Bay City, Flint, Grand Rapids, Jackson, Kalamazoo, Lansing/East Lansing, Muskegon, and Saginaw. WATS number for all other areas.

MINNESOTA
Fort Snelling Federal Bldg.
St. Paul 55111

MISSISSIPPI
1500 E. Woodrow Wilson Dr.
Jackson 39216
Local call also from Biloxi/Gulfport and Meridian.

MISSOURI
601 E. Twelfth St.
Kansas City 64106

1520 Market St.
St. Louis 63103
Local call also from Columbia, Kansas City, St. Joseph, and Springfield. WATS number for all other areas.

MONTANA
Fort Harrison 59636
Local call also from Great Falls.

NEBRASKA
220 S. Seventeenth St.
Lincoln 68508
Local call also from Omaha/Council Bluff.

NEVADA
1201 Terminal Way
Reno 89502
WATS number for all other areas.

NEW HAMPSHIRE
497 Silver St.
Manchester 03103
WATS number for all other areas.

NEW JERSEY
20 Washington Pl.
Newark 07102

249

Local calls also from Atlantic City, Camden, Clifton/Patterson/Passaic, Long Branch/Asbury Park, New Brunswick/Sayreville, Perth Amboy, and Trenton. WATS number for all other areas.

NEW MEXICO
500 Gold Ave., S. W.
Albuquerque 87101
WATS number for all other areas.

NEW YORK
Executive Park,
N. Stuyvesant Plaza
Albany 12201

111 W. Huron St.
Buffalo 14202
Local call also to Buffalo from Binghamton, Elmira, Rome, and Utica. WATS number for other areas to Buffalo.

252 Seventh Ave.
New York City 10001
Local call also to New York City from Hempstead, Poughkeepsie, and Scarsdale. WATS number for other areas to New York City.

100 State St.
Rochester 14614

809 S. Salina St.
Syracuse 13202

NORTH CAROLINA
Wachovia Bldg.
Winston-Salem 27102
Local call also from Asheville, Charlotte, Durham, Fayetteville, Gastonia, Greensboro, High Point, Raleigh, and Wil-

mington. WATS number for all other areas.

NORTH DAKOTA
21st Ave. & Elm St.
Fargo 58102
WATS number for all other areas.

OHIO
550 Main St.
Cincinnati 45202

1240 E. Ninth St.
Cleveland 44199
Local call also to Cleveland from Akron, Canton, Cincinnati, Columbus, Dayton, Elyria, Lima, Lorain, Mansfield, Springfield, Toledo, Warren, and Youngstown. WATS number for other areas to Cleveland.

360 S. Third St.
Columbus 43215

OKLAHOMA
Second & Court St.
Muskogee 74401
Local call also to Muskogee from Lawton, Oklahoma City, Tulsa, and Stillwater. WATS number for other areas to Muskogee.

200 N. W. Fourth St.
Oklahoma City 73102

OREGON
426 W. Stark St.
Portland 97204
Local call also from Eugene/Springfield and Salem. WATS number for all other areas.

THE RIGHTS OF VETERANS

PENNSYLVANIA
5000 Wissachickon Ave.
Philadelphia 19101
Local call also to Philadelphia
from Allentown/Bethlehem/
Easton, Harrisburg, Lancaster,
Reading, Scranton, Wilkes-
Barre, Williamsport, and York.
WATS number for all other
areas to Philadelphia.

1000 Liberty Ave.
Pittsburgh 15222
Local call also to Pittsburgh
from Altoona and Johnstown.
WATS number for all other
areas to Pittsburgh.

19-27 N. Main St.
Wilkes-Barre 18701

PHILIPPINES
1131 Roxas Blvd.
Manila 96528

PUERTO RICO
GPO Box 4867
San Juan 09936

RHODE ISLAND
Federal Bldg., Kennedy Plaza
Providence 02903

SOUTH CAROLINA
1801 Assembly St.
Columbia 29201
Local call also from Charles-
ton and Greenville.

SOUTH DAKOTA
2501 W. Twenty-Second St.
Sioux Falls 57101
WATS number for all areas.

TENNESSEE
110 Ninth Ave. South

Nashville 37203
Local call also from Chat-
tanooga, Knoxville, and Memphis. WATS number for all
other areas.

TEXAS
1100 Commerce St.
Dallas 75202

2515 Munworth Dr.
Houston 77054
Local call also to Houston
from Beaumont, Bridge City/
Port Arthur/Orange, Browns-
ville, Corpus Christi, Edin-
burg/McAllen/Pharr, Laredo,
Harlingen/San Benito, San
Antonio, and Texas City/
Galveston. WATS number for
all other areas to Houston.

1205 Texas Ave.
Lubbock 79401

410 S. Main St.
San Antonio 78285

1400 N. Valley Mills Dr.
Waco 76710
Local call also to Waco from
Abilene, Amarillo, Austin,
Bryan/College Station, Dallas,
El Paso, Fort Worth, Killeen,
Lubbock, Midland/Odessa/
Terminal, San Angelo, Tem-
ple, Tyler, and Wichita Falls.
WATS number for other areas
to Waco.

UTAH
125 S. State St.
Salt Lake City 84111
Local call from Ogden and
Provo/Orem. WATS number
for all other areas.

VERMONT
White River Junction 05001
WATS number for all other
areas.

VIRGINIA[6]
211 W. Campbell Ave.
Roanoke 24011
Local call also from Hampton,
Norfolk, and Richmond.

WASHINGTON
915 Second Ave.
Seattle 98174
Local call also from Everett,
Richland / Kennewick / Pasco,
Spokane, Tacoma, and Yaki-
ma.

WEST VIRGINIA
502 Eighth St.
Huntington 25701
Local call also from Charles-
ton.

WISCONSIN
342 N. Water St.
Milwaukee 53202
Local call also from Green
Bay, Madison, and Racine.

WYOMING
2360 E. Pershing Blvd.
Cheyenne 82001
WATS number for all other
areas.

NOTES

1. Residents of Alpine, Lassen, Modoc, and Mono Counties in California use Reno, Nev., office: WATS number to Reno.
2. Residents of Rock Island and Moline in Illinois use Des Moines, Iowa, office; local call.
3. Residents of Lake, LaPorte, and Porter Counties in Indiana use Chicago, Ill., office. Residents of Gary/Hammond/East Chicago area can place local calls to Chicago office.
4. Residents of Montgomery and Prince Georges Counties in Maryland use the Washington, D.C., office; local call.
5. Residents of Fall River and New Bedford in Massachusetts use Providence R.I., office; local call. Residents of Dukes, Nantucket, Barnstable, Plymouth, and Bristol Counties also use Providence office; WATS number.
6. Residents of Arlington and Fairfax Counties and Alexandria, Falls Church, and Fairfax Cities in Virginia use the Washington, D.C., office; local call.

Appendix IV

Revised Separation Program Numbers and Definitions*

21L   Enlisted personnel—separation for good and sufficient reason when determined by Secretarial authority.

21T   Enlisted personnel—release of REP 63 trainees due to emergency conditions. (Does not apply to active duty.)

21U   Separation for failure to demonstrate adequate potential for promotion.

28B   Unfitness, frequent involvement in incidents of a discreditable nature with civil or military authorities.

28E   Financial irresponsibility.

28F   Unfitness, an established pattern showing dishonorable failure to pay just debts.

28G   Unfitness, an established pattern for showing dishonorable failure to contribute adequate support to dependents or failure to comply with orders, decrees, or judgments of a civil court concerning support of dependents.

28I   Unsanitary habits.

38A   Desertion/trial deemed inadvisable (WWII). Rescinded.

38B   Desertion/trial deemed inadvisable (peacetime desertion). Rescinded.

38C   Desertion/trial deemed inadvisable (Korean War). Rescinded.

41A   Apathy, lack of interest.

41C   To accept a teaching position.

41D   Discharge of enlisted personnel on unspecified enlistment who completed 20 years' active federal service, do not submit application for retirement; Commander

---

* If your code is not listed, see pp. 55-56 for the address to write to, to find out what your code means. (Assistant Secretary of Defense Finneran memorandum of December 28, 1976.)

determines discharge will be in best interest of the government.

41E Obesity.

46A Unsuitability, apathy, defective attitudes, and inability to expend effort constructively.

46B Sexual deviate.

46C Apathy/obesity.

46D Sexual deviate.

77E Mandatory retirement—surplus in grade after 30 years' service, removal from active list (Regular Army).

77J Voluntary retirement—placement on retired list at age 60.

77M Mandatory retirement—permanent retirement by reason of physical disability.

77N Mandatory retirement—placed on Temporary Disability Retired List.

77P Voluntary retirement—in lieu of or as a result of elimination board proceedings. Regular Army and Reserve commissioned officers and warrant officers.

77Q Mandatory retirement—Temporary Disability Retirement in lieu of or as a result of elimination proceedings.

77R Mandatory retirement—permanent disability retirement in lieu of or as a result of elimination proceedings.

77S Voluntary retirement—Regular Army and Reserve commissioned officer.

77T Voluntary retirement—Regular Army and Reserve warrant officers.

77U Voluntary retirement—Regular Army commissioned officers with 30 or more years of service.

77V Voluntary retirement—enlisted personnel, voluntarily retired as a commissioned officer.

77W Voluntary retirement—enlisted personnel, voluntarily retired as a warrant officer.

77X Voluntary retirement—warrant officer voluntarily retired as a commissioned officer.

77Y Mandatory retirement—retirement of Director of Music, USMA, as the President may direct.

77Z Mandatory retirement—Regular Army commissioned officers with WWI service.

771   Mandatory retirement—commissioned officers, unfitness or substandard performance of duty.

772   Mandatory retirement—warrant officers, unfitness or substandard performance of duty.

78A   Mandatory retirement—formerly retired other than for disability, who while on active duty incurred a disability of at least 30%.

78B   Mandatory retirement—formerly retired for disability, who while on active duty suffered aggravation of disability for which individual was formerly retired.

79A   Voluntary REFRAD—as USAR warrant officer (aviator) to accept USAR commission (aviator) with concurrent active duty.

79B   Resignation—as RA WO (aviator) to accept USAR commission (aviator) with concurrent active duty.

201   Enlisted personnel—expiration of term of service (includes personnel on ADT as initial trainees).

202   Expiration of term of enlistment.

203   Expiration of term of active obligation service.

205   Release from active duty and transferred to Reserve.

212   Honorable wartime service subsequent to desertion.

213   Discharge for retirement as an officer.

214   To accept commission as an officer in the Army, or to accept recall to active duty as an Army Reserve officer.

215   To accept appointment as warrant officer in the Army, or to accept recall to active duty as Army Reserve warrant officer.

217   To accept commission or appointment in the armed forces of the United States (other than Army).

219   Erroneous induction.

220   Marriage, female only.

221   Pregnancy.

222   Parenthood.

225   Minority.

226   Dependency.

227   Hardship.

229   Surviving family members.

230   Retirement after 20 years' but less than 30 years' active federal service.

231   Retirement after 30 years' active federal service.

238   Service retirement in lieu of other administrative action.

240   Unconditional resignation of enlisted personnel service on unspecified enlistment.

241   Resignation of enlisted personnel or unspecified enlistment in lieu of reduction for misconduct or inefficiency.

242   Resignation of enlisted personnel or unspecified enlistment for the good of the service.

243   Resignation of enlisted personnel on unspecified enlistment in lieu of board action when based on unfitness.

244   Resignation of enlisted personnel on unspecified enlistment in lieu of board action when based on unsuitability.

245   Resignation of enlisted personnel on unspecified enlistment in lieu of separation for disloyalty or subversion.

246   Discharge for the good of the service (in lieu of trial).

247   Unsuitability/multiple reasons.

248   Unsuitability.

249   Resignation of enlisted personnel on unspecified enlistment (homosexuality).

250   Punitive discharge, class I homosexual, general court-martial.

251   Punitive discharge, class II homosexual, general court-martial.

252   Punitive discharge, class I homosexual, special court-martial.

253   Discharged as a result of board action (class II homosexual). Rescinded.

255   Retirement in lieu of discharge under AR635-89 (homosexuality).

256   Acceptance of discharge in lieu of board action (class III homosexual). Rescinded.

257   Unfitness, homosexual acts.

258   Unfitness/multiple reasons.

260   Unsuitability/inaptitude.

261   Psychiatric or psychoneurotic disorder.
262   Unsuitability/enuresis.

263   Enuresis.

264   Unsuitability/character and behavior disorders.

265   Character disorders.

270   Placed on Temporary Disability Retired List.

271   Permanently retired by reason of physical disability.

273   Physical disability with entitlement to receive severance pay.

274   Physical disability resulting from intentional misconduct or willful neglect or incurred during period of unauthorized absence. Not entitled to severance pay.

276   Released from EAD and revert to retired list prior to ETS.

277   Physical disability, EPTS, established by medical board. Discharged by reason of physical disability upon application by individual. Not entitled to severance pay.

278   Physical disability, EPTS, established by physical evaluation board proceedings. Not entitled to severance pay.

279   Release from EAD and revert to retired list at ETS.

280   Misconduct/fraudulent entry into the Army.

282   Misconduct/prolonged unauthorized absence for more than 1 year of desertion.

283   Misconduct/AWOL, trial waived or deemed inadvisable.

284   Misconduct/convicted or adjudged a juvenile offender by a civil court during current term of active military service.

285   Initially adjudged a juvenile offender by a civil court during current term of active military service. Rescinded.

286   Repeated military offenses not warranting trial by court-martial.

287   Unclean habits, including repeated venereal disease.

288   Habits and traits of character manifested by antisocial, amoral trends.

289   Unsuitability/alcoholism.

290   Desertion (court-martial).

292   Other than desertion (court-martial).

293   General court-martial.

294   Special court-martial.

311   Alien without legal residence in the United States.

312   Separation of members of Reserve components on active duty who, due to age, would be precluded from attaining eligibility pay as provided by 10 U.S.C. 1331-1337.

313   To immediately enlist or reenlist.

314   Importance to national health, safety, or interest.

316   Release, lack of jurisdiction.

318   Conscientious objection.

319   Erroneous enlistment.

320   To accept employment with a legally established law enforcement agency.

333   Discharge of Cuban volunteers upon completion of specified training. Rescinded.

344   Release of Cuban volunteers upon completion of specified training. Rescinded.

361   Homosexual tendencies.

362   Unsuitability/homosexual tendencies, desires, or interest, but without overt homosexual acts, in service.

367   Aggressive reaction.

368   Antisocial personality.

369   Cyclothymic personality.

370   Released from EAD by reason of physical disability and revert to inactive status for the purpose of retirement under 10, USC, sections 1331–1337, in lieu of discharge with entitlement to receive severance pay.

375   Discharge because of not meeting medical fitness standards at time of enlistment.

376   Release from military control (void induction) because of not meeting medical fitness standards at time of induction.

377   Nonfulfillment of enlistment commitment.

380   Desertion/trial barred by 10, U.S.C., section 834 (Art. 34, UCMJ). Rescinded.

381   Desertion/trial deemed inadvisable (Spanish-American War/WWI) Rescinded.

383   Criminalism.

384   Unfitness/drug abuse.

385   Pathological lying.

386   Unfitness/established pattern for shirking.

387   Habits and traits of character manifested by misconduct.

388	Unfitness/sexual perversions, including but not limited to lewd and lascivious acts, indecent exposure, indecent acts with or assault upon a child, or other indecent acts and offenses.
411	Early separation of oversea returnee.
412	Enlisted members of medical holding detachments or units who, upon completion of hospitalization, do not intend to immediately enlist or reenlist in the Regular Army.
413	To enter or return to college, university, or equivalent educational institution.
414	To accept or return to employment of a seasonal nature.
415	Early release of inductees who have served on active duty prior to their present tour of duty.
416	Physical disqualification for duty in MOS.
418	Discharge of enlisted personnel on unspecified enlistment who complete 30 years' active federal service and do not submit application for retirement.
419	Discharge of enlisted personnel on unspecified enlistment over 55 years of age who have completed 20 years' active federal service and do not submit application for retirement.
420	Discharge or release of individuals with less than 3 months remaining to serve who fail to continue as students (academic failure) at service academies.
421	Early release at Christmas will be issued as appropriate by Army and has been included in separation edit table. Rescinded.
422	Early release at original ETS of enlisted personnel who have executed a voluntary extension. Rescinded.
423	Early release after original ETS of personnel serving on a voluntary extension. Rescinded.
424	Separation at ETS after completing a period of voluntary extension. Rescinded.
425	Discharge (inductees) to enlist for Warrant Officer Flight Training.
426	Discharge (inductees) to enlist to attend critical MOS School.
427	Discharge (inductees) to enlist for Officer Candidate School.
428	Discharge for failure to complete Officer Candidate School.

429   Discharge because of not meeting medical fitness standards for flight training.

430   Early separation of personnel denied reenlistment under Qualitative Management Program.

431   Reduction in authorized strength.

432   Early release to serve 1 year in an ARNG or USAR unit.

433   Involuntary release of personnel on compassionate assignment.

434   Early release of AUS and first-term RA personnel—phase down release programs. (Early out from Vietnam.)

436   Reduction in strength—USASA option first term.

437   AUS, RA first term, exempted from 90-day suspension of Early Release Program for reasons of intolerable personal problems.

440   Separation for concealment of serious arrest record.

460   Emotional instability reaction.

461   Inadequate personality.

462   Mental deficiency.

463   Paranoid personality.

464   Schizoid personality.

469   Unsuitability

480   Personality disorders.

482   Desertion/trial barred by 10, U.S.C., sec. 843 (Art. 43, UCMJ). Rescinded.

488   Unsuitability (general discharge separation).

489   Military Personnel Security Program (disloyal or subversive).

500   Resignation—hardship.

501   Resignation—national health, safety, or interest.

502   Resignation—completion of required service.

503   Resignation—enlistment in the Regular Army—Regular Officer.

504   Resignation—withdrawal of ecclesiastical endorsement.

505   Resignation—serving under a suspended sentence to dismissal.

508   Resignation—to attend school.

509   Resignation—in lieu of elimination because of substandard or unsatisfactory performance of duty.

510   Resignation—interest of national security (in lieu of elimination).

511   Resignation—in lieu of elimination (homosexuality).

518   Resignation—in lieu of elimination because of unfitness or unacceptable conduct.

522   Resignation—in lieu of elimination because of conduct triable by courts-martial or in lieu thereof.

524   Resignation—unqualified or other miscellaneous reasons.

528   Resignation—marriage.

529   Resignation—pregnancy.

530   Resignation—parenthood (minor children).

536   Voluntary discharge (substandard performance of duty).

537   Involuntary discharge—unfitness (unacceptable conduct).

539   Voluntary discharge—termination of RA or AUS warrant or member serving on active duty in RA or AUS warrant to retire in commissioned status.

545   Involuntary discharge—failure of selection for permanent promotion (commissioned officers).

546   Involuntary discharge—failure of selection for permanent promotion (warrant officer).

550   Involuntary discharge—reasons as specified by HDQA.

551   Involuntary discharge—administrative discharge, GCM.

552   Dismissal—general court-martial (homosexuality).

554   Dismissal—general court-martial.

555   Involuntary discharge—failure to complete basic, company officer, or associate company officer course —USAR officers.

556   Failure to complete basic, company officer, or associate company officer course—ARNGUS officers.

558   Voluntary discharge—conscientious objection.

586   Involuntary discharge—for reasons involving board action or in lieu thereof (homosexuality).

588   Involuntary discharge—reasons involving board action, or in lieu thereof—unfitness or unacceptable conduct.

589   Voluntary discharge—reasons involving board action,

or in lieu thereof, due to substandard performance of duty.

590   Involuntary discharge—interest of national security.

595   Involuntary discharge—pregnancy.

596   Involuntary discharge—parenthood (minor children).

597   Voluntary discharge—administrative.

599   Voluntary REFRAD—lack of jurisdiction.

600   Voluntary REFRAD—to enlist in Regular Army.

601   Voluntary REFRAD—to enlist in Regular Army for purpose of retirement.

602   Voluntary REFRAD—national health, safety, or interest.

603   Involuntary REFRAD—due to disapproval of request for extension of service.

604   Voluntary REFRAD—hardship.

606   Voluntary REFRAD—dual-status officer to revert to regular warrant officer.

609   Voluntary REFRAD—to attend school or accept a teaching position.

610   Voluntary REFRAD—marriage.

611   Voluntary REFRAD—expiration of active-duty commitment, voluntarily serving on active duty.

612   Voluntary REFRAD—expiration of active-duty commitment, involuntarily serving on active duty.

616   Voluntary REFRAD—selection for entrance to a service academy.

618   Voluntary REFRAD—in lieu of serving in lower grade than Reserve grade.

619   Voluntary REFRAD—by request, includes MC and DC officers.

620   Voluntary REFRAD—interdepartmental transfer of other than medical officers.

621   Voluntary REFRAD—in lieu of unqualified resignation.

623   Voluntary REFRAD—interdepartmental transfer of medical officers.

624   Voluntary REFRAD—release from ADT to enter on 24 months' active duty.

625   Voluntary REFRAD—annual screening, voluntary release prior to 90th day subsequent to receipt of notification.

627   Involuntary REFRAD—maximum age.

631 Involuntary REFRAD—failure of selection for permanent Reserve promotion (discharged).

632 Involuntary REFRAD—failure of selection for permanent Reserve promotion (commission retained).

633 Involuntary REFRAD—failure of selection for promotion, temporary.

640 Involuntary REFRAD—commissioned officer under sentence of dismissal and warrant officer under sentence of dishonorable discharge awaiting appellate review.

644 Voluntary and Involuntary REFRAD—convenience of government, or as specified by Secretary of the Army.

645 Involuntary REFRAD—annual screening, release on 90th day subsequent to receipt of notification.

646 Involuntary REFRAD—maximum service, warrant officers.

647 Involuntary REFRAD—maximum service, commissioned officers.

648 Involuntary REFRAD—completion of prescribed years of service.

649 Involuntary REFRAD—withdrawal of ecclesiastical endorsement.

650 Involuntary REFRAD—physically disqualified upon order to active duty.

651 Involuntary REFRAD—release of Reserve unit and return to Reserve status.

652 Involuntary REFRAD—release of unit of NG or NG(US) and return to state control.

655 Involuntary REFRAD—revert to retired list, not by reason of physical disability.

657 Involuntary REFRAD—physical disability. Revert to inactive status for purpose of retirement under Chapter 67, 10 U.S.C., in lieu of discharge with entitlement to receive disability severance pay.

660 Physical disability discharge—entitlement to severance pay.

661 Physical disability discharge—disability resulting from intentional misconduct, or willful neglect, or incurred during a period of unauthorized absence. Not entitled to receive disability severance pay.

662 Physical disability discharge—EPTS, established by

physical evaluation board. Not entitled to disability severance pay.

668 Dropped from rolls—AWOL, conviction and confinement by civil authorities.

669 Dropped from rolls—AWOL, desertion.

672 Involuntary REFRAD—medical service personnel who receive unfavorable background investigation and/or National Agency Check.

681 Voluntary REFRAD—to accept employment with a legally established law enforcement agency.

685 Resignation—failure to meet medical fitness standards at time of appointment.

686 Involuntary discharge—failure to resign under Chapter 16, AR 635-120, when determined to be in the best interests of the government and the individual.

689 Voluntary REFRAD—reduction in strength, voluntary release prior to 90th day subsequent to receipt of notification.

690 Involuntary REFRAD—reduction in strength, release on 90th day subsequent to receipt of notification.

70A Mandatory retirement—35 years' service/5 years in grade, Regular Army major general.

70B Mandatory retirement—age 62, Regular Army major general.

70C Mandatory retirement—age 60, Regular Army major general whose retirement has been deferred.

70D Mandatory retirement—age 64, Regular Army major general whose retirement has been deferred and each permanent professor and the Registrar of the U.S. Military Academy.

70E Mandatory retirement—30 years' service/5 years in grade, Regular Army brigadier general.

70F Mandatory retirement—30 years of service/5 years in grade, Regular colonels.

70G Mandatory retirement—28 years' service/Regular lieutenant colonels.

70J Mandatory retirement—age 60, regular commissioned officers below major general.

70K Mandatory retirement—more than 30 years' active service, professors U.S. Military Academy.

70L Mandatory retirement—30 years' or more active service, Regular warrant officers.

70M   Mandatory retirement—age 62, Regular warrant officers.

701   Enlisted separation—early release of personnel assigned to installations or units scheduled for inactivation, permanent change of station, or demobilization.

741   Mandatory retirement—failure of selection for promotion, established retirement date, commissioned officer.

742   Mandatory retirement—failure of selection for promotion, established retirement date, warrant officer.

743   Enlisted separation—early release of personnel upon release of unit of the ARNG or the ARNGUS from active federal service and return to State control.

744   Mandatory retirement—failure of selection for promotion, early retirement date, commissioned officers.

745   Mandatory retirement—failure of selection for promotion, early retirement date, warrant officers.

747   Mandatory retirement—failure of selection for promotion, retained for retirement, commissioned officer.

748   Mandatory retirement—failure of selection for promotion, retained for retirement, warrant officer.

749   Enlisted separation—early release of Puerto Rican personnel who fail to qualify for training.

753   Enlisted separation—early release of Reserve personnel upon release of Reserve units.

764   Enlisted separation—release of REP 63 trainees upon completion of MOS training.

941   Dropped from rolls (as deserter).

942   Dropped from rolls (as military prisoner).

943   Dropped from rolls (as missing or captured).

944   Battle casualty.

945   Death (nonbattle—resulting from disease).

946   Death (nonbattle—resulting from other than disease).

947   Current term of service voided as fraudulently enlisted while AWOL from prior service.

948   To enter U.S. Military Academy.

949   To enter any of the service academies (other than USMA).

971   Erroneously reported as returned from dropped from rolls as deserter (previously reported under transaction code GA).

972   Erroneously reported as restored to duty from dropped from rolls as military prisoner (previously reported under transaction code GB).

973   Erroneously reported as returned from dropped from rolls as missing or captured (previously reported under transaction code GC).

976   Minority, void enlistment or induction—enlisted personnel.

Appendix V
Code of Patient Concern

The Veterans Administration is committed to providing high-quality medical care for its patients. It is also committed to providing this care in a climate in which the human needs and concerns of the patient are met, and in which his interests are protected. This climate must be based on respect for the dignity of the patient as an individual, and on care which is provided in a courteous, concerned, and compassionate manner. In order to achieve these goals, the dedication of each employee to the principles outlined in this document is essential. It is only through the willing assumption of this responsibility on the part of the staff that the hospital or clinic will be able to provide the kind of patient care to which it is committed. To this end, this Code of Patient Concern reaffirms the commitment of the Veterans Administration.

1. Each patient must be accorded dignity as an individual, and treated with compassion and respect.
2. Each patient seeking advice or assistance will be helped in a prompt, courteous, responsive manner.
3. Every effort should be made to make the patient feel that all employees care about him as an individual.
4. In all cases, the needs and feelings of the patient and his family will be given primary consideration.
5. Each employee, in his contacts with patients and their families, is responsible for creating and fostering an atmosphere of mutual acceptance and trust.
6. The physician responsible for the care of the patient, or the employee designated by him, will provide the patient with information concerning his diagnosis, treatment, and prognosis in terms the patient can reasonably be expected to understand. When it is not medically advisable or feasible to give such information to the patient, the information should be made available to the next-of-kin,

or other person designated by the patient upon acceptance for care, except when existing law does not permit the release of information without written consent of the patient.

7. The physician responsible for the care of the patient, or the employee designated by him, will make certain that the patient is aware of the person who is responsible for coordinating the patient's care.

8. The physician will, prior to the initiation of any procedure with a recognized element of risk, provide the patient with sufficient information for the patient to form the basis of a reasonable request for such procedure. Except in emergencies, such information should include the specific procedure and/or treatment, the medically significant risks involved, and the probable duration of incapacitation. Where medically significant alternatives for care and treatment exist, or when the patient requests information concerning medical alternatives, this information will be provided. The patient also will be told the name of the person responsible for the procedure and/or treatment. In the case of a patient who is considered mentally incapable of making a rational decision and request for a procedure, the sponsor or legal guardian will be provided with sufficient information to form the basis of a reasonable request for such procedure to be performed on the patient.

9. The patient may elect to refuse treatment. In this event, he must be informed of the medical consequences of this action. In the case of a patient who is mentally incapable of making a rational decision, approval will be obtained from the guardian, next-of-kin, or other person legally entitled to give such approval.

10. The privacy of the patient, including matters concerning his own medical care program, will be respected. Case discussion, consultation, examination, and treatment are confidential and should be conducted discreetly.

11. All records and communications pertaining to the care of the patient must be treated as confidential.

12. The hospital or clinic, within its capacity, will be responsive to the request of a patient for service, as determined to be medically appropriate.

13. In the event any investigative (research) procedures are contemplated involving a patient, the patient will be fully advised and informed consent secured. The patient will not be included in the investigative procedures if such informed consent is not given. Any exception to the rule must be submitted to review by an approved mechanism

268

which clearly provides protection of the patient's interest (i.e., Ethical Review Committee). No attempt will be made to influence the patient to give consent if he is reluctant to do so. In the case of patients who are considered mentally incapable of executing an informed consent, approval will be obtained from the guardian, next-of-kin, or other person legally entitled to give consent.

14. The patient will be provided continuity of care within the applicable laws and policies which govern the Veterans Administration and within the resources available. The patient's physician, or the employee designated by him, will provide appropriate guidance and recommendations for further medical care to the patient who is being discharged from the Veterans Administration medical care program.

15. In the hospital setting, the physician responsible for the care of the patient, or the employee designated by him, will ensure that discharge planning is initiated early in the period of hospitalization. The patient will be assisted, where necessary, in making appropriate plans for his care after his episode of hospitalization.

16. The patient will be provided with those hospital or clinic rules and guidelines which apply to his responsibility as a patient.

17. It is important that each employee recognize that the veteran patient has, in effect, prepaid hospital and medical coverage by virtue of service in the armed forces of this country, and has fully earned the right to his care.

No set of guidelines alone will ensure that the patient receives the kind of care and treatment that the Veterans Administration wants him to have. It is imperative, therefore, that each employee be concerned about each patient as a human being, and so conduct himself that the spirit and intent of this Code of Patient Concern is carried out.

ACLU HANDBOOKS

THE RIGHTS OF GOVERNMENT EMPLOYEES Robert O'Neil	38505	1.75
THE RIGHTS OF CANDIDATES AND VOTERS B. Neuborne and A. Eisenberg	28159	1.50
THE RIGHTS OF MENTAL PATIENTS Bruce Ennis and Richard Emery	36574	1.75
THE RIGHTS OF THE POOR Sylvia Law	28001	1.25
THE RIGHTS OF PRISONERS Rudovsky, Bronstein, and Koren	35436	1.50
THE RIGHTS OF STUDENTS (Revised Ed.) Alan H. Levine and Eve Cary	32045	1.50
THE RIGHTS OF SUSPECTS Oliver Rosengart	28043	1.25
THE RIGHTS OF TEACHERS David Rubin	25049	1.50
THE RIGHTS OF WOMEN Susan Deller Ross	27953	1.75
THE RIGHTS OF REPORTERS Joel M. Gora	38836	1.75
THE RIGHTS OF HOSPITAL PATIENTS George J. Annas	39198	1.75
THE RIGHTS OF GAY PEOPLE E. Boggan, M. Haft, C. Lister, J. Rupp	24976	1.75
THE RIGHTS OF MENTALLY RETARDED PERSONS Paul Friedman	31351	1.50
THE RIGHTS OF ALIENS David Carliner	31534	1.50
THE RIGHTS OF YOUNG PEOPLE Alan Sussman	31963	1.50
THE RIGHTS OF MILITARY PERSONNEL (Revised Ed. of THE RIGHTS OF SERVICEMEN) Robert R. Rivkin and Barton F. Stichman	33365	1.50
THE RIGHTS OF VETERANS David Addlestone and Susan Hewman	36285	1.75

Wherever better paperbacks are sold, or direct from the publisher. Include 25¢ per copy for postage and handling; allow 4-6 weeks for delivery.

Avon Books, Mail Order Dept.,
250 West 55th Street, New York, N.Y. 10019

ACLU 4-78

Are you
a member?

The ACLU needs the strength of your membership to continue defending civil liberties. If you have not renewed, we urge you to do so today. If you are not a member, please join.

Fill out the membership form below and send, with the mailing label on the right, to: **American Civil Liberties Union, 22 East 40 Street, New York, N.Y. 10016. Att: Membership Dept.**

If you have already renewed, give this issue to a friend and ask them to join.